The International History of East Asia, 1900–1968

This book provides a broad account of the international history of East Asia from 1900 to 1968 – a subject that is essential to any understanding of the modern epoch. Whereas much of the scholarship on this subject has focused purely on the immediate origins and consequences of violent events such as wars and revolutions, this book demonstrates the importance of also considering other forces such as ideology, trade and cultural images that have helped shape East Asian international history. It analyses how the development of the region was influenced by ideological competition and 'orientalism', by both multilateral and unilateral efforts to instil order, and by the changing nature of international trade. It considers a number of important topics such as the concept of the 'open door'; the rise and influence of progressive internationalism in the forum of the League of Nations; the development of anti-colonial nationalism and anti-Western internationalism in the shape of pan-Asianism; and the onset of the Cold War. It also includes detailed case studies of subjects including the administration of the Chinese Maritime Customs Service; the international effort to regulate the trade in opium; and the significance of intra-Asian trade. Overall, this book constitutes an impressive account of the international history of East Asia, and is an important contribution to the interpretive study of this crucial period of history.

Antony Best is Senior Lecturer in International History at the London School of Economics, UK. He is the author of *Britain, Japan and Pearl Harbor: Avoiding War in East Asia, 1936–1941* and *British Intelligence and the Japanese Challenge in Asia, 1914–1941*.

Routledge studies in the Modern History of Asia

The International History of East Asia, 1900–1968

Trade, ideology and the quest for order

Edited by Antony Best

Routledge
Taylor & Francis Group

LONDON AND NEW YORK

First published 2010
by Routledge
2 Park Square, Milton Park, Abingdon, Oxon OX14 4RN

Simultaneously published in the USA and Canada
by Routledge
711 Third Ave, New York, NY 10017

Routledge is an imprint of the Taylor & Francis Group, an informa business

© 2010 Antony Best for selection and editorial matter; individual
contributors, their contribution

Typeset in Times by Wearset Ltd, Boldon, Tyne and Wear

British Library Cataloguing in Publication Data
A catalogue record for this book is available from the British Library

Library of Congress Cataloging-in-Publication Data
The international history of East Asia, 1900–1968: trade, ideology and the
quest for order/[edited by] Antony Best.
p. cm. – (Routledge studies in the modern history of Asia)
Includes bibliographical references and index.
1. East Asia–Foreign relations. 2. East Asia–History–20th century. I. Best,
Antony, 1964–
DS518.I49 2010
327.5009′041–dc22

2009026449

ISBN13: 978-0-415-40124-1 (hbk)
ISBN13: 978-0-203-86207-0 (ebk)
ISBN13: 978-0-415-62504-3 (pbk)

Contents

Illustrations

Contributors

Professor Shigeru Akita is a professor in the Department of Letters at Osaka University. He is the author of *Igirisu teikoku to Ajia kokusai chitsujo* [The British Empire and the Asian International Order] (Nagoya, 2003) and editor of *Gentlemanly Capitalism, Imperialism and Global History* (Basingstoke, 2002).

Dr Antony Best is a senior lecturer in the Department of International History at the London School of Economics. He is the author of *Britain, Japan and Pearl Harbor, Avoiding War in East Asia, 1936–1941* (London, 1995) and *British Intelligence and the Japanese Challenge in Asia, 1914–1941* (Basingstoke, 2002).

Professor Robert Bickers is a professor in the Department of History at the University of Bristol. He is the author of *Britain in China: Community, Culture and Colonialism, 1900–1949* (Manchester, 1999) and *England Made Me: An Englishman Adrift in Shanghai* (London, 2003).

Professor Harumi Goto-Shibata is a professor of International History in the Department of Advanced Social and International Studies, Graduate School of Arts and Sciences, at the University of Tokyo. She is the author of *Japan and Britain in Shanghai, 1925–31* (Basingstoke, 1995) and a contributor to K. Sugihara (ed.), *Japan, China and the Growth of the Asian International Economy, 1850–1949* (Oxford, 2005).

Professor Akira Iriye is emeritus professor in the Department of History at Harvard University. He has published extensively on the international history of East Asia and on transnational history as a distinct historical discipline. His latest book (co-edited with P. Saurier) is *Palgrave Dictionary of Transnational History* (London, 2009).

Dr Tomoki Kuniyoshi is associate professor in the Foreign Relations of Postwar Japan at the School of Political Science and Economics, Waseda University. He was previously a doctoral research student in the Department of International History at the London School of Economics where he recently completed his thesis on Britain and the Japanese peace treaty.

Dr Peter Lowe was until his recent retirement a reader in the Department of History at Manchester University. He has published extensively on Anglo-Japanese relations. His latest book is *Containing the Cold War in East Asia: British Policies Towards Japan, China and Korea, 1948–1953* (Manchester, 1997).

Dr Joseph A. Maiolo is a senior lecturer in international history in the War Studies Department of King's College London. He is the author of *The Royal Navy and Nazi Germany, 1933–39: A Study in Appeasement and the Origins of the Second World War* (Basingstoke, 1998) and co-editor (with Robert Boyce) of *The Origins of World War Two: The Debate Continues* (Basingstoke, 2003).

Professor Masataka Matsuura is a professor in the Law Faculty at Hokkaido University. He is the author of *Ni chū sensoki ni okeru keizai to seiji* [Economic and Political Dynamics during the Sino-Japanese War (Tokyo, 1995) and *Zaikai no seiji-keizai shi* [The Financial World and Political-Economic History] (Tokyo, 2002).

Professor Ian Nish is an emeritus professor of international history at the London School of Economics. He has published extensively on Anglo-Japanese relations and Japanese foreign policy. His latest book is *Japanese Foreign Policy in the Interwar Period* (Westport, 2002).

Professor Hans van de Ven is a professor in the Centre for Oriental Studies at the University of Cambridge. He is the author of *From Friend to Comrade: The Founding of the Chinese Communist Party, 1920–1927* (Berkeley, 1991) and of *War and Nationalism in China, 1925–1945* (London, 2003).

Dr Nicholas J. White is a reader in the Department of History at John Moores University, Liverpool. He is the author of *Business, Government and the End of Empire, 1942–1957* (Kuala Lumpar, 1996) and *British Business and Post-Colonial Malaysia, 1957–70: Neo-Colonialism and Disengagement* (London, 2003).

Acknowledgements

It is a pleasure on behalf of all of the contributors to this volume to show appreciation to those who have assisted us in the writing of this book. First I would like to thank the staff at the following institutions for their kind assistance: the Bank of England Archive, London; the British Library, London; the library of Daitō Bunka Daigaku, Saitama; the Gaimushō gaikō shiryōkan (The Diplomatic Record Office of the Ministry of Foreign Affairs), Tokyo; Guildhall Library, London; Harvard University Archives; Houghton Library, Harvard University; the Modern Records Centre, University of Warwick; the National Archives, Kew; the National Archives and Records Administration, Washington DC; the Ocean Archive of National Museums Liverpool; the Russian State Archive for Socio-Political History; the Second Historical Archives of China (Nanjing); and the archives of the School of Oriental and African Studies, London. Records from the Public Record Office appear by permission of the Controller of Her Majesty's Stationery Office.

This book originated with a conference that I had the pleasure of organizing at the London School of Economics in July 2004. The conference drew on funds left over from the Anglo-Japanese History Project and was intended to provide a forum within which Anglo-Japanese relations in the twentieth century could be seen against a broader regional context. I would like to thank the contributors to this volume for their interesting and provocative chapters, which often highlight aspects of East Asian political and economic relations that have been unjustly neglected. In addition, I would like to thank those who actively participated over the two days: Richard Aldrich, John Darwin, Toshi Hasegawa, Yoichi Kibata, Rana Mitter, Keith Neilson, Kaoru Sugihara, Takahiko Tanaka and Odd Arne Westad. I would also like to thank my editor at Routledge, Peter Sowden, for his interest in this project and for his patience as this volume came together.

My greatest debt, however, is to those who helped with the administration of the conference. I would therefore like to record my gratitude to the staff of STICERD (Suntory Toyota International Centre for Economics and Related Disciplines) and of the LSE Catering Department for their help, and wish to acknowledge the kind financial assistance provided by the International History Department. Above all, though, I wish to thank the staff of the Japan Society and the Anglo-Japanese History Project steering committee, and especially Captain Robert Guy and Jill Brooks, and above all the late Lew Radbourne. Those involved with the Anglo-Japanese History Project will know how much we all owed to Lew's enthusiasm and commitment and it is a matter of great sadness that he is not here to see this final volume come into print.

Abbreviations

This book follows the Japanese style of putting the family name first (except in the acknowledgements and when referring to the Japanese authors of work in English); Chinese names are given in Pinyin. The following abbreviations appear in the text and endnotes.

ANZUS   Australia, New Zealand and the United States mutual security pact
BOE   Bank of England Archive
BOT   Board of Trade
BCL   Borneo Company Ltd
BDFA   British Documents on Foreign Affairs: Reports and Papers from the Foreign Office Confidential Print
BMC   British Motor Corporation
CCP   Chinese Communist Party
CMCS   Chinese Maritime Customs Service
CO   Colonial Office
DNZER   Documents on New Zealand External Relations
FO   Foreign Office
FRUS   Foreign Relations of the United States
GATT   General Agreement on Trade and Tariffs
GMD   Guomindang
IA   Inchcape Archives, Guildhall Library, London
LNd   League of Nations documents
NARA   National Archives and Records Administration, United States
NGB   Nihon gaikō bunsho
NYK   Nippon Yusen Kaisha
OA   Ocean Archive, National Museums Liverpool, Maritime Archives & Library
OSSCo   Ocean Steam Ship Company
OAC   Opium Advisory Committee
OPA   Open Payments Agreement
ONC   Overseas Negotiations Committee
OUP   Oxford University Press

PRC   People's Republic of China
SHAC   Second Historical Archives of China (Nanjing)
SPA   Sterling Payments Agreement
SCAP   Supreme Commander for the Allied Powers
TNA   The National Archives, Kew

Introduction

East Asia and international order, 1900–68

Antony Best

The international history of East Asia in the twentieth century is a subject that is essential to any understanding of the modern epoch. Its significance for modern world history can most obviously be explained in two ways: first, that the region was from the 1890s onwards the scene of fierce competition between the European Powers for access to its markets, and, second, that the interest displayed by Europe led the leading indigenous states in the region, Japan and China, to fear for their security and provoked them into co-opting modernity and transforming themselves into Great Powers in their own right. As a result of this Great Power competition for influence, East Asia became for much of the twentieth century a flash-point of national rivalries second only to Europe itself and thus exerted a profound impact on international politics. For example, the battle for control of the region played a major role in shaping the two conflicts, the Second World War and the Cold War, which defined the nature of the second half of the century. Thus to comprehend why the Second World War proved to be the pivotal event in the collapse of European hegemony one must look at the rise of imperial Japan and the threat that its quest for regional predominance posed to the British, French and Dutch presence. Furthermore, to grasp why the Cold War became such a dangerous conflict in the 1950s and 1960s one has to study the emergence of Communist China and its poisonous rivalry with, first, the United States and, then, the Soviet Union.

The fascination with the rise of Japan and China as Great Powers and with their frequently turbulent interaction with the West has naturally meant that international historians of East Asia have tended to focus their attention almost exclusively on the conflicts that marked the rise of these states to this exalted status. They have therefore studied eruptions of violence such as the Russo-Japanese War, the Pacific War and the Korean War from every conceivable angle. However, the tendency to concentrate on the immediate origins, course and consequences of wars can produce a simplistic reading of regional history, where national security and military outcomes are the sole determinants. The obvious danger in this is that one can lose sight of other significant forces, such as ideology and trade, which helped to shape the history of the region. This is important for it is clear that the potent challenge that the region posed to European imperialism existed in political and ideological as well as military forms, for the rise of nationalism and modernization in Japan and China as a form of resistance to European imperialism had a galvanizing influence on nationalist movements across Asia. In addition, the development of economic growth in East Asia, first in Japan and then in China, soon eroded the domination that the European powers exercised over regional trade and had the effect of stimulating the development of complex trading networks that linked the region with the indigenous merchants of Southeast and South Asia.

Moreover, the inevitable focus on the conflicts that have scarred East Asia means that another aspect of regional politics has been largely overlooked, namely the efforts by states and non-governmental organizations to cooperate together to regulate various aspects of international interaction in the region.[1] It is important to rectify this deficiency and not to focus solely on realpolitik because this region, largely because it was such a clear source of potential instability, witnessed a number of significant international innovations and initiatives that had broader repercussions for the world as a whole. For example, it was largely the dangers posed by Great Power naval competition in East Asia in the wake of the Great War that gave rise to the world's first serious effort to introduce arms limitation in the shape of the five-power treaty of 1922.[2] Around the same time, concern about the dire internal condition of China led to states and activists coming together to attempt to regulate or even suppress the opium trade and to an international organization, the League of Nations, engaging in what, in retrospect, could be termed the world's first development programme.

This does not, of course, mean that these attempts at cooperation were all successful, far from it. However, the fact that the Powers felt the necessity, in the face of regional instability, to engage in such efforts provides an important commentary on how international politics and norms of behaviour evolved in the twentieth century. Moreover, these developments show that the idea, inspired by the inability of the League of Nations to resolve the Manchurian crisis of 1931–33, that internationalism had no place or influence in East Asia is fundamentally unsound. If anything the problem in East Asia in the inter-war period was not that internationalism had failed to set root in the region, but that too many different orders existed, with the Washington system, based on the 'open door', competing with, rather than complementing, the League of Nations. Here too, the course of events in the region has important implications for understanding the more general history of the inter-war period, for if internationalism only complicated the task of resisting Japanese aggression, what conclusions might be drawn for Europe in the same years?

Inspired by the need to examine more closely the broad forces that shaped the region, this volume brings together a range of British, Japanese and North American scholars to provide a different history of East Asia from 1900 to 1968. Instead of concentrating on war origins, the chapters in this book analyse how the development of the region was influenced by ideological competition, by both multilateral and unilateral efforts to instil order, and by the changing nature of international trade. The topics scrutinized include the concept of the 'open door', the rise and influence of progressive internationalism in the form of the

League of Nations, the development of anti-Western internationalism in the shape of pan-Asianism, the European retreat from empire, and the significance of intra-Asian trade. In order to show how these forces influenced East Asia, the volume focuses on their effect on one of the key relationships that shaped the region, namely the complex ties that existed between Britain and Japan.

In the first chapter Ian Nish sets the scene for the book by reviewing the state of the existing literature on Anglo-Japanese relations in the first half of the twentieth century. In particular, he does this in the light of the recent completion of the Anglo-Japanese History Project whose conclusions were published in five volumes by Palgrave-Macmillan between 2000 and 2003.[3] This project decided to go beyond studying the traditional area of politics and diplomacy and dedicated volumes to economic, strategic and cultural themes in order to demonstrate the breadth of the interaction between the two countries. The result was that the five volumes created a far richer picture than had existed hitherto in which it became clear that competition in one area of mutual activity was usually balanced by relative cordiality elsewhere. In addition, Nish provides an expert overview of the failed quest for regional order in East Asia, which began with the signing of the Anglo-Japanese alliance in 1902 and ended with the outbreak of the Pacific War in 1941.

International order in East Asia in the period of European hegemony arguably began with the development of the treaty-port system in China and its attendant 'open door' for commerce. To a degree, one might say that this nineteenth-century construction had an internationalist progressive aspect to it, for, as the child of the British ideology of free trade, it stood opposed to territorial gain and used law and regulation to ensure open access for all to the China market. By the end of the nineteenth century, however, its star appeared to be waning as the British predominance in Western relations with China came to be challenged by the European Great Powers, and in particular Russia. The second chapter by Antony Best in this volume provides a fresh interpretation of the moment in which the treaty-port system came under challenge by assessing the degree to which the Anglo-Japanese alliance was designed not merely to contain Russia but also to protect the 'open door' order. It argues that the British perceived the alliance as an essential underpinning to the 'open door' in China and as a way of ensuring that the latter country was not divided into spheres of influence. In contrast, Japan saw the alliance largely in terms of national security against the Russian threat. Over time these conflicting interpretations and interests led the alliance into a period of prolonged decline. Accordingly, by the end of the Great War Britain sought a new way of defending its interests and was drawn to working with the similarly inclined United States to uphold the 'open door' and contain Japanese ambitions in China. The international order established at the Washington Conference in 1921–22 should therefore be seen not merely as an expression of American internationalist thinking in the wake of its failure to join the League of Nations but also a reflection of a long-standing British and American interest in an order based on the 'open door'.

Complementing this emphasis on the 'open door' as an international order, Robert Bickers in the third chapter focuses on the machinery that underpinned the Western semi-colonial regime in China. He begins by outlining the mechanisms by which British power was projected into China after 1842 and then looks at how the integration of Japan into the concert of Powers from the 1890s onwards gradually undermined its influence. The chapter concentrates on one key manifestation of the British presence: the Chinese Maritime Customs Service. Bickers examines the evolution of this unique multilateral institution and how the desire to get Japan to accept the 'open door' order led to Japanese being recruited into the service. He demonstrates that the subsequent Anglo-Japanese rivalry for supremacy over the Customs Service, down to the appointment on 11 December 1941 of Kishimoto Hirokichi as Inspector-General, acts as a parallel commentary on the growing competition for influence between the two Powers. He argues that the challenge posed by Japan in this field mirrored other struggles for influence, such as that for control over the Shanghai Municipal Council.

The threat to the 'open door' was not, however, restricted to the rivalry that existed between the Great Powers and the preference of some for 'spheres of influence'. Somewhat ironically, opium, the very commodity that had originally propelled the West into forcing its own commercial rules on to East Asia, was itself a source of disorder for it threatened to dissolve the political and social glue that held China together. From the late nineteenth century onwards there were calls in the West to regulate and ultimately suppress the international trade in opium and in Chapter 4 Harumi Goto-Shibata looks at this largely neglected and perhaps surprising area of international cooperation. Goto-Shibata outlines the pre-Great War origins of the movement to control the production and use of this drug and how this then developed in the 1920s into a concerted effort by the League of Nations to create a formal committee mechanism to regulate trade and restrict domestic use of opium. She analyses why this attempt to establish international supervision proved difficult to establish and outlines why the system collapsed in the 1930s. In doing so, she points to one of the most striking developments of the inter-war period, namely the way in which, just as Japan began to eschew international cooperation, China began very consciously to adapt itself to the rules and language of internationalism. This was, of course, a political calculation, for this strategy was designed to curry favour with the West and bring international pressure to bear on Japan, but, in itself, it provides a clear demonstration of the importance of internationalism in shaping East Asian history in this turbulent period.

In the fifth chapter Joseph A. Maiolo explores another aspect of inter-war international cooperation, namely how naval competition between the Great Powers evolved from the Washington Conference of 1921–22 up to the outbreak of the Second World War. He shows that quantitative naval limitation came about in 1921–22 in the form of the Five-Power Treaty because Britain and Japan shared a powerful common interest in preventing the United States from outbuilding their respective fleets, something that was well within the capabilities of American industry and finance. By the mid-1930s, however, this arms limitation order began to break down. Crucial to its demise was the fact that the

Japanese naval leadership was no longer prepared to accept the inferior status that they perceived the Five-Power Treaty as imposing on Japan. Thus, while Britain attempted further revision of the naval arms limitation order by introducing qualitative controls, the Japanese rejected it altogether in actions that mirrored their withdrawal from the League of Nations and refusal to honour the 'open door'.

Japan's move away from cooperation with the Western powers should not, however, be seen as an outright rejection of internationalism, for some of the tenets of that approach to international affairs were evident in its attempts to reconstruct the East Asian order in its own image in the 1930s and 1940s. In Chapter 6 Masataka Matsuura illuminates Japanese thinking about international order in the 1930s by studying one of the most controversial issues relating to Japanese foreign policy, namely the degree to which it was influenced by pan-Asian thought. As Matsuura rightly observes, the effect of pan-Asianism on policy formulation has been largely neglected by historians, because scholarship has often approached the subject from the perspective of intellectual history, while studies of the political events that led to the 'Greater East Asian War' have concentrated on bureaucratic politics and the decisions of 'rational actors'.[4] Through an investigation of the activities of pan-Asian pressure groups such as the Greater Asia Society and of the links between pan-Asianists and the business community in the Kansai region, Matsuura provides one of the first studies of the way in which this ideology influenced Japanese foreign-policy making in the 1930s and suffused society as a whole. He shows that the rise of pan-Asianism was a reaction to a number of disturbing phenomena including perceived Western hypocrisy over internationalism, growing trade rivalry with the West, and fear of the revival of the Chinese state under the Guomindang. He concludes that an understanding of pan-Asianism is essential in any attempt to come to terms with why Japan went to war with China and the West and that it should not be dismissed as mere propaganda designed to justify expansion.

To argue that pan-Asianism exerted influence on Japanese policy is, of course, not the same as saying that Japan's war effort consisted in practice of a progressive campaign to liberate Asia from Western oppression. Clearly in reality Japan pursued a most brutal form of warfare and nowhere was this more apparent than in the war with China between 1937 and 1945. In Chapter 7 Hans van de Ven looks at the evolution of Western perceptions of East Asia in the first half of the twentieth century and draws attention to the way in which the Sino-Japanese War brought about a marked change in the way in which China and Japan were perceived. He outlines how Japan's use of mass aerial bombing of Chinese cities in the first months of the war helped to concentrate attention in the West on what was seen as the barbarity of the Japanese. This accordingly led Western journalists to begin to praise Chinese resistance and stoicism in the face of suffering, thus replacing the negative images of China that had pervaded thought for the past century with more positive ones.

The Pacific War was a disaster both for Japanese and British power in East Asia. It might therefore seem strange that four of the chapters in this volume deal with the post-1945 period when one might logically assume that Anglo-Japanese interaction carried ever less weight. One should not, however, predate Britain's decline, for while after 1945 it only played a small direct role in Chinese, Korean and Japanese affairs, its influence remained in Southeast Asia until the 1960s. This was important, for in seeking to protect its interests in the region, Britain was able to exert a considerable degree of influence on the post-war order in Asia in terms of security, finance and trade. Greatly assisting this process was the fact that the peculiar circumstances of the Cold War, in which Japanese trade with mainland China was severely restricted, meant that Southeast Asia was the logical focus of Japanese commercial expansion.

The first two chapters look at the role that Britain played in regard to regional security. Tomoki Kuniyoshi in Chapter 8 looks at Britain's role in the process leading to the post-war settlement with Japan in 1951. Kuniyoshi deals first with the development of the British government's attitude towards both the timing and terms of the peace treaty and the security arrangement that it envisaged accompanying the end of the occupation. In doing so, he places the British view in the context of its broader security and economic concerns for the region and in particular its desire to safeguard its interests in Southeast Asia. Second, he discusses whether Britain exerted any influence upon American thinking about the peace treaty and concludes that it played a more significant role than has been thought hitherto in shaping the broad international order in the region, which has been termed the 'San Francisco Peace Treaty regime'. Britain, he argues, achieved its goals through its persistent lobbying for the conclusion of a bilateral American–Japanese security pact, its insistence that Soviet involvement in any peace treaty was not necessary, and its strenuous opposition to any multilateral pact that would commit the antipodean Dominions to Japan's defence.

In Chapter 9 Peter Lowe shifts the focus to Southeast Asia itself and shows that between 1948 and 1960 Britain executed a skilful retreat from its colonial responsibilities in the region, while at the same time helping to establish a framework for regional stability. Lowe argues that the key to British policy was that from 1953 it saw the main threat to regional security as coming not from a conventional attack by China, but rather as arising from the possibility of subversion. Arguing that this could be defeated by a combination of good governance and economic and social reform, it worked hard to develop a strong Western commitment to the Colombo Plan and the Southeast Asian Treaty Organization (SEATO). Important to its pursuit of stability was that it tried to downplay Cold War tensions by eschewing anti-Chinese rhetoric and limiting SEATO's geographical scope so that it did not extend into East Asia, which inadvertently had the effect, once again, of shoring up the San Francisco system. In addition, it sought to restrict Japanese influence in Southeast Asia by ensuring that the latter's activities remained limited to the commercial field.

The last two chapters outline the ways in which Britain contributed to the development of the post-war economic order in East and Southeast Asia in the 1950s and by doing so helped bring about Japan's recovery. In Chapter 10 Shigeru Akita shows that the argument that intra-Asian trade and the interests of

Western finance were complementary can be extended into the post-1945 period. He demonstrates that the priority that the British government and the Bank of England put on the need to re-establish sterling as an international trading currency meant that Britain had a considerable interest in stimulating Japan's economic recovery. The result was that Japan was quickly able to restore its trading ties to Britain's colonies in Southeast Asia and take advantage of the status of Hong Kong as an entrepôt port. Akita concludes that the trading system that developed played an important part in Japan's later emergence as a global economic superpower.

In Chapter 11 Nicholas J. White takes a slightly different approach, for while he agrees that Britain played a major role in encouraging the re-establishment of Japan's commercial links to Southeast Asia, he argues that this derived largely from geopolitical rather than financial concerns. He contends that British ministers and mandarins were primarily preoccupied with the management of decolonization and of the Cold War. As such, encouraging Japanese trade with Southeast Asia had two major benefits, it prevented Japan from becoming over-reliant on mainland China for trade and it provided Malaya, Indonesia, Thailand and Burma with investment, aid and affordable consumer goods, thus reducing the attraction of communism. White goes on to point out, however, that away from state-driven concerns about the threat from communism, a previously overlooked set of 'complementarities' did exist between Japanese industrial/commercial enterprises and British businesses. The agency houses, which still dominated the commanding heights of the maritime Southeast Asian economies, increasingly sought out competitive Japanese consumer goods and/or burgeoning Japanese markets for Malaysian primary production. Meanwhile, the Liverpool-based Ocean/Blue Funnel shipping group, a key agent of intra-Asian linkages between Japan, China and Southeast Asia, established enduring connections with Nagasaki shipyards during the 1960s.

The chapters in this volume thus show that there is more to the international history of East Asia than conflict. The very fact that the region was prone to violence meant that in the political sphere there were continual attempts to instil order and stability. In the late-nineteenth and early-twentieth centuries the main focus of activity was ensuring the smooth running of the treaty-port system in China as the only practical alternative to a drift towards a spheres of influence approach that might only precipitate war. In the inter-war years internationalism temporarily peaked after the horrors of 1914–18 and raised hopes that the 'open door' could be strengthened and deepened, but this proved a false dawn in the face of the turmoil created by the Great Depression. For the Japanese, in particular, Western internationalism came to be seen by the time of the Manchurian crisis of 1931–33 to be a self-serving and hypocritical phenomenon that existed to perpetuate Western power and to deny Japan its legitimate goal of equality with the West. Japan thus sought to develop its own international order based on pan-Asianism, but came to be enmeshed in the same contradictions that compromised the West. In the Cold War era the desire for international order did not disappear but had to exist in a very different environment. The aim now was not to provide an overarching structure that would dampen all international tension, but rather to help create stability within the non-communist bloc in order to deny the Soviet Union and the PRC the means to engage in subversion. The irony here was that the most logical way in which to achieve this goal was to encourage the recently vanquished Japan to invest and trade in Southeast Asia. The West thus, in an echo of the period of the Anglo-Japanese alliance, sought to manipulate the Japanese into contributing to the international order, but this time in a way that meshed with Japan's long-term interests. As such, Britain and the United States paved the way for the Japanese 'economic miracle' and the rise of ASEAN, which provide the foundations of stability to the present day.

Notes

1 Recently some historians have begun to focus on internationalism in East Asia; see, for example, Naoko Shimazu, *Japan, Race and Equality: The Racial Equality Proposal of 1919*, London: Routledge, 1998; Tomoko Akami, *Internationalizing the Pacific: The United States, Japan and the Institute of Pacific Relations in War and Peace, 1919–45*, London: Routledge, 2002; Dick Stegewerns (ed.), *Nationalism and Internationalism in Imperial Japan: Autonomy, Asian Brotherhood, or World Citizenship?* London: Routledge, 2003; and Sagako Ogata and Asahiko Hanzawa (eds), *Guroubalu govanansu no rekishiteki henyo; kokuren to kokusai seijishi* [Global Governance in Historical Perspectives; The United Nations and International History], Kyoto: Minerva Publishing Co., 2007.
2 Roger Dingman, *Power in the Pacific: The Origin of Naval Arms Limitation, 1914-1922,* Chicago: Chicago University Press, 1976.
3 Chihiro Hosoya and Ian Nish (eds), *The History of Anglo-Japanese Relations, 1600–2000* (General Editors,), Basingstoke: Palgrave-Macmillan, 2000–03; vol. 1, *The Political–Diplomatic Dimension, 1600–1930*; vol. 2, *The Political–Diplomatic Dimension, 1931–2000* (both edited by Yoichi Kibata and Ian Nish); vol. 3, *The Military Dimension* (edited by Yoichi Hirama and Ian Gow); vol. 4, *Economic and Business Relations* (edited by Shinya Sugiyama and Janet Hunter); and vol. 5, *Social and Cultural Perspectives* (edited by Chihiro Tsuzuki and Gordon Daniels).
4 See, for example, Sven Saaler and J. Victor Koschmann (eds), *Pan-Asianism in Modern Japanese History: Colonialism, Regionalism and Borders*, London: Routledge, 2007, and Eri Hotta, *Pan-Asianism and Japan's War, 1931–1945*, Basingstoke, Palgrave-Macmillan, 2007, which despite their titles still focus primarily on intellectuals.

1 Forty years of diminishing cordiality

Anglo-Japanese relations, 1902–41

Ian Nish

Introduction

Myths and stereotypes exist in all inter-state relations. Historians have a role to re-examine these myths from time to time in order to clear up misunderstandings. In the case of international history it is best if this can be done by collaboration between scholars of the states concerned. It is to be hoped that historians of the two countries will jointly study their sources with sensitivity and formulate their views after listening to arguments on both sides and sharing their insights.

I was involved as the British coordinator of one such endeavour, the Anglo-Japanese History Project, which existed from 1995 to 2003. It produced ten volumes covering the history of relations between Britain and Japan between 1600 and 2000.[1] It originated in 1995 as the fiftieth anniversary of the end of the Pacific War approached. Murayama Tomiichi of the Japan Socialist Party was presiding over a coalition cabinet with the Liberal Democratic Party. There was much controversy within the government and the country about the need to make an appropriate apology for the Pacific War. Murayama made his apology and simultaneously announced his Peace, Friendship and Exchange Programme which in part read as follows:

> While this Initiative will focus primarily upon neighbouring Asian countries and areas where Japan's past actions have left deep scars to-day, I also want to include other regions as appropriate in the light of the Initiative's objectives.[2]

While it has taken time for the Murayama Initiative to be taken up with neighbouring countries, Britain came within the project from the start, presumably on the grounds that it was one of those 'other regions' where Japan's past actions had 'left deep scars'. Groups of historians with an interest in the theme came forward in roughly equal numbers from Japan and Britain and proceeded to undertake their researches. In each of the five years that the project lasted they met in conference in order to discuss their ideas with one another when there was often lively argument. They also exchanged individual correspondence and criticism when meeting was not possible.

At an early stage it was decided that it would not be feasible to reach consensus on a mutually acceptable interpretation of Anglo-Japanese relations. There would inevitably be occasions when Japanese interpretations differed from British ones. It could not therefore be our prime objective to present a story line to which all seventy scholars from these countries could agree. We therefore set about gathering source materials conscientiously in the hope that we could make it available in published form on which readers could make up their own minds. It was our intention to clarify historical points for future generations and assuage disagreements that affected the general public, and present a balanced account which would spread a better knowledge of history in the two countries affected. As Murayama's statement expressed it, 'While almost half a century has passed since the end of the war, a vast majority of the people to-day have not experienced war.... It is all the more essential in this time of peace and abundance that we reflect on the errors in our history.'

As regards methodology, it seemed to us that we should not confine our attention to conventional diplomatic history and should not look at Anglo-Japanese relations purely in terms of politics and diplomacy, the areas of rhetoric between any two countries, where nationalist attitudes tend to emerge. Since earlier assessments of this subject had tended to focus too much on state-to-state relations, it was felt that we should try to focus more on people-to-people relations by adopting a broad inter-disciplinary, multi-archival approach. In any case, it was felt that a respectable literature already existed on political–diplomatic aspects of the subject. We therefore interpreted our mandate widely and devoted some of the project to Anglo-Japanese relations from the standpoint of commerce, social-cultural issues and military–strategic thinking, areas which had been under-researched in the past. It was accepted that some of these areas, being innovative fields of inquiry, would require new basic research and would take time for completion.

Administration of the project was conducted through two committees based on the Japan Society in London and on the Diplomatic Record Office, Tokyo where it was coordinated by Professors Hosoya Chihiro and Tanaka Takahiko. After consensus had been achieved, the findings of the two groups were published in five volumes in English through Palgrave-Macmillan and in Japanese through Tokyo University Press between 2000 and 2003. It should be emphasized that there was at no stage any attempt at government interference or censorship of the finished product, though the whole project was generously funded by the Japanese government. In effect the historians involved published their individual views as part of a consortium of independent scholars.

As we subsequently learnt, the list of countries included by the Japanese government in the Murayama Initiative extended to the Netherlands, New Zealand and Australia. Each of these countries has published an account of its bilateral relationship with Japan based on the widest amount of documentation available. In the case of New Zealand, it published a multi-author study, Roger Peren (ed.), *Japan and New Zealand 150 Years*, Palmerston North, Massey University, 1999. In the Australian case, there was an exhibition of historical materials in Sydney accompanied by a single-authored study by Professor Neville Meaney, entitled *Towards a New Vision: Australia and Japan through 100 Years*, East Roseville, Kangaroo Press, 1999. A similar publication is Remco Raben (ed.), *Representing the Japanese Occupation of Indonesia*, Amsterdam, Netherlands Institute for War Documentation, 1999. This accompanied an exhibition in the Rijksmuseum.

While the Murayama Initiative was primarily undertaken in response to the calls for reinterpretation of the events of 1941–45, it also reflected a current political problem that had afflicted Japanese governments of whatever political complexion for a decade. That is the so-called 'history war'. The foreign aspect of this so-called war has to be seen against the background of Chinese and Korean complaints that textbooks authorized for Japanese junior high schools have distorted events relating to their countries. These vocal protests have been heard since the mid-1980s and have never ceased, though they have risen to a crescendo whenever a new textbook has been licensed by the Japanese government for use in schools. The Japanese government has been drawn into this contentious issue since these textbooks go through a scrutiny process and emerge with a mark of government approval.[3]

These two related issues have made it hard for the Japanese government to apply the same methods as were used with Britain to the cases of China and South Korea. This is not to say that nothing has been done because historical scholars have held conferences, colloquia and informal exchanges of views and there has in fact been a conscientious exchange of visits and opinions.

In view of this sensitive environment, the Tokyo government acted slowly. Against the background of territorial disputes and complaints about the Japanese prime minister visiting Yasukuni Shrine in Tokyo, the Japan–South Korea joint history research project (*Rekishi kyōdo kenkyūkai*) was launched in the summer of 2002 on the basis of an agreement reached between the leaders of both countries. Its object was to promote mutual understanding on 'the accurate facts and recognition of historical records on both sides'. It released its report in June 2005.[4]

A similar situation has obtained with China. Since the sharp confrontation between the public in China's major cities and Japan over textbooks in May 2005, a joint research project involving Chinese and Japanese historians has been launched. It is suggested that the sheer fierceness of the antipathy manifested worried the Chinese government and made it more ready to sanction a historical initiative of this kind. Certainly it also alarmed the Japanese government, which recognized that the extent of the unpopularity of its policies in China was growing. Moves were made towards launching a joint Sino-Japanese research project. For the future tranquillity of East Asia it is important that these two large countries should explore sources together, listen to each other and debate sympathetically.[5]

In addition to the problem of achieving bilateral dialogue between countries with different perceptions of their histories, there have also been domestic political concerns. It is difficult for politicians to offer apologies (as China, Korea and others have been calling for) if people of all generations are unaware of the issues and are unconvinced of the need for apology. It is politically important that the Japanese people should be informed about how foreigners view Japanese history, and consider how the Japanese should view the same history. One of the problems has been that the teaching of the modern period of Japanese history tends to be neglected in Japan's schools. Now the Society for History Textbook Revision has entered the lists and stoked up the controversies over the twentieth century. This leaves, as Professor Ishii writes, 'a pending question for Japan in the 21st century'.[6]

These early steps taken by governments to enlist historians to set the record straight are important and highly desirable. But historians are fallible and open to the criticism of Douglas Hurd, the former British foreign secretary, who describes them in his memoirs as 'professors of hindsight'. They do not have all the answers; indeed they cannot give the answers that politicians, the public or the media want. They can at best direct attention to considerations that strike them as relevant to their generation. Moreover, the dissemination of their ideas takes time. One cannot assume that the message percolates to the people at large in the short term.[7]

Diversity of interpretation

How far does the richer story, which we sought to offer in the project by using a broader inter-disciplinary treatment than usual, lead us to reinterpret the current orthodoxy of the political–diplomatic story? The richer exploration of Anglo-Japanese relations did not drastically alter the traditional view of their deterioration over the first half of the twentieth century. But it showed that there were greater divergences than might have been imagined if one feeds in issues from commerce, culture and strategy. It is relatively easy to define 'policy' in political terms but it is difficult to define national attitudes taking account of the trading, intellectual and military communities on both sides.

Britain and Japan were from the start mercantile, not to say mercantilist, states. It was perhaps for this reason that we were asked to start the project from 1600 when the pilot, Will Adams, sailed to Japan and, after settling there, assisted the English East India Company, which established a short-lived trade link that came to an end in 1623.

When we turned to consider the modern period from the Meiji Restoration in the 1860s, we found that were contradictory trends in evidence. At one level, Professors Ian Gow and Hirama Yoichi, the editors of the volume on 'The Military Dimension', could see it as a cordial time when education and training were the order of the day and Japan, content to learn from abroad, especially from Britain, moved from being a pupil to being a partner.[8] But, at another level, the Japanese were distrustful of the West and wary that they might not suffer the same fate as China. The outside powers had been able to impose treaties, which meant that until 1898 the trade of the Japanese treaty ports was carried on according to a tariff regime that favoured the foreign traders. The result was that the Japanese branded the treaties as unfair almost from the moment they were signed. The battle for renegotiation of the 'unequal treaties' lasted from 1870 to 1898 or even 1911. If Japan was thankful for the know-how being acquired from the West, it was nonetheless bitter over the unfairness of a system which it saw as retarding its economic progress. It was especially bitter about the actions of Britain, which, more than other countries, was holding back the treaty revision negotiations. So much so that at the very moment when Japan was looking around for a potential political ally, it was seething with anger over its failure to get full recognition as a world power.

Eventually Japan found its ally in Britain in January 1902. Throughout the period 1902–23 the alliance was the flagship policy of both governments. But there were complaints that the alliance was not yielding any substantial increase in trade or any commercial improvement to either side. Indeed Ayako Lister has shown that, by arranging the Japan–Britain Exhibition of 1910 in London, Japan was hoping to expand sales in order to alleviate its debt but had only meagre results.[9] Indeed after 1914 there was increased trade rivalry as Japan took possession of markets that had been vacated by the European powers which were fighting in Europe. On the other hand, there were cases in the 1920s where British and Japanese business leaders in Shanghai and elsewhere favoured Britain and Japan standing together in the face of Chinese nationalistic boycotts and other anti-foreign riots.[10] While Japanese businessmen, both in Shanghai and Japan, were eager to cooperate and show goodwill to the British, Shidehara and the foreign ministry were unwilling to do anything. By the 1930s there was serious competition over cotton, shipping and investments, affecting not only Britain but also the British Empire, including Malaya, India, Australia and South Africa.[11] But some British businessmen were not unsympathetic to Japan's arguments about over-population and had a different agenda from their government.

Thus, the Federation of British Industries mission under Lord Barnby went to Japan in 1934 and more critically to 'Manchukuo' in the hope of improving markets – and without the backing of the London government. Japanese historians are inclined to interpret this as an indication that Britain in the mid-thirties was ready for 'economic appeasement' and was making soundings to that end. Certainly it was regarded by some contemporary Japanese officials as sufficiently credible for them to arrange an audience with the Emperor, which the Barnby mission was granted in Japan. In the highly competitive markets after the world depression, British industrialists thought they must follow any avenues for business even if these were frowned upon by the British government. While this may have been true of some influential business leaders, it does not appear that it had Cabinet or government support. In short, there is evidence on the British side of contradictions between the attitudes towards Japan of traders and bankers and on the other hand of traditional industrialists like those from Lancashire. The background to the Leith–Ross mission of 1935–36 was a further illustration of the lack of cooperation between government and British commercial circles in China and of the difficulty the British government had in reconciling political and commercial objectives.[12]

If Japan was perplexed by Britain's conduct over China, it was positively alarmed by the activities of the League of Nations there. These formed part of a programme of humanitarian assistance inspired by Dr Louis Rajchmann, director of the health section of the League secretariat, and involved the strengthening of technical cooperation with the Guomindang government of China. There was an undercurrent of Japanese hostility to interference by supra-national bodies in this economic arena, which was so closely related to the political.[13] But these were only part of the workings of international semi-governmental organizations which were affecting the political–diplomatic process. Organizations as diverse as the International Labour Office, the Institute of Pacific Relations and the League of Nations Union also played their part in influencing public opinion globally. They may as yet not have affected events dramatically but they did have the effect of making governments more transparent in their dealings.

If one turns to the strategic side, there were signs that the Japanese military became disenchanted with the British connection certainly after 1911. Senior army figures, such as Yamagata Aritomo, wanted to diversify by entering into strategic arrangements with others, notably Russia with whom Japan concluded an alliance in 1916. So their commitment to the British alliance lessened as the influence of the military in the Japanese state grew. Another puzzle is that by the early 1930s, there were calls from time to time from senior Japanese army officers, notably General Araki Sadao, a former war minister, for a return to the Anglo-Japanese alliance. Evidently the Japanese thinking was that army leaders on both sides shared common ground in their hatred of world communism and the Soviet menace and might be willing to revert to the old alliance. While it was brought to the notice of the London government, the proposal was too intangible to proceed.[14] What this seems to confirm is the often-made claim that Britain and Japan were each following a dual diplomacy in the 1930s, with cliques seeking the upper hand in the absence of strong, coordinating leadership and in the atmosphere of tension sometimes pushing through their plans.[15]

Prolonged quest for East Asian stability

One of the shortcomings of a purely bilateral endeavour like the Anglo-Japanese History Project was that it might be too narrow in scope. We tried to avoid confining ourselves too much to the two states directly concerned and downplaying the role of third parties. This was particularly important since the United States played such a large part in influencing the international politics of East Asia in association with Britain and Japan and trying to preserve stability and fairness in the conduct of East Asian affairs. We tried also to pay sufficient attention to Japan's relations with its Asian neighbours. Inevitably Britain looked at Japan in the context of China, while Japan looked at Britain in the context of the latter's empire, especially in East and Southeast Asia.

Since the end of the nineteenth century statesmen had to consider how to deal with China whose weakness had come to the fore in its war with Japan in 1894–95. China had been humbled and was only saved by the *Dreibund* – that combination of Russia, France and Germany which came into being during the special circumstances created by China's defeat. These same powers – whether as part of the *Dreibund* or not – seemed to reassert themselves in 1898 when the powers made inroads into China's territory. In order to prevent further erosion of China, the powers under the initiative of the US exchanged 'Open Door' notes by which they guaranteed the territorial integrity of China. Despite the incursion of armed units from many countries during the Boxer uprising in 1900, these guarantees held good except in the case of Manchuria; but it was probably a close run thing.

When the Anglo-Japanese alliance came into being in January 1902 it naturally used the wording of the 'Open Door' doctrine. The preamble proclaimed the independence and territorial integrity of China and Korea, though it admitted elsewhere that Japan was interested 'in a peculiar degree politically as well as commercially and industrially in Corea'. Thus, while the two allies had their own objectives, they had also a sense of keeping the status quo. Both signatories consulted the United States in the remote hope that it might be tempted to join their compact; but without success.

The Russo-Japanese War drew the United States further into East Asia as the backstairs manipulator of the peace treaty of Portsmouth, which brought that conflict to an end in September 1905. President Theodore Roosevelt used his influence to try to steer things towards a balance of power of sorts by getting Japan to accept a settlement without receiving a monetary indemnity or acquiring the whole of the island of Sakhalin which her armies had over-run. The Japanese people, who did not gain what they expected from the war, distrusted the American president thereafter because of his partisanship. Yet the treaty, for all its faults, gave the region an international settlement which lasted twenty-five years.[16]

Did this mean that the US was looking for a leadership role in the east? There is a widespread debate about the extent of involvement that the United States wanted in the years ahead. On the one hand, the American emphasis on the 'Open Door', its concern with Manchurian railways and the cruise of the Great White Fleet, all suggested a desire to take a positive role but one heavily weighted in favour of America's national interest. On the other, over the Twenty-One Demands crisis of 1915, the Lansing–Ishii agreement and the island of Yap at the Paris Peace Conference, the United States took a mild, if not ambiguous, position. If Washington had great aspirations, they were not to be implemented yet awhile. By this stage, there was little evidence of Anglo-American coordination between the two devotees of the 'Open Door' ideology; and Japan was no longer regarded as an 'Open Door' adherent.[17]

At the Paris Peace Conference of 1919 the regional powers, Japan and China (even Korea), had high hopes. They had long-term goals inconsistent one with the other; but they were not adopted. The major regional problem of Sino-Japanese relations was not addressed adequately for reasons of time and inadequate expertise. Understandably the younger members of the Japanese delegation in Paris greeted the outcome as an example of an Anglo-American conspiracy.

While senior figures like Makino Nobuaki held that Japan's destiny lay in cooperation with Britain and the United States, some juniors at Paris, such as Konoe
Fumimaro, saw the outcome as the result of the Pax Anglo-Americana which
was trying to exclude Japan from international decisions. The post-war prescrip-
tion for East Asia pleased neither China nor Japan.[18]

A different atmosphere prevailed when the Washington conference assembled
in November 1921. First Japan presented itself unwillingly; China had a divided
delegation; and Korea was again unhappily on the periphery. It was widely
recognized that, after its brief but decisive intervention in the First World War,
America had great capacity for speedy mobilization and great potential for activity, if aroused. The United States had the ability to take on the mantle of world
leadership if it wanted; and the new Republican administration showed American power at the Washington conference with some good results. The 'wicked'
Anglo-Japanese alliance was despatched, with some regret from the original
partners. Late in life Lord Hankey, the secretary to the British delegation, looked
back as follows:

> At the Washington Naval Disarmament Conference at which I was present,
> there was no one, either in the British Delegation or in the Japanese Delega-
> tion who wanted to end the Anglo-Japanese Alliance. On the contrary, both
> parties felt deep foreboding of the consequences. They hated the breach so
> much that they could hardly speak of it, even together.[19]

This demonstrates that, as the delegates signed the four-power pact discarding
the alliance, they were not sure that the formula reached for other considerations
was really appropriate to the East Asian region. The atmosphere of the alliance
lingered for a while but the two allies gradually fell apart. In the nine-power
treaty of 6 February 1922 the 'Open Door' formula for China was reiterated: the
nine signatories undertook to 'refrain from taking advantage of conditions in
China in order to seek special rights'.[20]

But as happened with President Woodrow Wilson after the Paris conference,
the US leaders went into retreat over eastern questions for the rest of the twenties,
when there was in the east a distinct lack of any sense of international cooperation.
When would the new internationalism, the Pax Anglo-Americana of Washington,
be put to the test? The first challenge came from Japan's actions in Manchuria.
America's response can be seen in the note issued by Henry L. Stimson on 7
January 1932 which stated that Japan was in breach of the 'Open Door' and the
Washington treaties, which were both part of the American holy grail. Moreover,
the United States 'would not recognize any treaty which may impair the treaty
rights of the US ... including those which relate to the sovereignty, independence
or territorial and administrative integrity of the Republic of China'.[21]

We had earlier tried to address the Anglo-American aspect of this question of
stability in East Asia during the 1979 conference in London when we felt that
Anglo-Japanese relations could best be studied within a triangular structure in
association with the United States. Professor Hosoya Chihiro, the senior Japa-

nese historian at that conference, entitled his keynote address 'Britain and the United States in Japan's view of the international system'. It appeared that Japan's leaders were by the 1930s drawing a sharp distinction between its standpoint towards the two Western powers. In the case of the US, there were no big issues which could not be sorted out between them. Thus, there was no major threat to Japan in the American presence in the Philippines. Moreover, Japan felt America to be preoccupied with domestic issues and non-interventionist, until the war with China began. The reverse side of this perception was that Japan had real conflicts of interest with Britain and that the possibility of war between the two could not be ruled out. Since Britain and Japan were geographically poles apart, the points of tension were less visible in metropolitan Britain than in the British Empire in Asia where trade policies seemed to represent a barrier to Japanese commerce. Britain's existing stake in China was anathema for those anxious to pursue Japan's ambitions there. Moreover, Japanese historians are inclined to take the events of the mid-1930s as an indication that Britain was ready for 'economic appeasement' and was making soundings to that end.[22]

This interpretation continued to be discussed in our project. Kibata Yoichi, in a significant essay, argued that the British government wanted to be conciliatory to Japan over 'Manchukuo', though less so over Shanghai. It might have been willing to contemplate a non-aggression pact at this time. But Antony Best argued in response that 'Britain steered a middle course neither engaging in outright appeasement nor leaning towards the construction of an anti-Japanese bloc with the US'. In short, there was no agreement except on the fact that both sides were prepared to keep the dialogue open without any definite hopes of reward.[23]

Any thought of rapprochement between Japan and the West blew away in July 1937 with the start of the undeclared Sino-Japanese War. Britain wanted to act in concert with the League and with Washington. President Franklin Roosevelt's quarantine speech of 5 October 1937, the reaction to the sinking of the USS *Panay* in December, and the threats over renouncing the American–Japanese trade agreements were steps in a deteriorating relationship between Washington and Tokyo. Were they to be seen as the normal tussle of bilateral relations or as part of a serious ongoing campaign to restrain Japan? Bit by bit the United States was taking a firm and independent policy line. Britain would have wished that it was less independent and more cooperative with her. But, as Sir Robert Vansittart summed up the position in epigrammatic form, 'the Japanese are more afraid of the US than of us, and for the obvious reasons. At present, however, they share our low view of American fighting spirit.'[24]

Fortunately for Britain, the Japanese regarded the Pax Anglo-Americana as having more substance than it did (as viewed from London). Japan's navalists were worried that the US might be prepared to go to war in support of Britain, because the interests of the two seemed to be similar and it could be that policies were synchronized. The issue was debated in the naval hierarchy without consensus being reached. Admiral Suetsugu Nobumasa, the leader of the fleet faction, wrote in 1937 that it was 'inconceivable America would willingly be made a cat's-paw of the British. Since we have no conflict of interest with the

Americans, I just don't think it is possible.'[25] But others thought that such a view was too optimistic. The likelihood of America's associating with Britain continued to mystify Japan's leaders though it is probably true that the United States grew more likely to respond to Britain's appeals after 1939.

Pax Anglo-Americana as a supranational solution to East Asian problems lapsed. The baton effectively passed from Britain to the United States at the time of the Tianjin crisis in July 1939. But there is the problem with relay teams – and indeed with athletic metaphors – that the baton, once passed, may not be grasped and may be fumbled. At any rate it was firmly grasped by 1941 when America negotiated with Japan alone. By that autumn, it was the Tokyo–Washington axis that counted, not the London–Tokyo one. Ambassador Shigemitsu was tellingly withdrawn from London in June at the behest of Foreign Minister Matsuoka. Since he despaired of the progress being made in negotiating with Washington, one of his first jobs on returning was to egg on the British Ambassador Sir Robert Craigie to open a second line of diplomatic approaches for peace. Craigie responded evasively that he favoured a negotiated settlement; but, when he asked London, they insisted on leaving negotiation to the Americans.[26]

After parting company with the West in 1937, Japanese politicians were not without ideas for improving relations with their neighbours. It was a time when the axis powers, Germany and Italy, were declaring their 'New Orders'; and it was not unnatural for Japan, their associate in the Anti-Comintern Pact, to follow suit. In November 1938 Prime Minister Konoe announced his 'New Order in East Asia' (*Tō-A Shinchitsujo*), an attempt to win over the goodwill of the Chinese, but it did not formally come into being until September 1940. Once Japan made her declaration of war on the West in December 1941, the rhetoric of Japan's foreign policy changed. When the invasion of Southeast Asia took place, the idea of a 'New Order' took on a new resonance. The initial stage was set for Prime Minister Tōjō Hideki to say that Japan was acting for reasons of self-defence but wanted to secure permanent peace for Greater East Asia by creating a new order and eradicating the odious rule of the United States and Britain, especially the British colonies of Hong Kong and Malaya.[27]

This was swiftly followed by the so-called Greater East Asia Co-prosperity Sphere (*Dai Tō-A kyōeiken*) whose draft planning paper was leaked out in January 1942. In its early formulations it had been largely an economic and commercial doctrine but it now spoke the language of anti-imperialism and anti-colonialism, dwelling on the need of Asia 'shaking off the yoke of Europe and America'. But, as Komatsu Keiichi has shown, it was vaguely drawn and deliberately avoided being specific.[28]

The final stage was to emphasize Japan's pan-Asianism, her mission of liberating Asia from America, Britain, France and the Netherlands. But this idea was in fact a late-comer for Japan. It was the result of finding out how weak the resistance was from the colonial territories its armies had conquered in the first six months of war but also discovering how difficult it was going to be to act as an occupying power, bearing in mind its shortage of manpower. At the special wish of Prime Minister Tōjō a Greater East Asian Conference was held in Tokyo on 5–6 November 1943, attended by leading figures from Japanese occupied territories. A 'Greater East Asian Declaration of Cooperation' (*Dai Tō-A kyōdō sengen*) was passed. It spoke of the need for the construction of an order of co-existence and co-prosperity. It deliberately played down the idea of the Co-prosperity Sphere, which would have implied Japanese dominance in the relationship with her partners and smacked of colonial intentions. It was the symbol of one strand of Japan's foreign relations during the war. The change was the handiwork of Tōjō but also of Shigemitsu Mamoru, the foreign minister between March 1943 and March 1945. Given Japan's parlous situation, it was an adroit tactic to change the image of Japan's approach towards China and Asia from one of conqueror to one of liberator. It gave the Japanese people a sense of mission which had hitherto been lacking. More important, however, was its value in inspiring her soldiers at the front. Again it was an attempt to convince the people of the occupied territories to become compliant and cooperative with Japan. To give credibility to the Declaration, Japan had granted independence to Burma and Indonesia beforehand. But there were sceptics also who thought that it was merely a grand gesture in which Japan was able to exult after it had come to a realization that the war was lost. Like the Atlantic Charter of 1941, the Declaration was idealistic and had an unrealistic quality, bearing in mind the harsh war that was still being fought.[29]

This chapter has attempted to throw light on the Anglo-Japanese History Project, which engaged the attention of some seventy professional historians over an eight-year period. It was primarily an attempt to review Anglo-Japanese relations fifty years after the end of the Asia-Pacific war. We uncovered many new facts and new documents. We tried to widen the scope of our enquiry to include people-to-people relations rather than merely state-to-state relations and not to consider issues in too narrowly bilateral terms. We emerged without agreement on some salient points; but there was a broad consensus on the central themes. This was salutary because historians have the reputation for failing to reach the same conclusion even when examining the same historical document.

Notes

1 *The History of Anglo-Japanese Relations, 1600–2000* (General Editors, Chihiro Hosoya and Ian Nish), Basingstoke: Palgrave-Macmillan, 2000–03, vol. 1, *The Political–Diplomatic Dimension, 1600–1930*; vol. 2, *The Political–Diplomatic Dimension, 1931–2000* (both edited by Yoichi Kibata and Ian Nish); vol. 3, *The Military Dimension* (edited by Yoichi Hirama and Ian Gow); vol. 4, *Economic and Business Relations* (edited by Shinya Sugiyama and Janet Hunter); and vol. 5, *Social and Cultural Perspectives* (edited by Chihiro Tsuzuki and Gordon Daniels). [Hereafter referred to by the volume title].
2 Statement by Prime Minister Murayama Tomiichi, 31 August 1994.
3 Caroline Rose, 'The Textbook Issue: Domestic Sources of Japan's Foreign Policy', *Japan Forum*, 11 (1999) and Mutsumi Hirano, 'Revisiting the 1980s Textbook Issue in Japan', in *International Studies* (STICERD), IS/00/403, pp. 29–67.
4 Kimura Kan, 'Historical Perspectives and South Korea's Changing Identity', *Japan Echo*, October 2005, pp. 11–15.

5 Kawashima Shin, 'The History Factor in Sino-Japanese Ties', *Japan Echo*, October 2005, pp. 16–17.
6 Ishii Shiro, 'Traditions of Narrative History and the Recent Historical Textbook Debate', in *Journal of Law and Politics* (University of Tokyo), I (2004), pp. 3–24.
7 Douglas Hurd, *Memoirs*, London: Little, Brown, 2003, p. vii.
8 *Political Dimension*, vol. 1.
9 Ayako Hotta-Lister, *The Japan–British Exhibition of 1910*, Richmond: Japan Library, 1999, ch. 6.
10 Harumi Goto-Shibata, *Japan and Britain in Shanghai, 1925–31*, Basingstoke: Macmillan, 1995, pp. 24–5, 144.
11 *Nihon gaikō bunsho (NGB)*, Shōwaki II-2–2 (1933), Tokyo: Gaimushō, 1998, pp. 724–80.
12 Kibata in *Political Dimension*, vol. 2, quoting work by Inoue Toshikazu and Masuda Hiroshi. See also Jurgen Osterhammel, *Britischer Imperialismus im Fernen Osten, 1932–7*, Bochum: Brockmayer, 1983, pp. 406–22.
13 *NGB*, Shōwaki II-2–2 (1933), pp. 340–69.
14 M.D. Kennedy, *The Estrangement of Great Britain and Japan, 1917–35*, Manchester: Manchester University Press, 1969.
15 Ann Trotter, *Britain and East Asia, 1933–7*, Cambridge: Cambridge University Press, 1975, pp. 210–13.
16 Okamoto Shumpei, *The Japanese Oligarchy and the Russo-Japanese War*, New York: Columbia University Press, 1970, pp. 218–21, for a balanced account.
17 Akira Iriye, *Pacific Estrangement, 1897–1911*, Cambridge, MA: Harvard University Press, 1972; F.R. Dickinson, *War and National Reinvention: Japan in the Great War, 1914–19*, Cambridge, MA: Harvard University Press, 1999.
18 Hosoya Chihiro in Ian Nish (ed.), *Anglo-Japanese Alienation, 1919–52*, Cambridge: Cambridge University Press, 1982, pp. 4–7. The Japanese version of these papers edited by Professor Hosoya was published as *Nichi-Ei kankeishi, 1917–49*. Hereafter cited as '*Alienation*'.
19 Speech by Lord Hankey in the House of Lords, 29 November 1951.
20 *US Relations with China, 1944–9*, Washington, DC, State Department, 1949, p. 440, Art.1
21 Ibid., pp. 446–7.
22 Hosoya in *Alienation*, ch.1 and ch. 3.
23 Kibata in *Political Dimension*, vol. 2, pp. 6–7; Best in *Political Dimension*, vol. 2, pp. 31–3 and Hugh Cortazzi (ed.), *Britain and Japan: Biographical Portraits*, vol. 4, Richmond: Japan Library, 2002, p. 103.
24 Rohan Butler, Douglas Dakin and M.E. Lambert (eds), *Documents on British Foreign Policy, 1919–29*, series 2, vol. ix, London: HMSO, 1965, no. 238fn.
25 Hosoya in *Alienation*, p. 59.
26 Best in *Political Dimension*, vol. 2, pp. 43–4.
27 Tōjō's speech to the Japanese Diet, December 1941.
28 The most authoritative version of the secret planning paper is found in T. de Bary (ed.), *Sources of Japanese Tradition*, New York: Columbia University Press, 1958, pp. 801–5; Komatsu Keiichi, *Origins of the Pacific War and the Importance of 'Magic'*, Richmond: Japan Library, 1999, pp. 218–21. 'Greater' is used here because that is the form used by the Japanese government in its English-language publications at the time.
29 Gotō Kenichi, *Tensions of Empire: Japan and Southeast Asia in the Colonial and Postcolonial World*, Athens: Ohio University Press, 2003, pp. 57–9; Akira Iriye, *Power and Culture: The Japanese–American War, 1941–5*, Cambridge, MA: Harvard University Press, 1981, pp. 118–21.

2 The Anglo-Japanese alliance and international politics in Asia, 1902–23

Antony Best

The creation of the Anglo-Japanese alliance in 1902 was one of the most signi-ficant developments in shaping the history of East Asia in the twentieth century. Coming into being at a moment of great instability, this powerful naval and mili-tary Great Power combination dominated the region for the next twenty years, allowing Japan and Britain to survive both Russian and German challenges to their regional interests. This apparent success meant that after the alliance's demise, and particularly in the troubled years leading up to the outbreak of the Pacific War, many politicians and commentators in Britain and Japan looked back on these days as a halcyon period in which the two countries had co-operated to their mutual advantage.[1] There was in this nostalgic assessment an assumption that the alliance had rested on broad common interests and that it had brought a much needed element of stability and order to the region's volatile politics. This positive image of the alliance is interesting for it naturally raises the question of whether the original Anglo-Japanese alignment and its sub-sequent revisions were consciously intended to construct a regional order. Could it be said, for example, that the Anglo-Japanese alliance was deliberately designed to bring about a strategic balance of power encompassing all of East Asia and which would contain any challenge to regional stability? To go even further one might, in addition, ask whether the emergence of the alliance reflected the existence not just of military imperatives but also of the larger polit-ical, economic and ideological forces that were shaping the region's destiny. In other words, was the alliance a strategic manifestation of the liberal 'open door' regime in China favoured by Britain and the United States and did it stand in opposition to the more overtly imperialist ideology of the continental European Great Powers? Finally, in contradistinction to those who later romanticized the alliance, one might ask whether it was Anglo-Japanese differences over these very issues that eventually led to the alliance's termination and its replacement by the treaty system that was agreed at the Washington Conference of 1921–22.

The 'open door' and the origins of the Alliance

In order to understand the relationship between the alliance and international order in East Asia, it is necessary to look first in some detail at why the initial treaty came about in January 1902. The orthodox answer to this question is that in 1901–02 Britain and Japan shared a common interest in containing Russian imperialism in northeast Asia, as the latter threatened, if given full rein, to establish exclusive control over Manchuria and Korea. The two powers therefore combined primarily to bring home to Russia the potential for its actions to end in war in the hope that the Tsarist regime would retreat from its more extreme goals. The alliance was thus an attempt to contain Russian ambitions and as such it was intended to establish a strategic balance of power in East Asia. From the British perspective, this, in turn, was a reflection of its continent-wide competition with Russia in Asia and the growing Franco-Russian challenge to its naval predominance.[2] Indeed, one of the great attractions of the alliance for the British government was that the pooling of Anglo-Japanese naval resources in the West Pacific would allow the Royal Navy greater flexibility in global fleet distribution.[3]

However, in addition to this, one must look beyond the immediate strategic concerns and outline the interests that Britain and Japan sought to defend in East Asia. After all, the Russian threat did not emerge in a vacuum; it was a danger because it menaced specific interests that the alliance signatories maintained in the region. For Britain, China had been seen as an important market for its goods ever since the mid-nineteenth century. It had sought to enhance this potential for trade and investment in two ways. First, through the development of the treaty-port system with its emphasis on providing an 'open door' for international commerce, it had attempted to codify and expand trade in a manner that benefited not only itself but also the other Western states with an interest in the China market. Second, it had tried to encourage the Qing dynasty to introduce Western-style political and economic reforms in order to turn China into a viable trading partner. As such, Britain had come to possess the most important voice among the Western states that forced a semi-colonial regime on China.[4] However, the Qing proved remarkably obdurate about reform, lost a disastrous war with Japan in 1895, and by the late 1890s presented an image to the world of a doomed empire mired in decadence. As Germany, Russia and France moved in 1897–98 to acquire naval ports and spheres of influence, it appeared that China was on the verge of being partitioned in a 'scramble' that would mirror recent events in Africa. Britain was thus faced with a situation where it could either acquiesce to this drift towards spheres of influence or stand firm in support of the multilateral 'open door' regime. The British government's general preference was for the latter, but it was prepared, if standing firm only threatened to bring about dangerous complications in its relations with the European Great Powers, to accept partition as long as its own spheres of influence, the Yangzi valley and the area adjoining Hong Kong, remained safely in its hands.[5]

This dilemma over which policy to pursue was reflected in the alliance discussions. One of the first Foreign Office memoranda proposing an agreement stipulated that it should take the form of an assurance that the British would respect Japan's interests in Korea, while the Japanese would agree to uphold Britain's stake in the Yangzi valley and south China. In other words, it appeared to propose an arrangement based on mutual recognition of spheres of influence. However, the document also referred to the need to uphold both the 'open door' and the territorial integrity of China.[6] The final text of the alliance maintained this ambiguity. In keeping with the 'open door', its preamble expressly recognized China's territorial integrity and the right of the Powers to equal commercial opportunity, but article one then referred to the 'special interests' of both Powers.[7] The alliance can therefore be seen as straddling the boundary between the 'open door' and spheres of influence. It was merely the latest round in Britain's intermittent effort since 1897 to safeguard and prevent the division of China into spheres of influence if at all possible, but contained within it the means to hedge the bet and retain the richest prize if this proved impracticable.

In this context, it is, of course, worth noting that, although not a signatory, the United States implicitly approved of the alliance on the grounds that this alignment was intended to defend the 'open door'. As in the British case, American policy was driven by a belief in the infinite potential of the China market and the fear that this would be compromised if the imperial powers gave up on the multilateral treaty-port system and sought unilateral spheres of influence.[8] Indeed, it was the American secretary of state, John Hay, who had explicitly set out in two statements made in 1899 and 1900 the main tenets of the 'open door' and called for them to be universally recognized.[9] It is tempting to conclude from this that it is accurate to say that the alliance was a manifestation of a broader constituency of support for the 'open door' and that there is mileage in the idea that the United States was an undeclared adherent to the Anglo-Japanese combination. It is important though not to make too much of this, for in reality the United States was as ambivalent about the 'open door' as Britain. For both it undoubtedly constituted the optimum policy, but their ability to commit to it outright was compromised by strategic and political concerns.[10]

Moreover, whether Japan had any real concern for the 'open door' is a moot point, for its attention was focused squarely on Korea rather than on China. To some degree this was for commercial reasons, but its over-riding concern was national security. Its goals were to get international recognition of its special interests in Korea and to prevent that country from falling under the influence of any other power. Some, such as Inoue Kaoru and Itō Hirobumi, were even content to suggest that, in exchange for Russian recognition of Japanese predominance in Korea, Japan should allow Russia to establish a sphere of influence in Manchuria. Others, notably the army and the Prime Minister, Katsura Tarō, felt that this idea was simply not feasible, for as long as Russia occupied Manchuria then Korea would never be completely safe. It was this second group that strongly supported the alliance, believing that this combination provided the only sure diplomatic means of forcing a Russian retreat, while at the same time providing a way of 'keeping the ring' if war become necessary. Japan therefore may have committed itself to upholding the 'open door' in China, but it was clearly not its priority.[11]

It is therefore possible to say that, while the allies may have shared an enemy, they did not necessarily share a common vision of the region. The divide was not as stark as suggesting that Britain supported the 'open door' while Japan did not, but it does seem clear that the latter had less interest in the concept of perpetuating equal access to the China market than the former. What this meant is that while the alliance was sound in regard to shared short-term strategic interests, this was not necessarily the case in regard to longer-term political visions of the future. This is a vital point, for to see the differences in the two states' political priorities is to understand why the alliance was to be dogged by problems in the future.

The above description might suggest that the signing of the alliance simply constituted a traditional act of diplomacy. However, it is also important to see that in one sense it was a revolutionary move, for it was an alliance between a European and an Asian power. It is important then to ask why Britain and Japan decided to cross the racial divide in search of an ally. Of course, the seriousness of the situation in 1901–02 provides much of the answer, but one must also note that ever since its victory over China in 1895 Japan's international standing had greatly improved. Accordingly, at the diplomatic level the West had displayed a greater desire to engage with Japan than hitherto, perhaps the greatest sign of the latter's acceptability being its role in suppressing the Boxers in 1900. This willingness to treat Japan as a significant entity represented not only recognition of its newly acquired military prowess, but also the degree to which the Japanese government had successfully adopted European diplomatic methods. This stood in stark contrast to China, which in the midst of its decadence maintained its pretensions to moral superiority.[12]

The alliance therefore in part came about because the British political elite viewed Japan as an important player whose approach to international politics broadly conformed to European practice. In other words, they perceived that the two countries shared a common diplomatic language, and that Japan could therefore be trusted. However, it would be going too far to say that Britain saw Japan entirely as an equal, for there was some racial calculation in its thinking. In particular, the British feared that if Japan was left to its own devices in the face of the Russian threat, its 'oriental' outlook on international affairs might lead it to make unsound decisions, such as suddenly opting for war, or, conversely, seeking a compromise deal, with Russia. As one British diplomat put it, 'it is difficult to say what a country and especially an oriental state may do when it finds itself without funds or reliable friends'.[13] British influence was thus seen as an essential injection of common sense and backbone that would steady Japan and deliver it from temptation. In this context, one might say that the alliance constituted a means through which Britain could cement and expand upon Japan's gradual adoption of Western diplomatic practice.

Britain's willingness to align with 'oriental' power met, in turn, with enthusiasm and relief in Japan, which had its own reasons beyond simple strategy for wishing to construct an alliance that crossed the racial frontier. After all, based on the experience of the Triple Intervention of 1895, which had denied it the full fruits of its victory over China, it had feared that the Europeans would perpetually unite against Japan in the spirit of opposing the 'yellow peril'. To sign an alliance with Britain removed that concern, as it ended Japan's racially-imposed isolation. In addition, there was some hope that this alignment might go some way towards addressing an increasingly troublesome issue that had its own racial angle, namely that it might ameliorate the tensions arising from Japanese trade with and emigration to the British Empire.[14] Lastly, of course, Japan was simply pleased at this affirmation that its efforts at reform and its striving to be treated as an equal had not been in vain. The alliance was, after all, the ultimate sign that Fukuzawa Yukichi's goal of leaving 'decadent' Asia behind and joining 'enlightened' Europe had been achieved.[15]

The Anglo-Japanese alliance was then at its birth an understanding with many different facets. At its heart it was an attempt to create a local balance of power that would contain Russian expansion. It was certainly linked to some degree to a desire to uphold the 'open door' in China, but that cannot be seen as the sole motive, for both signatories were unclear about what exactly that expression entailed and how far they were committed to it. Lastly, it was a gamble that seemed to work, for, despite some concern expressed about whether an interracial alliance could function effectively, it met, at least in Britain and Japan, with a relatively warm reception and, at least initially, did lead to a limited Russian retreat in Manchuria.

The Alliance and the Russo-Japanese War

If the primary aim of the alliance was to establish a permanent balance of power that would contain the Russian menace, it has to be said that it was far from a complete success, for within two years of its being signed Japan and Russia were at war. Why then did order break down? The answer lies very largely in the fact that Russia's policy-making was too diffuse for the alliance to act as a sufficient deterrent and that, in addition, its political elite badly under-estimated Japan's military capabilities. Accordingly, in February 1904, faced with the failure of Russia to fulfil its promise to retreat from Manchuria and its continual refusal to provide Japan with a 'free hand' in Korea, the Katsura government felt that it had no choice but to go to war as the Japanese could never feel secure so long as Russian power was entrenched in northeast Asia. For its part, Britain had no interest in restraining Japan, for to do so might risk alienating Japanese opinion, thus possibly endangering the alliance and leaving the British alone to bear the weight of upholding the 'open door'.

The alliance therefore was not able in the end to achieve its primary goal of deterring conflict, but once the Russo-Japanese War started it did play an important role in shaping the nature of that conflict. Its most significant impact was that its very existence restricted the ability of the war to escalate into a fundamental challenge to the 'open door' order in China. It was able to do this because the terms of the alliance stipulated that if France came to Russia's aid and joined in the war, then Britain would enter the fray on Japan's side. Faced with this possibility, France settled on acting as a benevolent neutral towards Russia but no more than that, for it could not risk a global war with Britain. As a result, the war remained limited both in a geographical and material sense. In addition, it might be said that the alliance also provided indirect sustenance to the Japanese cause. Its existence, for example, facilitated Japan's access to loans from the City of London.[16] Moreover, the link with Britain added substantial credence to the argument that underpinned Japanese wartime propaganda in the West, namely that Japan was fighting in order to uphold progressive values such as the 'open door', while Russia represented the forces of 'reaction'.[17]

The war, of course, ended in a Japanese victory and in the Treaty of Portsmouth, signed in September 1905, Russia was forced to retreat from south Manchuria and to forego its say in Korea – interests which Japan duly inherited. Japan's triumph clearly brought about a change in the regional balance of power, but it is important to see that this development was, in turn, reinforced by the contemporaneous renewal and re-negotiation of the terms of the alliance. The new revised version of the alliance was signed in August 1905, just as the Portsmouth conference was about to convene. It was directed primarily at deterring the Russians from launching a war of revenge. It did this by stipulating that if Russia attacked Japan in northeast Asia or Britain in India, it would find itself at war with both powers.[18] Japan's success in war and the new strengthened terms meant that, by virtue of the naval and military power at the alliance's disposal, it now undoubtedly constituted the key strategic alignment in East Asia. Indeed, such was the alliance's air of invincibility that in 1907 Russia signalled an end to its policy of expansion in Asia by agreeing to sign pacts with both Britain and Japan.

The new alliance's ability to shape East Asia, however, rested on more than this strategic arrangement, for it also advanced the process whereby Japan was brought firmly within the European states system. In a display that the alliance was one of equals, Britain followed its formal signature by raising the status of diplomatic representation between the two countries to ambassadorial level. This was a relatively rare privilege in international relations at the time, as ambassadors were only exchanged between Great Powers. Moreover, in 1906 King Edward VII bestowed Britain's highest honour, the Order of the Garter, on Emperor Meiji. The alliance therefore became a self-conscious Great Power alignment, and as such acted as an anchor that tied Japan to the European states system by providing an incentive to eschew any 'return to Asia'.[19]

This was an important achievement, because in the wake of the victory over Russia, much concern existed in European circles about Japan's increasing influence over East Asia. This anxiety focused on two distinct threats. The first was that, influenced by pan-Asian sentiment, Japan might try to stimulate its fellow Asians to throw off the Western colonial yoke and, through that means, oust the Europeans and unite the region under its leadership. The second threat was that Japan, imbibing the spirit of realpolitik, might simply use its new military and political power to construct its own hegemonic control over East Asia. In particular, it was feared that Japan might use its influence to negotiate a preferential position for itself in Beijing. The Japanese government was, of course, aware that its newly found power had aroused these suspicions. Moreover, it had its own concerns in this area, for it had no wish to see fear of its Asian identity provoking the re-emergence of a European combination against it.[20] The alliance therefore proved to be a useful tool, as it could be used to demonstrate that Japan was a reasonable diplomatic partner wedded to co-operation and that therefore the European fears had no basis in fact.

This aspect of the alliance exerted a particular attraction for France, which feared that Japan might provide not just inspiration but also direct encouragement to the Vietnamese nationalists who were beginning to challenge colonial rule.[21] As an insurance policy France therefore signed its own pact with Japan in April 1907, which saw the latter declare its respect for French control over Indochina and its willingness to co-operate in policy towards China. Enthused by this development, Auguste Gérard, the French ambassador in Tokyo, revealingly declared his satisfaction that Japan 'brings henceforth to the examination and treatment of Chinese question the attitude and pre-occupations not only of an Asiatic but, if I may so, of a world power'.[22] The alliance therefore acted as a vehicle which demonstrated that there was little substance to the 'yellow peril' alarms that still reverberated in the West, and which brought Japan closer to the Concert of Europe.

It is tempting, based on the above, to argue that the alliance now became the arbiter of the region and that it shifted East Asian international politics away from a balance of power regime towards a more co-operative international order. There is some basis for such an argument. After all, those powers that had hitherto tried to undermine the 'open door' now appeared once again to acquiesce to the British-dominated treaty-port regime. This was exemplified by the emergence of the China Consortium in 1909–12. Moreover, even though China was rocked by the turbulent collapse of the Qing dynasty in 1911–12, it is noticeable that this dramatic event did not sound the tocsin for its partition, and this is certainly not what one might have predicted in 1900. The alliance might therefore be construed as a positive force in that its strategic strength inhibited any of the Great Powers from posing an effective challenge to the 'open door'. As such, in this period the alliance might appear to live up to the reputation that its supporters constructed for it after its demise.

However, it is important to qualify any such judgement, for there are other factors that help to explain the survival and further evolution of the 'open door' in China. One important point to make is that the development of international co-operation in China between 1905 and 1914 reflected not so much the strength of the alliance but Britain's relative strategic weakness. In this period, fearing the effect that any aggressive defence of its extensive rights in China might have on its entente partners, France and Russia, and not wishing to add further fuel to Anglo-German antagonism, the Foreign Office, in essence, followed a policy of appeasement in East Asia. Just as in the late 1890s, when it had also feared the effect that a resolute defence of its interests would have on European Great Power politics, it was therefore consistently amenable to co-operation with the other powers in regard to the financing and construction of railways and followed this line even when this went against its own commercial interests. This, on balance, had the effect of maintaining the 'open door', but that was not the primary motive. Indeed, the frustrated British minister in China, Sir John Jordan, became so enraged that he engaged in a series of complaints to the Foreign Office about what he saw as the selling-out of British interests for the sake of 'international compacts which tie our hands in competing with unscrupulous opponents'.[23]

Moreover, some events during these years indicated that the alliance proved at times to be actively detrimental to the 'open door'. British policy-makers had hoped that, in line with the terms and spirit of the alliance, Japan's victory over Russia in 1905 would lead to the revival of the 'open door' in Manchuria. Indeed, Jordan's predecessor in Beijing, Sir Ernest Satow, tried in November of that year to reassure the Chinese in regard to Manchuria's future by arguing that the signing of the revised alliance showed that 'Japan harboured no sinister intentions'.[24] However, it did not take long for this optimism to be shattered, for very soon Japan began to collaborate with Russia to divide Manchuria between themselves, and, in particular, to monopolize railway construction in their respective spheres of influence. Although this ran completely counter to one of the fundamental principles of the alliance, Britain on the whole acquiesced to this development. Once again it was European factors that led to British weakness. The problem was simple. With Russia vanquished, the strategic rationale of the alliance had changed. For Britain, it had now become a necessary element in the containment of the German menace, for if the defence of East Asia could be entrusted to Japan, then the Royal Navy could concentrate more ships in the North Sea in order to contain Germany. As Valentine Chirol, the foreign editor of the *Times*, noted to G.E. Morrison, the newspaper's correspondent in Peking, 'the importance of preserving the A.J. alliance in the present position of world politics would incline me to assent to a much weaker case than Japan is able to make for herself'.[25] The need from a global strategic perspective to continue the alliance thus ironically had the effect of undermining Britain's regional political and commercial interests.

The Great War and the alliance

As Japan's ambitions became clearer this inevitably had an effect on the evolution of the alliance. Clearly, due to the European situation, Britain could not afford to abrogate the arrangement and Japan itself had much to gain from its extension, as it provided both status and access to financial capital and naval technology. This did not though prevent changes to its terms and to the way in which it was perceived. For example, in 1911, when the alliance was revised for the second time, Britain insisted on a new clause being added that implicitly prevented it from being activated in the case of a Japanese–American war.[26] In part, this move reflected Britain's antipathy towards the idea of any conflict arising with the United States, and such a war was not impossible as American–Japanese tensions had been rising steadily since 1906.[27] In addition, however, it can be seen as an implicit acknowledgement that with Japan's regional ambitions now more readily apparent, it appeared that Britain and the United States had more in common in regard to China than was the case between the two allies. As the foreign secretary, Lord Lansdowne, had recognized as early as 1905, there was little substantial difference between British and American interests in East Asia, for both were strong supporters of China's territorial integrity and the 'open door'.[28]

The manner in which Britain handled the alliance also changed in another way at the time of the second revision, for it now began to be justified as an inexpensive way of containing Japan itself.[29] This new interpretation had a particular audience in mind, namely the prime ministers of the British Dominions bordering on the Pacific – Canada, Australia and New Zealand. These countries perceived Japan very differently from Britain, because to them it posed a dual threat, first, as an expanding regional naval power, and second, as a country keen to encourage emigration in order to relieve its growing population pressure. The Dominions were convinced that Japan had predatory designs on them and that one day the Japanese fleet might be used to coerce them into moderating their discriminatory immigration policies that restricted entry to Europeans alone. They therefore needed reassurance from Britain that the Japanese threat was under control, particularly as the Pacific, in the face of the German threat in the North Sea, was virtually denuded of the Royal Navy's presence.[30] Accordingly the alliance was given yet another face, but in so doing it entered into dangerous territory, for it now came to represent not just an arrangement that assimilated Japan into the European order, but also one that underpinned racial discrimination against it. The contradiction could not be sustained for long.

Thus when the alliance was activated at the start of the Great War it was already in a fragile state. It is therefore no surprise that during that conflict both it and the 'open door' came under great strain, for Japan, now freed from the watchful eye of the Europeans, sought to advance its imperial interests in China through the Twenty-One Demands and the Nishihara loans. This image of an unshackled Japan not only caused concern about the future of China, but also reinvigorated fears that the former might use pan-Asianism as a means of facilitating its drive for continental leadership.[31] Criticism of the alliance was not, however, limited to just one of its signatories, for dissatisfaction was also evident in Japan. Here critics objected to what they saw as Britain's senior status within the alliance, which confined Japan to a position of permanent inferiority. Added to this was the belief that Britain was acting to inhibit Japan's natural expansion and obstructing it from achieving its natural role as leader of the region. Those resentful of British influence espoused the cause of new alignments with other Great Powers, such as Russia or Germany, or even argued that Japan should put itself forward as the head of a pan-Asian crusade of liberation from the West.[32]

The result was that by the end of the war, the alliance was badly damaged. The differences over the 'open door' that had been finessed in the 1900s were now all too apparent. Britain and Japan clearly held very different views about the political future of China. Furthermore, the strategic glue that had held the alliance together was also breaking down and this made the situation even worse. The simple fact of the matter was that with Germany now vanquished and Russia lost in the chaos of its civil war, there was no substantial threat to Britain in Europe or East Asia bar the menace posed by Japan itself. Thus the strategic constraints that had forced Britain to walk a cautious line in the pre-1914 period and to accept an ambiguous interpretation of the 'open door' had largely disappeared. The only remaining strategic reason for continuing the alliance was that it might provide a means of restraining Japan. The Japanese meanwhile faced their own strategic dilemma, which was that the alliance did not protect them from the only power that they had cause to fear – the United States.

As if this were not enough, the greatly changed ideological environment that had come to exist by 1918 also challenged the alliance's future. The Great War had given a substantial boost to progressive and internationalist ideas. In a general sense this led to criticism of the concept of Great Power alliances, which were seen as having been responsible for the descent into war in 1914. As a means of instilling order therefore alliances came to be perceived as anachronistic. In addition, naked imperialism came to be seen as morally questionable. In the context of East Asian politics, this meant an increased emphasis on the moral underpinnings of the 'open door' in contrast to the selfish imperialist desire for spheres of influence. This shift towards a more moralistic attitude in foreign policy had dire consequences for Japan, for, in the light of its continued adherence to imperialist expansion, it was perceived as a state imbued with distinctively German militarist traits and came to be christened the 'Prussia of the East'.[33] Those British diplomats who had wrestled with the contradictions and obstructions caused by the alignment with Japan revelled at the prospect of collaboration with the United States. For example, Jordan in June 1918 looked forward to the time when, 'We shall have no more of these artificial and unnatural Alliances resting on no community of interest or national ideals ...'[34]

In this environment it was virtually inevitable that the alliance would not continue in its past form. As Ian Nish has persuasively argued in his definitive history of the alliance, both countries recognized after the Great War that in its current guise it had completely lost its raison d'être.[35] The question, of course, was what should take its place. For Britain and the United States the priority was to bring in an arrangement that would stabilize the region and safeguard the 'open door' in China. The problem though was whether it was possible to get more than Japan's reluctant acquiescence to such an international order. Fortunately change was under way in Japan. The government of Hara Takashi was aware that the recent unilateral policy of trying to gain a preferential position in China threatened to return Japan to the isolation that the alliance had originally been signed to counteract. Moreover, some Japanese diplomats, such as the ambassador to the United States and future foreign minister, Shidehara Kijurō, believed that Japan had to adapt to, and could benefit from, the internationalist spirit that now pervaded diplomacy. In addition, it was recognized that Japan, due to its proximity to China and its success as a producer of cheap cotton textile goods, had much to gain from the 'open door' and much to lose should Britain seek to use its power to penalize its rivals for the Yangzi valley market, which included Shanghai.

As a result of the change of thinking in Britain, the United States and Japan, the fate of the alliance was finally sealed in the autumn of 1921 at the Washington Conference, where it was replaced by the Four-Power Treaty, a multilateral consultative pact to respect the status quo in the Pacific that did not include any security commitments, and by the Nine-Power Treaty, which was designed to uphold the 'open door' and China's territorial integrity. With the alliance's demise it looked as if finally a coherent regional order was being established which would have one shared political vision of the future at its core. That, however, was to prove to be a false dawn, for the Washington order was to be as divided as the alliance had been in terms of its signatories' interpretation of and commitment to the 'open door'. Most noticeably, the agreements at Washington had elided over one of the key issues in regional politics, namely to what degree the 'open door' was considered to apply to Manchuria. This was, in turn, to lead to the collapse of the order between 1931 and 1933.[36]

Conclusion

What then should one make of the arguments used in the inter-war period by those who lamented the loss of the Anglo-Japanese alliance? Had the alliance really been a golden age that had brought order to East Asia? In some senses, one can say that the alliance made a positive contribution to regional order. It created a balance of power that helped to constrain the Russian threat to the region, and by providing this strategic stability it stopped the general drift towards the sphere of influence approach to the region, which seemed so prevalent in the 1890s. Moreover, it acted as a vehicle through which Japan was able to transcend its Asian roots, elevate its international status and join the European Great Power club. Building on these elements, the alliance brought an element of order to East Asia, which naturally affected the strategic calculations of the other Great Powers.

However, it would probably be a mistake to say that its influence on the international order went any further than this, for though the strategic rationale was strong, Britain and Japan had little in common when it came to the political future of the region. It may be tempting to say that the alliance was a strategic manifestation of the 'open door', but this is probably to read too much into it. In reality, the signatories were not by any means equally committed to the perpetuation of that concept and the alliance's ensuing ambivalence towards China threatened on a number of occasions to undermine rather than to reinforce the 'open door'. It may be true to say that Britain wished that the alliance could provide a strategic underpinning to the 'open door', but it was not enough for only one of the signatories to take this view. With this divide steadily opening up over what was to Britain a key interest, it is not surprising that the alliance, as Ian Nish has noted, began to decline from 1908 onwards. From this point on, beneath the formal surface of the alliance, which was marked by royal pageantry and declarations of undying friendship, gratitude and respect, the ties that had brought Britain and Japan together began to unravel as their strategic, political and ideological interests diverged. Indeed, one might argue that it only continued after the late 1900s due to the fact that it grew into one element in Britain's attempt to contain the German threat to its interests.

The alliance was then the result of a transient commonality of strategic interests between Britain and Japan, but it was not a meeting of minds. This existed elsewhere, most notably in the Anglo-American relationship. The dilemma here, however, as time was to show, was that while Britain and the United States were interested in the same kind of political future for East Asian politics based on the 'open door', their strategic commitment to this international order was limited. With so many other more vital priorities to consider and domestic constituencies to satisfy the governments in London and Washington were reluctant to fight over East Asian issues. In this problem lay Japan's opportunity to create its own international order.

Notes

1 For the retrospective glow given to the alliance, see Antony Best, 'The "Ghost" of the Anglo-Japanese Alliance: An Examination into Historical Mythmaking', *Historical Journal*, 49/3 (2006), pp. 811–31.
2 The standard text is Ian Nish, *The Anglo-Japanese Alliance: The Diplomacy of Two Island Empires, 1894–1907*, London: Athlone, 1966, but see also Keith Neilson, *Britain and the Last Tsar: British Policy and Russia 1894–1917*, Oxford: Clarendon, 1995, and T.G. Otte, *The China Question: Great Power Rivalry and British Isolation, 1894–1905*, Oxford: Oxford University Press, 2007.
3 The National Archives, Kew (TNA) CAB37/58/81, 'Balance of Naval Power in the East', Selborne memorandum, 4 September 1901.
4 Jurgen Osterhammel, 'Britain and China, 1842–1914', in A.N. Porter (ed.), *The Oxford History of the British Empire: The Nineteenth Century*, Oxford: OUP, 2000, pp. 146–69, and James Hevia, *English Lessons: The Pedagogy of Imperialism in Nineteenth Century China*, Durham: Duke University Press, 2003.
5 E.W. Edwards, *British Diplomacy and Finance in China 1895–1914*, Oxford: Clarendon, 1987, pp. 16–27, and T.G. Otte, 'Great Britain, Germany, and the Far Eastern Crisis of 1897–8', *English Historical Review*, 90 (1995), pp. 1157–79.
6 TNA FO46/547 Bertie memorandum, 22 July 1901.
7 The main tenets of the 'open door' are set out in the preamble to the alliance; see Nish, *The Anglo-Japanese Alliance*, p. 216.
8 Michael Hunt, *The Making of a Special Relationship: The United States and China to 1914*, New York: Columbia University Press, 1983, pp. 189–202, and Walter LaFeber, *The Clash: U.S.–Japanese Relations Throughout History*, New York: Norton, 1997, pp. 65–73.
9 For Hay's 'open door' notes, see Marilyn Young, *The Rhetoric of Empire: American China Policy, 1895–1901*, Cambridge, MA: Harvard University Press, 1968, pp. 123–36, 162–4.
10 For Anglo-American relations in East Asia, see Iestyn Adams, *Brothers Across the Ocean: British Foreign Policy and the Origins of the Anglo-American 'Special Relationship' 1900–1905*, London: Tauris Academic Studies, 2005, pp. 165–86.
11 See Akira Iriye, *Japan and the Wider World: From the Mid-Nineteenth Century to the Present*, London: Longman, 1997, pp. 15–18, Ian Nish, *Japanese Foreign Policy, 1869–1942*, London: Kegan Paul, 1977, pp. 64–71, and LaFeber, *The Clash*, pp. 73–7.

12 See Antony Best, 'The Role of Diplomatic Practice and Court Protocol in Anglo-Japanese Relations, 1867–1900', in Marcus Mosslang and Torsten Riotte (eds), *The Cultural History of Diplomacy, 1815–1914*, Oxford: OUP/German Historical Institute, 2008, pp. 231–53.
13 Lansdowne papers, BL, Lans (5) 78/1 Bertie memorandum, 22 July 1901.
14 Komura memorandum, 7 December 1901, reproduced in Nish, *The Anglo-Japanese Alliance*, p. 385.
15 Yoshitake Oka, 'The First Anglo-Japanese Alliance in Japanese Public Opinion', in Sue Henny and Jean-Pierre Lehmann (eds), *Themes and Theories in Modern Japanese History*, London: Athlone, 1988, pp. 185–93.
16 For the financial links between London and Tokyo, see Toshio Suzuki, *Japanese Government Loan Issues on the London Capital Market, 1870–1913*, London: Athlone, 1994, and Janet Hunter, 'Bankers, Investors and Risk: British Capital and Japan During the Years of the Anglo-Japanese Alliance', in Phillips Payson O'Brien (ed.), *The Anglo-Japanese Alliance, 1902–1922*, London: Routledge/Curzon, 2004, pp. 176–98.
17 For Japan's propaganda, see R.B. Valliant, 'The Selling of Japan: Japanese Manipulation of Western Opinion, 1900–1905', *Monumenta Nipponica*, 1974, pp. 415–38.
18 For the terms of the second alliance, see Nish, *The Anglo-Japanese Alliance*, pp. 331–3.
19 For royal diplomacy, see Yoshimura Michio, 'Nichi-Ei kyūtei kōryu shi no ichimen: sono seijiteki seikaku to hiseijiteki seikaku', in Kibata Yoichi, I.H. Nish, Hosoya Chihiro and Tanaka Takahiko (eds), *Nichi-Ei kōryu shi, vol. 1, Seiji-Gaikō*, Tokyo: Tokyo University Press, 2000, pp. 309–35, and Antony Best, 'Race, Monarchy and the Anglo-Japanese Alliance, 1902–1922', *Social Science Japan Journal*, 9/2, 2006, pp. 171–86.
20 See, for example, Nish, *The Anglo-Japanese Alliance*, p. 309, and Iriye, *Japan and the Wider World*, pp. 24–5.
21 M. Shiraishi, 'Indochina and the French Perception of the "Yellow Peril" After the Russo-Japanese War', *Journal of the Japan–Netherlands Institute*, 1990, pp. 77–97.
22 E.W. Edwards, 'The Far Eastern Agreements of 1907', *Journal of Modern History*, 26 (1954), p. 550.
23 Alston papers, TNA, FO800/247 Jordan (Beijing) to Langley (FO), 5 May 1913, and Edwards, *British Diplomacy and Finance*, passim.
24 Satow diary, 13 November 1905, in Ian Ruxton (ed.), *The Diaries of Sir Ernest Satow: British Envoy in Peking (1900–06)*, vol. 2, Morrisville: Lulu Press, 2006, p. 239.
25 Chirol to Morrison, 7 July 1909, in Lo (ed.), *The Correspondence of G.E. Morrison*, p. 496.
26 The standard texts on the third alliance are Peter C. Lowe, *Britain and Japan, 1911–15: A Study of British Far Eastern Policy*, London, 1969, pp. 33–57, and Ian Nish, *Alliance in Decline: A Study in Anglo-Japanese Relations, 1908–23*, London: Athlone, 1972, pp. 60–80.
27 See Akira Iriye, *Pacific Estrangement: Japanese and American Expansion, 1897–1911*, Cambridge, MA, Harvard University Press 1972.
28 Satow papers, TNA, PRO30/33 7/4 Lansdowne to Satow (Beijing), 3 August 1905.
29 See the statement by Sir Edward Grey on 26 May 1911, quoted in Keith Neilson, 'The Anglo-Japanese Alliance and British Strategic Foreign Policy, 1902–1914', in O'Brien (ed.), *The Anglo-Japanese Alliance*, pp. 58–9.
30 See Lowe, *Britain and Japan*, pp. 267–97.
31 For suspicion of Japan during the Great War, see Antony Best, *British Intelligence and the Japanese Challenge in Asia, 1914–1941*, Basingstoke: Palgrave, 2002, pp. 22–48, Nish, *Alliance in Decline*, pp. 256–60, and LaFeber, *The Clash*, pp. 99–127.
32 Frederick Dickinson, *War and National Reinvention: Japan in the Great War, 1914–1919*, Cambridge, MA: Harvard University Press, 1999, passim, and Nish, *Alliance in Decline*, passim.

33 Akira Iriye, *Across the Pacific: An Inner History of American–East Asian Relations*, New York, 1967, pp. 139–40, and Best, *British Intelligence*, pp. 45–6.
34 Jordan papers, TNA, FO350/16 Jordan to Macleay, 3 June 1918.
35 Nish, *Alliance in Decline*, pp. 392–7.
36 See Antony Best, 'Senkanki higashi ajia ni okeru kokusai renmei: kokusai kyōchō shugi, chiki shugi, nashonarizimu' [Internationalism, Regionalism and Nationalism in East Asia in the Inter-war Period], in Ogata Sadako and Hanzawa Asahiko (eds), *Guroubaru govanansu no rekishiteki henyō: kokuren to kokusai seijishi* [Global Governance in Historical Perspectives; The United Nations and International History], Kyoto: Minerva Publishing Co., 2007, pp. 25–48.

3 Anglo-Japanese relations and treaty port China

The case of the Chinese Maritime Customs Service

Robert Bickers

In China's nineteenth century the British Empire figured most prominently in the Qing state's encounter with overseas power. This is equally the case in terms of the projection of British power into China itself, and in terms of the experience of Chinese people in Southeast Asia. Some of these encounters were already underway before the mid-century wars that led to the establishment of the treaty ports. However, the development of new European communities in Chinese cities brought the 'foreign' home in ways that provided opportunity and trouble in equal measure. It also brought the British and their collaborators to China, to work in the treaty ports, in Chinese government service, and as missionaries. The culture which developed among foreign residents in China was dominated by the English language and by British ways, which were aped by all. And while there was no British grand colonial design, and no plan of attack, the Union flag flew high nonetheless in Shanghai, Tianjin, Hankou, on the Yangzi, in Burma, Hong Kong and in Tibet.

This chapter first sketches out the ways in which British power was projected into China, and then looks at how the interpolation of Japan into the China concert of the powers after 1900 undid one key sector of the British presence: the Chinese Maritime Customs Service. There are echoes of changes and challenges elsewhere – in such treaty port administrations as the Shanghai Municipal Council for example, although there is a key difference: whereas the Council ran a semi-autonomous private statelet, the International Settlement, the Chinese Maritime Customs Service was an agency of the Chinese state. British and Japanese interests met in such grey zones of interaction – leased territories, spheres of influence in Manchuria and the lower Yangzi, the seized German naval colony at Qingdao, and the international settlements: areas in which Chinese sovereignty was compromised to varying degrees. The Customs Service was one such.

British power in China

British hegemony in China was based on treaty and military force, and was reinforced over the decades by accumulated precedent and the ever-developing fact of settlement.[1] In practical terms the vectors of power included the various treaty ports, leased territories and the Crown Colony at Hong Kong. British merchants dominated the administration at the International Settlement of Shanghai. British concessions run by municipal councils developed at Tianjin, Hankou and Xiamen. These and other small pockets were incorporated into the normal world of British empire to varying degrees. Mostly, and most effectively, the centre of British gravity lay until the 1920s and 1930s with commercial Shanghai, rather than diplomatic Beijing, or the Crown Colony's Governor. Hong Kong was also drawn away into a wider orbit of colonial and Colonial Office practice and strategy. Official British activities in China proper were undertaken by representatives of the Admiralty, Board of Trade (merchant shipping), Colonial Office (the Weihaiwei leased territory), Foreign Office, War Office and the India Office (which ran the British Consulate at Kashgar). Less officially British and British Indian intelligence also maintained a presence.[2] In the twentieth century the Treasury could be added to the list. When the Foreign Office came in 1943 to consider the Chinese request to rescind the British claim to have a British national in the Customs Service Inspector General post, it referred its decision to the Treasury for approval.[3]

The official presence after 1861 was headquartered at the magnificent Legation in Peking, and co-ordinated from there, inasmuch as it could be co-ordinated. It projected British power through pomp and pretence, as much as through its ability to bluster, cajole and bully Qing officials and other members of the Diplomatic Body, and through its co-ordination of a national network of consular officers responsible for districts of varying sizes and British populations reporting to it.[4] Underpinning the workings of this presence was extraterritoriality, with British subjects required to register annually with their local consulate, and a Supreme Court for China and Japan established in 1865, together with company legislation which served to provide basic regulation and prevent abuses. Law was backed up by force. The British military presence was tangible. Army units were garrisoned at Beijing and Tianjin, and after 1927 at Shanghai. The Royal Navy's China Station operated river gunboats on the Yangzi and the West River, while the main fleet, headquartered at Hong Kong in winter and at Weihaiwei in summer, operated coastal patrols and anti-piracy activities. British naval and marine vessels passed each other on the rivers. Treaties had secured additional advantages for British business, such as inland navigation rights, coastal shipping rights and restrictions on Chinese tariff autonomy.

The relationship between British business interests and the Crown was hardly intimate in policy terms, but – all due class considerations taken into account – diplomats and consuls shared the treaty port social world with their commercial peers. They shared English too, and the language became rooted as the pre-eminent foreign tongue in China, in its orthodox and unorthodox forms – in pidgin (where English vocabulary was grafted on to Chinese sentence patterns) and in the Anglophone inflections discernible in treaty-port German or American speech. There were private 'civilising' projects too. Mission societies across the Christian spectrum ran evangelical, medical and educational initiatives, and mission personnel were present across rural and urban China. In the intellectual sphere Britons were involved in translating, describing and representing China, in varying degrees of accuracy, and with varying aims and ambitions.[5] Commercial imperatives and opportunities also saw an important British contribution to the development of Chinese newspapers, such as the involvement of the Major brothers in founding the *Shenbao* – China's first Western-style newspaper, and the *Dianshizhai huabao*.[6]

Each of these vectors had significant weaknesses. Most important treaty ports were international (so there was much scope for international rivalry), they were semi-autonomous (as institutions they were mostly not under any direct diplomatic or consular oversight), and they were often firmly parochial (their activists cared for local issues first). There was no guarantee that the merchants of Shanghai, however loyal, would toe the correct diplomatic line. They were also quite capable of local acts which had national consequences: for example, the 1905 Mixed Court incident, and most notably the 1925 May Thirtieth incident in Shanghai.[7] Extraterritoriality itself offered great scope for abuse, and abuse could lead to conflict – the Arrow incident in 1856 for example. Extraterritoriality was at times vulgarly extended to, variously and variably, British-owned, or leased, property, goods, employees, representatives. It was a habit of mind, as much as a legal convenience and it kept British diplomats and consuls busy, with a slowly decreasing enthusiasm until 1943.

Inland navigation rights offered further potential for conflict. At its softest there were new commercial rivalries, but new shipping lines and the opening of new ports saw the penetration of the foreign presence into new localities and disturbed the local status quo, whether through popular opposition to the arrival of a foreign presence, however small, or the opposition of local power holders.[8] The application of military power could backfire. Available British resources were ultimately weak in the face of determined and popular resistance, and there was a need for balance of power considerations. Missions invited conflict with Qing procedures, with local power holders and local society. Intellectual projects could be mired in chinoiserie silliness, or meshed with developing scientific racism to undermine understandings of Chinese society and politics.

There was also little official support for the private spheres of this activity. There was little by way of development of an infrastructure – such as language training programmes, or an organised credible research capacity. Chinese studies in Britain itself were accorded little support. Training programmes for consuls were fairly ad hoc. Privately religious diplomats might believe in principle that the conversion of Chinese was a good, but the presence and sometimes the actions of missionaries created no end of bother. Ultimately the biggest weakness actually underpinned the resilience of the British presence, itself a congeries of interests and initiatives: China was not very important for the British. The trade relationship was asymmetrical. Britain loomed large in China, in the balance sheets, and in some major cities and sectors of the economy, and at times in the anti-imperialist imagination. But China mostly loomed large only in the British imagination, and in some strategic anxieties. It was otherwise not very important. Disinterestedness on the part of the state gave scope for flexibility and innovation amongst British participants in the treaty ports, who could reinvent themselves when the situation changed.[9]

The 1890s destabilised this British-dominated treaty port world, ultimately introducing a host of factors that led the Qing state to declare war on imperialism in June 1900 at the height of the populist Boxer rising. The scramble for China – the rush for concessions after the Sino-Japanese War of 1894–95 – dramatically heightened the potential tensions of empires in China. The British themselves made two formal imperial advances (securing leases on Weihaiwei and in Kowloon's New Territories). This marked a strategic departure from existing practice, and whetted the appetite of the campaigning China hands, such as J.O.P. Bland. European and indeed global tensions and competitions were imported into the China sphere, and so then were the Japanese.

The institution which combined a great number of the above in its multifaceted activities, which stretched from a publication programme to construction of a navigation lights network for the China coast was the Imperial Maritime Customs Service, and this was British-dominated until 1941. The Customs was nonetheless an agency of the Qing state. Circular No. 8 of 1864 was clear: 'The first thing to be remembered by each is that he is the paid agent of the Chinese Government for the performance of specified work, and to do that well should be his chief care.'[10] Letters of appointment spelt this out in detail. The high tide of imperialism in the 1890s had an impact here too, as elsewhere in the treaty port world. This chapter will now explore how the arrival of Japan on the scene affected the British presence in the Customs, which for contemporary and modern friends and foes alike symbolised British hegemony in China. It follows the issue through until July 1945 when after three and a half years of Japanese leadership of the Service, all Japanese employees were paid off. The perspective is that of the British, the Customs Service itself (and the two should not be conflated), and Japanese interests as they represented themselves to the British, and to the Customs.

The Chinese Maritime Customs Service

The foreign inspectorate of the Customs was established in Shanghai in 1854 to deal with the impact on foreign trade of the twin crises of national and local rebellion around the city.[11] As the crisis passed the advantages of a system of contracting out to foreigners, the assessment of duties on foreign imports and exports led Qing officials to agree to a permanent foreign-staffed inspectorate. Robert Hart, Inspector General (IG) after 1863, turned this ad hoc innovation into a powerful, efficient and national agency of the Qing state. One measure of its expansion would be the numbers of new stations: by 1864 there were fourteen Customs stations, by 1877, nineteen. By 1905 there were thirty-six and by January 1931, forty-seven. Subject to caveat, each station represented a port, and sometimes a district, directly opened to international trade.

The Customs was always more than a tax agency. Hart and his team of administrators, engineers and marine staff, collected a wider and wider range of duties, developed navigation and lighthouse systems, ordered treaty port harbours, negotiated treaties, collected, collated and published reams of trade and other statistics (notably meteorological data), and sponsored the publication of works of geography, history, linguistics, medicine and even ethno-musicology. The Service represented China at international fairs, took on the Chinese Post Office, and was also a tool of Qing imperialism in Korea – the Korean Customs was reorganised under CMCS control from 1885 onwards.[12] Hart welded his cosmopolitan staff together into a body of men wedded to a strong service ethos and strong service loyalties. This was achieved as much by autocratic whimsy as by socialisation, and was the stuff of much legend and self-regard, but it had a tangible effect on the nature and efficiency of the Service.

Hart began as a consular official, switched to the Customs in 1859, was made IG in 1863, and remained at the helm in effect until 1908, and in name until 1911. He was a figure who dominated representations of British power in China. In one 1908 survey of Hong Kong and the treaty ports, portraits of Hong Kong Governor Lugard and British minister Sir John Jordan open the volume, as might be expected. But Hart gets a longer write-up than the minister at Peking. The British presence in China was thus represented by a comprehensive trinity of formal colonial governor, informal diplomatic proconsul and Hart.[13] The Customs aided the British presence in China, but not necessarily more so in practical terms than other trading treaty powers. It made trade with China for all physically safer, and procedurally rational.

From the start the Service was British dominated, but there were enough non-Britons for Hart and others to boast of its cosmopolitanism. In the earliest available staff list (1873), fifty-eight Britons worked on the 'indoor' staff alongside fourteen French, eleven Germans, eight Americans, two Norwegians and two solitary Swiss and Russian employees.[14] Between 1854 and the end of 1899, 2,983 foreign men served out whole careers: 1,697 of these were British, 361 American, 288 German, eighty-two French, with the remainder from a number of European states.[15] In 1900, of 1,733 staff, 689 were Chinese, 560 were British, 128 German, ninety-one American and fifty-three were French. Lower-ranking 'outdoor' posts were more likely to be recruited locally from the pool of foreign seamen that might be available, but appointments to the 'indoor' branch were more politicised. Decisions were taken at various times to appease specific national interests or pre-empt their expression. In 1874 four graduating students were recruited from Harvard. The previous year when Hart had sent a Customs team to the Vienna Exhibition he sent two Britons, one German and an American. The mixture sent a message.

The mixed (and balanced) composition of the staff remained important.[16] In 1894 Hart could boast that the 'cosmopolitan' senior staff at the Inspectorate included a Russian, German, Dane and a Frenchman.[17] In 1880 he noted that 'Russia begins to notice that there are many Russian merchants and no Russian Customs' employees, and I must get out of the difficulty this is preparing me for before the trap snaps'. '*[S]o, look alive*', he continued to J.D. Campbell in London, and find three Russians '*as quickly as possible.*'[18] In 1889 Hart ventured that there should be no British appointments for the next two years.[19] 'I want three Russians and *two* Germans' he wrote in a routine 1896 letter to Campbell.[20] Delay in despatch, he reported the following year, 'has caused some friction at the Russian Legation'.[21] By 1903 he declared the British position 'no longer what it was', but even so, half of the stations were run by Britons.[22] Hart took the initiative as much as possible, 'I prefer the men we select, and without them, have to take Legation candidates when the "balance of power" demands additions'.[23]

The balance of nationalities was a sop to great power rivalry and self-importance – and not just great powers: by 1937, 256 Norwegians had served or were still serving in the CMCS.[24] It also prevented it seeming too much a British service in Chinese eyes. The Service also defended itself as a Chinese govern-ment agency from outside pressures, and it made a virtue of transparency from the start by always publishing the nationality, and latterly the Chinese home province, as part of men's basic service details in the annual *Service List*. This multinational character was, for Hart, a key part in keeping the Customs inde-pendent. National favouritism was a regular complaint amongst personnel, but mostly amongst British personnel who felt that the balancing of national inter-ests cut across the disinterested assessment of individual talents and experience, and service requirements.

Japan joins the Customs world

The Japanese 'trap', as it were, snapped in February 1899 and Hart was wholly unprepared. 'Yesterday I felt very like throwing up and bolting: the Japs came and asked me to appoint a certain Japanese official to be *Commissioner at Amoy* right off! I said I could employ some Japs as *4th Assts.*, but could not at this date appoint *Commissioners.*'[25] A fourth assistant – the entry-level position into the 'indoor' staff – is what they got, with the appointment of Kurosawa Reikichi to the Amoy Customs.[26] Hart's letters show little interest in the Japanese factor, which for him, as for others, was overshadowed by German and Russian advances in China. Others were a little more alert. The earliest discussion of Japanese ambitions for overall control of the Customs appears to have come in some July 1899 rumours set off by W.V. Drummond, acting British Crown Advocate in Shanghai, and discussed by G.E. Morrison.[27] The introduction of the Japanese factor into the Customs caused pressure in three areas as calls grew for exclusive or dominant representation in designated ports (Japanese colonial acquisitions such as the Kwantung leased territory (Dalian), and Qingdao (held 1915–22), at Manchurian ports, and at Shanghai), for greater Japanese represen-tation amongst staff generally; and for greater representation of Japanese at senior levels (as Commissioners, Secretaries, and latterly the Inspector-Generalship).

Two further fundamental issues arising out of the Sino-Japanese War dislo-cated the Service. First there was the loss of revenue. Tainan and Keelung Customs stations were lost to Service control. Hart described the losses as 'crippling': in terms of revenue loss, and the concomitant decrease in the Office allowance which paid for the upkeep of the Service.[28] The combined loss in revenues of the two ports represented 4.95 per cent of total revenues of *c*.22 million Haiguan Taels at 1893 levels. This was significant enough, although the opening of new ports by 1899 saw revenues grow to 27 million Taels per annum, and the loss of the allowance was made up as early as 1896.[29] The second issue was the impact of new indemnities and loans on Customs practice and perceptions of its role. There was a loss of Qing government autonomy as revenues were used or pledged to serve the loans raised to pay the war indemnity imposed by the Treaty of Shimonoseki. At issue here were both the use of the Customs revenue as guarantee for the loans, and the recourse to the administration of the Customs Service itself as a factor in the loans – for example, the stipulation in the 1896 Anglo-German Second Indemnity Loan that 'the administration of the Imperial Maritime Customs of China shall continue as at present constituted during the currency of this loan'. Other loan palavers constantly revolved around reassigning control of the Service in some form to the French, the Russians or the Germans.[30] The British felt they brought this to an end with the extraction of a promise that the IG-ship would remain in the hands of a Briton as long as British trade predominated.[31]

Turning now to the impact of Sino-Japanese developments on the running of the Service itself, there were four stages in this development, but an underlying issue was the establishment of an exclusively German-staffed office of the Maritime Customs at the German naval port of Qingdao in 1899.[32] Over the next decade Russian and Japanese advances in Manchuria saw similar exclusive positions demanded at Lüshun (Port Arthur)/Dalian both basically on the Qingdao model. The 1907 Dalian Agreement, which opened the station in the Japanese Kwantung Leased Territory, used identical text in key clauses, with relevant substitutions.[33] One important issue in these agreements was control over the appointments. At Qingdao the Germans secured a veto – specifically that 'the Inspector General of Customs will come to an understanding with the German Legation in case of appointing a new Commissioner' – feeling a need to choose from the Germans on the established Customs staff who might be appointed. All other European staff were 'as a rule' to be German.[34]

The veto was used. Hart reported, for example, that in 1904 Germany did 'not want either' Gustav Detring or Ernst Ohlmer to be appointed to the station (the former possibly because of his close working relationship with Li Hongzhang).[35] The 1915 Qingdao Customs agreement replaced German privileges with Japanese ones – literally; the 1915 Agreement which Hart and Japanese Minister Hioki negotiated specified that the 1899 Sino-German agreement should be held to stay in force, subject to 'the replacement of the term "German" by "Japanese" wherever the principle of this Agreement demands such change'.[36] The situation had the potential to promote considerable tensions of empire loyalty within the treaty port communities, with prominent Britons, or Germans, French, or Japanese, working in the service of a power many of their peers treated as a colonised state, or latterly an enemy state.

Commissioner Tachibana Masaki's experiences at Qingdao highlight the difficulties. He reopened the Chinese Customs in September 1915, taking over from the Japanese military which still administered the former colony. In June 1916 he outlined various tensions that had developed with the Japanese community, and fault lines in the relationship between Japanese Customs staff and the military administration. The community, he wrote, comprised:

> ... a good number of petty traders, a greater number of those who failed in business in Japan, Formosa, Korea, and Manchuria, and also of a sort of adventurers who have flocked here since the commencement of the siege dreaming to make a large fortune.

Their cosy, sometimes, corrupt relations with the Japanese military customs had been queered by Tachibana, so that they looked at the Customs as 'their mortal foe', and plots of violence against the Commissioner and his staff, including Kishimoto Hirokichi, had been widely discussed. There was also pressure on Tachibana for the Customs to subscribe officially to the forthcoming coronation celebrations, and to decorate the office with Japanese flags and national emblems. 'A cry of non-national was raised' against him when he demurred.[37] The intimidation was directed at long-standing Service employees like him, rather than the more recent local Japanese appointments. Some new 'outdoor' staff had come straight from the Yokohama Customs, and found themselves already thereby connected to figures in the Japanese administration, and such ties threatened to affect their work.[38] The 'outdoor' men were also often men of compromised social standing (formerly subordinates of Japanese administration officials for example), and overall it proved 'very hard' to 'cause their full self-awakening to their true position, that is, that they are the employees of nothing but the Chinese Customs'.[39] Some seemed to act as if they were on secondment from the Japanese state, or acted 'like conquerors', 'dreaming of a strong backing from the Tokyo Finance Department'. And if all of this was not difficult enough, Tachibana's loyalty was assailed from the Chinese side, with later accusations that the Customs staff were 'mere puppets of the Japanese authorities'.[40] Tachibana's career advancement of course depended on his satisfactory performance as a Chinese Customs official, but there was much more to the anxieties he displayed than the mere restating of his credentials and of his credibility as a Customs man. The complex world of the treaty ports presented individuals with many such conflicting calls on their loyalties.

The Japanese in the Customs

Kurosawa Reikichi's appointment in 1899 presaged a modest development in numbers of Japanese in the Service (see Table 3.1). Another two were appointed that year. The recruits of 1905 were appointed to stations all over China, but the mass influx of 1907 was primarily for Dalian (thirty-four of the appointments). With one exception the men appointed before 1907 had been 'indoor' staff. In 1907

Table 3.1 Recruitment of Customs Japanese staff, 1899–1931

Year	No.	Year	No.	Year	No.
1899	3	1910	6	1921	18
1900	2	1911	9	1922	18
1901	1	1912	7	1923	12
1902	0	1913	13	1924	13
1903	5	1914	6	1925	11
1904	1	1915	66	1926	11
1905	9	1916	37	1927	2
1906	2	1917	19	1928	6
1907	42	1918	9	1929	5
1908	10	1919	7	1930	2
1909	11	1920	11	1931	8

Source: *China Maritime Customs Service List*, 1899–1931 (Shanghai: Statistical Department of the Inspectorate General).

twenty-three were Tidewaiters, and twelve were Watchers – all appointed to Dalian. The infusion of lower-grade Japanese staff was a significant development. The Japanese component reached a good size quite swiftly. By 1911 there were on the 'indoor' staff: thirty-two Japanese, compared to thirty-one French, fifteen Americans, fourteen Russians, thirty-eight Germans (who would all be gone by the end of 1917), and 152 Britons.[41] Another forty-nine Japanese served on the 'outdoor' staff. There was little overall impact on Customs culture and practice, but the politics and changes caused by the Russo-Japanese War had begun to make an issue out of Japanese representation. Kurosawa, 'the best man in my office here' for Hart in 1904, was fast-tracked to acting Deputy Commissioner that year and appointed to Niuzhuang in August – as the Japanese army had just occupied the city.[42] However, Japanese, like German diplomats or colonial authorities, did not overlook the fact that such fellow nationals were employees of a foreign government. The Japanese military authorities turfed him out in favour of their own man. In July 1907 he opened Dalian.[43] Japanese staff served two political purposes for the Customs: they apparently kept the Legation happy ('the Japanese are quite proud of having a Commissioner' Hart told Campbell in 1907, after Kurosawa was appointed to Dalian[44]), and it was hoped that they might ease local pressures in times of conflict, for example in just-occupied Niuzhuang, or at Qingdao in 1915–17.

In the second stage, during the First World War, as a result of the Japanese displacement of German authority in Qingdao, and because of shortages caused by European volunteering and recruitment, a greater number of Japanese personnel were introduced. The Japanese Legation and foreign ministry were involved in nominating candidates, and persuading men to accept the positions.[45] The IG Sir Francis Aglen appealed to Sir John Jordan not to 'unbalance' the Customs through military recruitment of British staff, and Sir John himself noted that the CMCS 'was largely a British interest in China' and promised not to upset it.[46] But like many other 'British interests' the personnel crisis was a problem, as might be its logical solutions (increased recruitment of Chinese ..., or for example, of Japanese) – in Shanghai, for example, the International Settlement police force recruited Japanese officers for the first time in 1915.[47]

British merchants and consuls complained about this, while Japanese chambers of commerce agitated in 1917 and 1918 for appointment of Japanese as Commissioners in routine Customs posts. The argument used was to become a familiar one: Japanese trading interests were now predominant locally. The 1898 undertaking about the IG-ship should logically apply in the localities. Niuzhuang and Andong should therefore have Japanese commissioners. The British disputed the figures, averred that if they were accurate then this was due to war conditions or other contingent disadvantages British traders were labouring under, and fell back on the need to avoid 'dislocating the whole Customs Administration'.[48] The Japanese Legation had broached the subject with Sir Francis Aglen in 1917, to no avail. C.A.V. Bowra, the acting IG in 1918, thought the whole idea of parcelling out posts on such lines preposterous and potentially crippling to the system. Moreover, the Japanese already had a privileged position in Dalian, and now – until 1922 – in Qingdao.[49]

A third stage developed after 1926 when a concerted diplomatic effort was made to introduce more Japanese personnel into the Service. Pressure was maintained on the Service to recruit more Japanese, and to forward the careers of Japanese staff. As Japan's representative in China, Yoshizawa Kenkichi, put it to the Officiating IG (OIG), A.H.F. Edwardes, that year:

> owing to the striking development of the Sino-Japanese trade of late years the services of able Customs officials, who are thoroughly conversant with the Japanese language and merchandise, have become, as you might perhaps be aware, so imperative to Japanese traders, that I am constantly demanded to see my way to effect in some or other realisation of putting efficient Japanese in the Customs Service at least in such ports of China as where our trade is mostly concerned.[50]

There was a further context: an internal power struggle, and the Nationalist revolution. Edwardes, and his rival Frederick Maze, both needed external support for their claims to the position, and both courted the Japanese. At Yoshizawa's request an examination was held in Tokyo in autumn 1926 to select candidates. 'Without the least pretension of trespassing on the authority of the IG in this matter', continued Yoshizawa:

> may I be permitted to take this opportunity of expressing on behalf of our trading interests in China our sincere desire that the future vacancies in the Customs service might as far as possible be allocated to Japanese candidates after taking due account of the proportionally great amount of trade in China.[51]

There were plenty of recruits – 276 men applied for the six positions.[52]

The issue began to switch, however, from overall representation almost wholly to specific posts: a DC at Harbin was requested (July 1927), a Commissioner at Wenzhou was offered ('we'd rather have a DC at Shanghai', said the Japanese Consulate there).[53] In 1927 foreign recruitment was suspended, and in

1929 ended completely (except for contract technical staff), and the principle of equality was also introduced into staff administration, breaking down the Chinese/foreign staff divide.[54] Although this cut short the issue of overall recruitment it threw the focus on location and seniority. In the treaty port administrations this continued to be driven by the numbers as well: the Shanghai Military Police had 200 Japanese police by 1930, and 250 five years later – this, combined with the relative size of the Japanese community there, led to growing demands for the allocation of more responsible positions to Japanese staff.[55]

The Customs context in 1927–28 was of course Aglen's dismissal, and the struggle for control between the OIG, Edwardes, backed by the British Legation, and Shanghai Commissioner Frederick Maze, who was backed by the Guomindang. As the British minister, Sir Miles Lampson, put it in October 1927, 'Japanese whole-hearted support is essential to save the Customs Administration'. He continued: 'to secure that support we have to pay a price, and all we can do is to keep that price sufficiently low to enable us still to draw a dividend on our original investment'. In London they were a little more phlegmatic. Out of forty-five stations there were only six with Japanese Commissioners, so 'It is no wonder if the Japanese press for increased representation'. 'If we want Japan's "wholehearted support"', minuted diplomat Frank Ashton-Gwatkin, 'they will probably have to be given a rather larger share in the high posts.'[56]

This was a portable bargaining chip: with Maze installed the Japanese minister was not slow to press on him the need to appease Japanese interests (and Maze was not the type to risk alienating any potential supporters). Japanese foreign ministry officials were apparently 'astonished' to find in October 1929 that training and advancement of Japanese appraisers and assistants was not developing more quickly, and pressed for intensification of such efforts.[57] At this stage there were no worries about loyalty: Edwardes, when OIG, told the Foreign Office that Japanese employees were 'on the whole very admirable and satisfactory both in their work and their attitudes [and] that they keep clear of all political issues and intrigues'.[58] Increased recruitment of Japanese was not a concern as long as the IG was British.

That last point of course slowly became an issue. In January 1928, with Zhang Zuolin still dominating Beijing, Lampson met Yoshizawa to resolve a misunderstanding over the probable future role of Kishimoto Hirokichi. Kishimoto, with twenty-two years in the Service, had first been appointed Chief Secretary in February 1927.[59] Yoshizawa's understanding of discussions that month, was that Lampson had recognised that with this position – seen as a Deputy IG post although the position itself had been unfilled since 1911 – Kishimoto was next in line and the logical successor to the Inspector-Generalship.[60] This was not at all Lampson's position. He had not intended to give any such impression. '[T]he Customs had been built up by British effort', he reminded his colleague, 'and was organised upon purely British lines, behind it lay British tradition, and I did not believe it would continue to function efficiently and satisfactorily under any but a British head.' This was 'plain fact'. Misunderstanding aside, Yoshizawa spoke plainly too. A number two in the Service was a number two, and if number one went he should move up. There were other issues: more Japanese recruits should be recruited overall, and a Japanese Deputy Commissioner appointed at Shanghai. They agreed to differ. They needed a note and Yoshizawa wrote one: Lampson 'insisting that a British subject will be Inspector-General for ever', Yoshizawa disagreeing. 'Fortunately' the issue did not arise, and both agreed on the need to back Edwardes.[61]

The long-term context of this was the British government's extraction in 1898 of the undertaking that the IG-ship would remain in the hands of a Briton as long as British trade predominated.[62] The spur to action had been the need to outmanoeuvre Russian attempts to tie control of the Customs to loan negotiations.[63] The issue was apparently initially raised by the Foreign Office in May 1897 'as there was reason to expect an attempt to appoint some foreigner'.[64] The bewildering array of negotiations and agreements over loans and indemnities from 1894–1905 saw much by way of airy proposals to redraw the Customs map or overthrow its structure by way of seeking additional security by installing multinational boards of control, or different nationals at the top. Little actually came of this, but for Hart, looking back in 1903, the 1898 agreement 'called too much attention to the post, and gave it a political character that I had always divested it of, and the intrigues for Boards, etc., have been the result'.[65] But justifications for Britons to succeed to the post changed over the years, and an emphasis came instead to be placed on the 'British' nature of the Service, its working practices, and the predominance of the English language. Trade predominance was, naturally, a hostage to the changing fortunes of British enterprise in China, and the logic could propel a Japanese candidate to the fore. In the meantime Japanese diplomats were not alone in suggesting that other senior posts should be allotted to specific nationals.

Hart initially welcomed the Chinese commitment in 1898, but thought it:

> a pity the Legation touched the question thus for every other Legation has a precedent and an opening: they can say 'all right – let your I.G. always be British!' But we demand that the Commissioner at Shanghai shall always be French – or at Tientsin German – or at Hankow Russian ... or that there shall be such and such a Deputy I.G. etc., etc.[66]

And so they did. British merchants called for a British Commissioner in Shanghai in 1903.[67] The Japanese demanded a Japanese Commissioner for Niuzhuang in December 1904.[68] In 1906–07, and in 1911, there were moves to suggest that a German should be appointed DIG.[69] Clarity on the issue was not helped by the fact that British diplomats in China and in London conducted two campaigns to prevent British individuals becoming IG. They successfully obstructed the appointment of Sir Robert Bredon, Hart's son-in-law, in 1903, and in 1907–10, although they failed in the second case to prevent the appointment of Sir Frederick Maze, Hart's nephew, instead of Arthur Edwardes.[70] Hart's complaints about the Foreign Office position were disingenuous – he had after all briefly accepted the position of British Minister to China in 1885, but turned it down stating that as IG he could 'be most useful to England and certainly to China'.[71] He knew how politicised the IG-ship was well before 1898.

By 1929 again Hirokichi had already held reasonably senior positions. His confirmation as Chief Secretary was raised as an issue in 1928–29 in private discussions between Maze and the Japanese Minister in Shanghai. At this stage Yoshizawa suggested, with apparent foreign ministry support, that if he secured that post there would be no pressure for a Japanese IG. Maze suggested that he needed substantive experience as a commissioner at a large port before such a promotion could be secured. Yoshizawa got this in writing. Kishimoto served again as Chief Secretary from 1 April 1931 onwards.[72] The position of the Japanese staff thereafter was complicated by the developing military assault on China. There were 206 Japanese staff on 1 July 1931, but only 86 two years later. The invasion of Manchuria, and the detachment of the Manchurian Customs stations with all but one of their Japanese staff, gutted the Service's complement. As Table 3.2 shows, no Japanese were recruited at all for three years, and twenty only in the years 1932–36. Although no new permanent foreign staff were being appointed, significant numbers of contract employees, especially marine staff, were still being taken on. The conflict also politicised routine staff transfers of Japanese, but this issue came into its own and dominated discussions after the outbreak of full-scale warfare in July 1937.

As Japanese forces advanced after the Shanghai campaign, and secured new ports, they moved to rehabilitate and re-open them to trade. Over the next four years Maze was presented with request after request and demand after demand. A 21 May 1938 memorandum from the Japanese consul-general in Shanghai sets the scene:

> it is highly desired that the Inspector General of Customs would first of all realise the urgent necessity of increasing Japanese staff in the customs service. Therefore, the Japanese Consul General proposes that the Customs Authority will quickly act to recruit at least 22 Examiners and 40 Tide-Waiters. These new officials must be appointed as permanent employees of the Customs for the following reasons; firstly, some of them may be transferred, when circumstances permit, to other ports in China where the necessity of employing Japanese staff [is] generally recognised, and secondly, qualified persons cannot be successfully recruited unless their positions are secured permanently.[73]

Table 3.2 Recruitment of Customs Japanese staff, 1932–44

1932	4	1937	13	1941	68
1933	0	1938	269	1942	207
1934	0	1939	200	1943	179
1935	0	1940	72	1944*	76
1936	16				

Source: *China Maritime Customs Service List*, 1832–1944 (Shanghai: Statistical Department of the Inspectorate General).

Note
* January–July only available. No details are available for recruitment in 1945.

The de facto power fished for bigger fry as well. In July 1938 the Japanese demanded the Xiamen Commissionership, in November they demanded the Statistical and Tariff Secretaryships, in January 1939 they suggested replacing the present Customs Revenue Guards in Shanghai with 100 collaborationist personnel, in March 1939 as Qiongzhou was now under Japanese control the Embassy demanded that a commissioner, an assistant, a tide-surveyor, an examiner and six tide-waiters be appointed from existing Japanese Customs staff, and that replacements be recruited to the Service to replace the men transferred.

As routine staff turnover opened up positions, the notes from the Japanese embassy became routine, and as well as demanding specific positions, they proposed named individuals from outside the Customs, often men with Japanese navy or consular experience, and always they demanded that as staff were transferred new Japanese appointments be added to replace them at their present posts.[74] Maze would counter-offer, relying on the pool of pre-1937 staff as more 'reliable' in Service terms, and on that 'loyalty' demonstrated by Tachibana in 1916 and by others. More fundamentally Maze also worried that the puppet regime would seek to formally control the Service, through engineering his 'dismissal' (by them) and 'replacement' by their own man. A precedent for this had been set by Manchukuo's appointment of Fukumoto Jinzaburō to the post of Dalian Commissioner in September 1932 (although in that case Fukumoto was already the Maze-appointed Commissioner). The Chinese government could hardly willingly acquiesce in the appointment of enemy nationals to positions in its own civil service, but recognised the difficulty of Maze's position, and informally supported his tactics.[75] Maze sought British and other diplomatic support as he resisted Japanese pressure, but over 612 Japanese were in fact appointed between the end of 1937 and Pearl Harbor.

The old guard was still there though, and Kishimoto got his promotion to the top job after all. Maze and the entire Customs senior staff were still based in Shanghai when the Pacific War broke out. He was formally 'dismissed' from his post by the collaborationist Wang Jingwei government, and replaced by Kishimoto on 11 December 1941. To all intents and purposes Kishimoto ran the legitimate Chinese Maritime Customs Service under the direction of the Wang Jingwei regime. It remained the foreign-administered Customs, though it was being run by senior Japanese, not British, administrators. Kishimoto's service recruited an additional 400 Japanese into the Customs between December 1941 and July 1944, who joined the 640 already in the Service at Pearl Harbor. At the end of the conflict they were paid off and sent packing. Unlike the German and Austrian staff in 1917, their withdrawals from the Service were not recorded in the *Service List*. Their service was expunged from the Customs record.

It is worth stressing that although senior outsiders were appointed, part of the core Japanese leadership consisted of Customs men, thoroughly immersed in its traditions and ethos. They might have been glad to see the back of the British, but there was probably much more ambivalence overall. Like many of their British counterparts these men had multiple calls on their loyalty: the Service itself, the Japanese state, notions of Japanese empire or imperial mission more broadly, and perhaps more parochially as members of, or participants in, Japanese treaty port China. In this they were very much like the treaty-port British, and it is easy to forget this.[76] Maze argued that his appointment of Akatani Yusuke as Shanghai Commissioner of Customs in November 1941 was a safe one, as Akatani 'had always been regarded as an efficient and loyal employee' of thirty-years' Customs standing, and that his retirement in 1942 was on account of his being suspected of being 'pro-Chinese'.[77]

Three Japanese servants of the Chinese Customs

Individual case studies offer further glimpses of the complexities of the position of Japanese in the Service. In a 1929 letter to Frederick Maze former Commissioner Kurosawa Reikichi, who had left under a cloud in 1919, made it clear that he made his family in Tokyo begin each day with a collective bow towards a photograph of Sir Robert Hart. 'The grateful memory of Sir Robert', he noted, 'has become a religion in my family.'[78] This might be a little extreme, but it was not much more an expression of the cult of Hart (contested to be sure) than the IG quietly cultivated, and which was perpetuated by his successors. Hart's photograph was ordered to be installed in each Commissioner's office in 1913, and was not replaced until 1942 with Sun Yatsen, while Aglen oversaw indirectly the installation of the Hart statue on Shanghai's Bund.[79] Maze referred incessantly to Hart. The cult of Hart was nurtured by the sense of loyalty to the Service that was instilled in all employees foreign and Chinese. Kurosawa exhibited that same Service loyalty, despite the unfortunate termination of his own career.

Fukumoto Jinzaburō had joined the Service in 1904. In 1931 he was appointed to Dalian. On 24 June 1932 he was dismissed for refusing to remit the Customs revenue to Shanghai. Two days later all but one of the sixty-two Japanese Customs staff at Dalian resigned, ostensibly in protest, and with Fukumoto formed a branch of the Manchukuo Customs operating in the leased territory. Fukumoto was damned in the official report on the 'Seizure of the Dalian Customs', circulated to Customs Commissioners and published in 1939.[80] However, this report concentrated on events following the resignation. An unpublished report throws more light on the predicament of Japanese personnel. Fukumoto was under great pressure. His attempts earlier in 1932 to head off a Manchukuo seizure by encouraging the new authorities to consider compromise arrangements with the National government – sincere, utterly unrealistic as they might seem in retrospect – left him 'in bad odour with his compatriots, who regarded him as a disloyal Japanese, and it affected his social relations with them'.[81] He told the IG that his interest lay in the 'prevention of interference with Customs integrity and the substitution of reasoned negotiations for arbitrary confiscation'.[82] But even this looked like treason to his fellow nationals. He told the senior British employee at the station, J.V. Porter, that if he did not accede to Manchukuo demands – and he felt that the de facto authority had its rights – then they would just bypass the Customs station and establish their own. If he did accede and then returned to China instead of joining the Manchukuo establishment, then he really feared for his life. Conversely, however, Porter also reported that Fukumoto also fully supported, personally, the Manchurian demarche.

Yoshida Gorō did not. He was also at Dalian and was the one Japanese who did not resign from the Service. 'George' Yoshida joined in 1915 as a Fourth Assistant, B, the standard 'indoor' staff entry point, and had risen to First Assistant by 1932. Yoshida still stayed on after the June 1932 demarche but in late February 1933 resigned from the Manchukuo Customs and later made his way to Shanghai where he was formally reinstated in the Chinese Service. His non-defection was prominent and newsworthy at the time. In 1942 he was compulsorily 'permitted to retire' at the insistence, he later wrote, of the commandant of the Japanese gendarmerie in Shanghai.[83] In April 1947 he wrote from Tokyo to L.K. Little, who had become IG in 1943, asking Little to allow him to rejoin the Customs as a special case, or, if that was impossible, to recommend him for employment with the occupation authorities. He was, he wrote, a 'loyal Japanese', that is loyal to the Customs and to his Chinese employers, and had opposed 'Tojo and his mad clique'. Little happily obliged with the recommendations, but re-employment with the Customs was impossible.[84]

Fukumoto's position accords with that of loyal imperial Britons in the Customs Service, men such as A.E. Hippisley, or J.O.P. Bland. They pledged allegiance to the Service, but they were also mostly and routinely loyal to the states to whose laws they were still subject. The only tangible difference here is that Japanese subjects were the only foreign employees ever really faced with the need to choose between the Service and their flag. More of them chose as Fukumoto had chosen, than as Yoshida did, but clearly it was not a position many relished finding themselves in. That was their predicament and tragedy. Kishimoto himself was perhaps in a different position. As the senior Japanese officer in the Service he was the focus of greater pressure. It is clear that he acted from early on in the 1920s as a conduit for communications between the Japanese Legation and foreign ministry. He talked with the minister; he talked with the ministry in Tokyo. That can hardly be surprising, and was part of the point of placing such men in senior positions. Senior customs officials had often made use of their Legation links to propel their own careers, but they were also potentially under pressure – of their loyalty as British, German or Japanese subjects, of their own ideological leanings, and they were sometimes under real threat, or felt that they were. The difference lay in the fact of Japanese ascendancy in China.

Conclusion

Although the new imperialism of the 1890s fundamentally disturbed the balance of power and character of foreign interaction in China, the shock of the Boxer War, and then the Russo-Japanese War, restored some sense to the situation. Imperialist ambitions in China seemed to have been reined in. For the Customs the arrival of the Japanese seemed at first normal. They were, for example, slotted into the existing balance of power games that Hart played with the composition of his staff. German particularities at Qingdao were adopted for the Japanese position at Dalian. Japanese Customs staff were considered traitors by some fellow nationals, just as British staff were in the early years of the Service. At the same time socialising and networking with fellow nations was as much a feature of the Japanese Customs experience as it was for the British or the Americans. But a key difference did develop, in that the Japanese role in the Customs grew as Japan's power in China was aggressively expanded. However normal Japanese behaviour was, however much, for example, Commissioner Tachibana worked to impress upon the Japanese in Qingdao (and in his staff) that the 'Customs is a Chinese not a Japanese institution', their loyalty to their foreign employer was constantly compromised by the actions of the Japanese military.[85]

The Manchukuo Customs episode finally demonstrated to the Service, and to its superiors in the Ministry of Finance, that the era of the apolitical world of Customs work was finally over. Although the Service had always been the site of international tensions, it had not previously been the case that an entire cohort of nationals had defected en masse. Senior French staff were sent on emergency leave in 1884.[86] In 1917 all German and Austrian nationals had been dismissed when China entered the war on the allied side. But in the early 1920s the Ministry of Finance and the Service had worked to ameliorate the plight of these loyal employees. The Manchukuo Customs defection marked, more than any single episode, the point at which the foreign character of the Service had truly become a liability. And here the issue was not restricted to the Japanese staff. The man who accepted the position of Adviser to the Manchukuo Customs, and who spent the next nine years lobbying British industry and government on behalf of Japan, was A.H.F. Edwardes, formerly OIG of the Service, and a Briton.[87]

In the twentieth century the British position in the Customs was degraded by the growth of the Japanese component in the Service, and in particular by the systematic politicisation of Customs appointments after the mid-1920s. But its character was also undermined by the reforms introduced by Maze, by the Sinicization of the Customs after 1929 in the face of triumphant Chinese nationalism, by tariff autonomy, and by the consolidation of National Government control over the Service, which was brought much more fully to heel under Chinese Ministry of Finance control under Maze than ever before. In fact Japanese pressure prolonged nominal British dominance: Maze stayed in command of the Service longer than might have been the case. He reached sixty in 1934 and should have retired at that point, but the Japanese invasion of Manchuria and the resulting acceleration of Japanese demands on the Customs meant that it was easier for the Nationalist government to have him stay on, than to open up the position for any successor. Overall, the British found their Customs hegemony undermined by Japanese competitors who sought the same privileges within the Service, and argued for a share of the Customs staff and of senior positions using arguments that the British had themselves originated in 1898. As Hart had predicted, no good was to come out of the claim for a British national to hold the IG post as long as British trade predominated. British trade did not long predominate. It did, however, devise new strategies for operating in China after the victory of the nationalists, and making an issue of the Customs became unnecessary.

For the pre-1937 Japanese personnel of the Customs, as for the Japanese of treaty port China more generally, the Pacific War was a complete disaster. Their participation as individuals in the internationalised world of the treaty ports was undermined by the arrival in China of the Japanese state in the shape of the military, which bagged up allied and other treaty port assets, and destabilised the existing state of affairs. It was further undermined by the wartime diplomacy which necessitated the handing to formal (collaborationist) Chinese control of the institutions underpinning that world – the Shanghai Municipal Council for example, retroceded to Chinese control from 1 August 1943. Japanese businessmen and treaty port residents no more wanted municipal affairs in Shanghai run by Chinese administrators than did British Shanghailanders, or German residents. The Japanese world of the Chinese Maritime Customs highlights the complexities and contradictions of the treaty port world in China. The examples of Tachibana, Kishimoto, Kurosawa, Yoshida and Fukumoto show how impossible it is to stereotype Japanese actors, and how wide the range of motives and loyalties was that operated even among Japanese members of the Chinese Maritime Customs Service.

Notes

1 For surveys see Robert Bickers, *Britain in China: Community, Culture and Colonialism, 1900–49*, Manchester: Manchester University Press, 1999; Jürgen Osterhammel, 'Britain and China 1842–1914', in Andrew Porter (ed.), *The Oxford History of the British Empire, vol. 3: The Nineteenth Century*, Oxford: OUP, 1999, pp. 146–69; and 'China', in Judith M. Brown, and Wm Roger Louis (eds), *The Oxford History of the British Empire, vol. 4: The Twentieth Century*, Oxford: OUP, 1999, pp. 643–66.
2 Richard J. Aldrich, *Intelligence and the War against Japan: Britain, America and the Politics of Secret Service*, Cambridge: Cambridge University Press, 2000; and Antony Best, *British Intelligence and the Japanese Challenge in Asia, 1914–1941*, Basingstoke: Palgrave/Macmillan, 2002.
3 The National Archives, Kew (TNA), FO371/31622, F7765/828/10 Brenan minute, 18 November 1942, on Seymour to FO, 14 November 1942 no. 1551.
4 J.E. Hoare, *Embassies in the East: The Story of the British Embassies in Japan, China and Korea from 1859 to the Present*, Richmond: Curzon, 1999; and P.D. Coates, *The China Consuls: British Consular Officers, 1843–1943*, Hong Kong: OUP, 1988.
5 See, for example, James L. Hevia, *English Lessons: The Pedogogy of Imperialism in Nineteenth-Century China*, Durham, NC: Duke University Press. 2003; Lydia Liu, *the Clash of Empires: The Invention of China in Modern World Making*, Cambridge, MA: Harvard University Press, 2004; and Norman Girardot, *The Victorian Translation of China: James Legge's Oriental Pilgrimage*, Berkeley: University of California Press, 2002.
6 Barbara Mittler, *A Newspaper for China?: Power, Identity and Change in Shanghai's News Media (1872–1912)*, Cambridge, MA: Harvard University Press, 2004; and Rudolf G. Wagner, 'The Shenbao in Crisis: The International Environment and the Conflict Between Guo Songtao and the Shenbao', *Late Imperial China* 20:1 (1999), pp. 107–43.

7 Richard W. Rigby, *The May 30 Movement: Events and Themes*, Folkestone: Dawson, 1980; Nicholas R. Clifford, *Spoilt Children of Empire: Westerners in Shanghai and the Chinese Revolution of the 1920s*, Hanover, NE: Middlebury College Press, 1991; and Robert Bickers, *Empire Made Me: An Englishman Adrift in Shanghai*, London: Allen Lane, 2003. On the Mixed Court riot see Bryna Goodman, *Native Place, City and Nation: Regional Networks and Identities in Shanghai, 1853–1937*, Berkeley: University of California Press, 1995, pp. 187–95.

8 Judith Wyman, 'The Ambiguities of Chinese Antiforeignism: Chongqing, 1870–1900', *Late Imperial China*, 18:2 (1997), pp. 86–122; and Anne Reinhardt, 'Navigating Imperialism in China: Steamship, Semicolony, and Nation, 1860–1937' (unpublished PhD thesis, Princeton University, 2002).

9 Jürgen Osterhammel, 'Imperialism in Transition: British Business and the Chinese Authorities, 1931–1937', *China Quarterly*, 98 (1984), pp. 260–86.

10 *Documents Illustrative of the Origin, Development and Activities of the Chinese Customs Service* (Shanghai: Statistical Department of the Inspectorate General of Customs, 7 volumes, 1936–40), hereafter *Documents Illustrative*), vol. I, p. 37.

11 Three good introductory surveys: Thomas P. Lyons, *China Maritime Customs and China's Trade Statistics 1859–1948*, Trumansberg: Willow Creek Press, 2003; S.F. Wright, *The Origin and Development of the Chinese Customs Service, 1843–1911: An Historical Outline*, Shanghai: privately printed, 1939; and L.K. Little, 'Introduction', to John King Fairbank, Katherine Frost Bruner and Elizabeth Matheson (eds), *The I.G. in Peking: Letters of Robert Hart, Chinese Maritime Customs, 1868–1907*, 2 vols, Cambridge, MA: Harvard University Press, 1975, vol. 1, pp. 1–34.

12 Wright, *Origin and Development*, pp. 46–7.

13 Arnold Wright (ed.), *Twentieth Century Impressions of Hong Kong, Shanghai and Other Treaty Ports of China*, London: Lloyds, 1908, preface.

14 A list of the Commissioners, Deputy Commissioners, 30 June 1873, Enclosure 2 in Circular 20, 1873, 1 December 1873, *Inspector General's Circulars. First Series: 1861–1875*, Shanghai, Statistical Department of the Inspectorate General, 1879, pp. 468–73.

15 Figures extrapolated from a dataset of all Service-listed Customs careers compiled from Customs Service Lists, 1854–1948.

16 Cf. Campbell to Hart, 24 April 1896, in Chen Xiafei and Han Rongfang (eds), *Archives of China's Imperial Maritime Customs: Confidential Correspondence between Robert Hart and James Duncan Campbell 1874–1907*, four vols, Beijing: Foreign Languages Press, 1990, vol. III, letter 2482, on the composition of staff accompanying Li Hongzhang's mission. This edition of the Hart–Campbell correspondence contains Campbell's side of the correspondence, as well as other additional materials.

17 *I.G. in Peking*, letter 946, 30 September 1894.

18 *I.G. in Peking*, letter 309, 14 December 1880.

19 *I.G. in Peking*, letter 694, 30 March 1889.

20 *I.G. in Peking*, letter 1026, Archives, 5 July 1896.

21 *I.G. in Peking*, letter 1135, 5 September 1897.

22 *I.G. in Peking*, letter 1289, 15 July 1903.

23 *I.G. in Peking*, letter 1346, 9 October 1904.

24 S. Hopstock, *Norwegian Members of the Chinese Customs Service*, Shanghai: privately printed, 1937.

25 *I.G. in Peking*, letters 1131, 1132, 12 and 26 February 1899.

26 Born in 1868, and a Methodist, Kurosawa had spent ten years in the United States (1884–94), Lo Hui-min (ed.), *The Correspondence of G.E. Morrison*, 2 vols, Cambridge: Cambridge University Press, 1976–78, vol. II, p. 345, n.2. Another Japanese employee, Sugi Ikaturo, also has a claim to be the first recruited. Appointed in March 1898 to the Education Department, as a professor at the Tongwenguan, he transferred to the mainstream indoor staff in August 1900 as 3 Assistant A. He died, however,

after a long illness in 1905 in England: NRS desp. no. 3455, 10 November 1905. See the correspondence in Second Historical Archives of China (Nanjing), Maritime Custom series [hereafter SHAC], 679(3), 1592, 'Non-Resident Secretary Despatches Nos 3446–3470'. See also NRS Despatch 3427, LO no. 61,921, 2 June 1905, in 679(3), 1591, Non-Resident Secretary Despatches Nos 3421–3445.

27 Morrison to Bland, 14 July 1899, in Lo, *Correspondence of G.E. Morrison*, vol. I, pp. 122–3.

28 *I.G. in Peking*, letter 969, 21 April 1895. His gloomy assessment was based on the proposed cession of Niuzhuang as well, which was not followed up.

29 Chinese Maritime Customs Project, Customs Revenue Dataset.

30 See *I.G. in Peking*, letter 1011, 8 March 1896. J.D. Campbell claimed to have originated this stipulation: Campbell to Hart letter 2477, 3 April 1896, Chen and Han (eds), *Archives of China's Imperial Maritime Customs*, vol. III.

31 English text in *Documents Illustrative*, vol. VI, pp. 597–8. There was less clarity, it seems, in the Chinese translation: Morrison to Chirol, 25 June 1907, in Lo (ed.), *Correspondence of G.E. Morrison*, vol. I, pp. 420–1.

32 The text is in Circular no. 894, 5 May 1899, *Documents Illustrative*, vol. II, pp. 193–212.

33 Text in *Documents Illustrative*, vol. II, pp, 575–86. The Russian negotiations are summarised in the note on p. 575.

34 Text in *Documents Illustrative*, pp, 193–212, quotation from p. 194.

35 *I.G. in Peking*, letter 1384, 8 October 1905. They accepted Ohlmer in the end.

36 Text in *Documents Illustrative*, vol. III, pp. 266–72; the agreement itself survives in: SHAC, 679(9) 1308, 'Agreement for the Re-opening of the Chinese Maritime Customs Office at Tsingtau'. The negotiations are summarised in *Documents Illustrative*, vol. VII, pp. 229–32.

37 SHAC, 679(1), 32014, 'Tsingtao s/o 1915–20', Tachibana to Aglen, 10 June 1916.

38 SHAC, 679(1), 32014, 'Tsingtao s/o 1915–20', Tachibana to Aglen, 13 September 1916.

39 SHAC, 679(1), 32014, 'Tsingtao s/o 1915–20', Tachibana to Aglen, 18 October 1916.

40 SHAC, 679(1), 32014, 'Tsingtao s/o 1915–20', Tachibana to Aglen, 20 December 1918.

41 Wright, *Origin and Development of the Chinese Customs Service*, p. 32.

42 *I.G. in Peking*, letter 1319, 28 February 1904.

43 *I.G. in Peking*, letter 1525, 15 December 1906.

44 *I.G. in Peking*, letter 1433, 17 February 1907.

45 SHAC, 679(1) 32783, 'Letters from Legations: Austria, Belgium, Chile, Denmark, France, Germany, Italy, Japan'.

46 SHAC, 679(9) 32767, 'Letters from British Legation, 1907–1917', Jordan to Aglen, 10 January 1916.

47 Thirty men joined the SMP from Tokyo that year. By 1925 there were fifty-seven, and by 1930 200, by which point they formed close to a third of the non-Chinese and non-Indian personnel.

48 TNA, FO228/3497, Peking no. 461, and enclosures, 9 October 1918.

49 Ibid. Bowra to Head, 7 October 1918.

50 SHAC, 679(1) 32783, 'Letters from Legations: Austria, Belgium, Chile, Denmark, France, Germany, Italy, Japan', Yoshizawa to Edwardes, 23 July 1926.

51 Ibid. See also: SHAC, 679(9) 15028, 'Examination in Japan of Japanese candidates for Assistantships in 1926'.

52 Ibid.

53 Various in SHAC, 679(1) 32783, 'Letters from Legations: Austria, Belgium, Chile, Denmark, France, Germany, Italy, Japan'.

54 Semi-official Circular 54, 24 February 1927, and Circular 3873, 14 March 1929, in *Documents Illustrative*, vol. IV, pp. 126–7, 174–90.

55 Bickers, *Empire Made Me*, p. 256.
56 TNA, FO288/3950, Lampson to FO, Peking no. 1159, 21 October 1927.
57 SHAC, 679(1) 'IG Confidential correspondence with Port Commissioners, 5 Jan.–Dec. 1929', Kishimoto [Tokyo] to Maze, 12 October 1929.
58 TNA, FO371/12465, F9202/630/10, Mounsey minute, 15 December 1927, on Peking no. 1159, 21 October 1927.
59 *Documents Illustrative*, vol. IV, p. 609.
60 After Bredon stepped down it was held by Aglen for a few months in 1910–11. Maze was appointed to it in December 1928, spending nine days in the post: *Documents Illustrative*, vol. IV, pp. 143–5. Ding Guitang was to be the next, and final, one in 1936.
61 TNA, FO228/3740, Lampson memorandum, 24 January 1928.
62 English text in *Documents Illustrative*, vol. VI, pp. 597–8. There was less clarity, it seems, in the Chinese translation: Morrison to Chirol, 25 June 1907, Lo (ed.), *The Correspondence of G.E. Morrison*, vol. I, pp. 420–1.
63 L.K. Young, *British Policy in China, 1895–1902*, Oxford: Clarendon, 1970, pp. 51–63.
64 TNA, FO288/3740, 5A 1928, 'British objections to Sir R. Bredon's appointment as Inspector-General of Customs', Sterndale Bennett note, 21 May 1928. This is a useful, if ultimately baffled, survey of the whole affair, prepared as a weapon in the fight against Maze. The legation was unable to pin down why the FO had turned so strongly against Bredon after having supported him in 1897.
65 *I.G. in Peking*, letter 1278, 18 April 1903.
66 *I.G. in Peking*, letter 2697, 22 May 1898.
67 Chen and Han (eds), *Archives of China's Imperial Maritime Customs*, vol. III, Campbell to Hart, letter 3144, 10 April 1903.
68 *I.G. in Peking*, letter 1354, 11 December 1904.
69 Morrison to Braham, 26 September 1911, Lo (ed.), *Correspondence of G.E. Morrison*, vol. I, p. 631.
70 TNA, FO288/3740, 5A 1928, 'British objections to Sir R. Bredon's appointment as Inspector-General of Customs', Sterndale Bennett note, 21 May 1928.
71 Telegram to Sir Julian Pauncefote, 31 August 1885, *Documents Illustrative*, vol. VII, p. 116.
72 TNA, FO 228/3741, 5A 1928, 'Customs situation and Tariff negotiations and Japanese debate, Interview with Japanese chargé re', tel. to FO, 28th December 1928; FO 228/3943, 1929 5A, Newton to Lampson, 17 April 1929.
73 SHAC, 679(1), 32781, 'Japanese embassy correspondence 1938–40, 21 May 1938', Consul General for Japan to Maze.
74 See various letters in SHAC, 679(1), 32781, 'Japanese embassy correspondence 1938–40, 21 May 1938'.
75 Of course, this issue was intertwined with arguments over the collection and disbursement of revenue: see Nicholas R. Clifford, 'Sir Frederick Maze and the Chinese Maritime Customs, 1937–1941', *Journal of Modern History*, 37:1 (1965), pp. 18–34.
76 On the Japanese in Shanghai see Joshua A. Fogel, ' "Shanghai–Japan": The Japanese Residents' Association of Shanghai', *Journal of Asian Studies*, 59/4 (2000), pp. 927–50; and Christian Henriot, ' "Little Japan" in Shanghai: An Insulated Community (1875–1945)', in Robert Bickers and Christian Henriot (eds), *New Frontiers: Imperialism's New Communities in East Asia 1842–1952* (Manchester: Manchester University Press, 2000), pp. 146–69; on the British see Robert Bickers, 'Shanghailanders: The Formation and Identity of the British Settler Community in Shanghai, 1843–1937', *Past and Present*, no. 159 (1998), pp. 161–211.
77 Harvard University Archives, 12.28, Fairbank papers, Box 3, 'English translation of Inspector General's report to His Excellency the Minister of Finance and two Vice-Ministers of Finance', enclosure in Maze to Cubbon, 31 December 1942. For a survey

of the Customs during the Pacific War see my: 'The Chinese Maririme Customs at War, 1941–45', *Journal of Imperial and Commonwealth History,* 36:2 (2008), pp. 295–311.

78 School of Oriental and African Studies archives, Sir Frederick Maze papers, Vol.III, R. Kurosawa to Maze, 28 December 1929. Kurosawa had been accused of misappropriating Customs property for his personal use. He denied the charge, but was nonetheless required to resign.

79 IG circular 2907, 13 September 1913; on the cult of Hart see Robert Bickers, 'Purloined Letters: History and the Chinese Maritime Customs Service', *Modern Asian Studies,* 40/3 (2006), pp. 691–724.

80 *Documents Illustrative,* vol. V, pp. 179–96.

81 SHAC, 679(9) 168, J.V. Porter, 'Report on Events Leading to the Seizure of the Dalian Customs', 8 September 1932.

82 SHAC, 679(9) 168, Fukumoto to Maze, Confidential S/O, 19 March 1932.

83 Harvard University, Houghton Library, Lester Knox Little papers, Am 1999.4, 'LK Little Personal (spine), IG Personal correspondence', Little to Atcheson, 3 June 1946.

84 Ibid., Ms Am 1999.16, II IGS Confidential correspondence with Foreign embassies, Naval and Military Authorities, 1946–1947, Yoshida to Little, 22 April 1947.

85 SHAC, 679(1), 32014, 'Tsingtao s/o 1915–20', Tachibana to Aglen, 10 June 1916.

86 *I.G. in Peking,* letter 495, 21 September 1884.

87 Antony Best, ' "That Loyal British Subject"? Arthur Edwardes and Anglo-Japanese Relations, 1932–41', in J.E. Hoare (ed.), *Britain and Japan: Biographical Portraits, vol. III,* Richmond: Japan Library, 1999, pp. 227–39.

4 The League of Nations, Washington and internationalism in East Asia

With special reference to the League's attempt to control opium

Harumi Goto-Shibata

The first and foremost objective of the League of Nations was to maintain peace, but it should not be forgotten that it also played a significant role in promoting international collaboration in social and humanitarian fields. Indeed, the League was actually more successful in this role, which was later taken up and expanded by the United Nations to the extent that some 8 per cent of the latter's budget is spent on social, economic and humanitarian activities. This chapter examines one aspect of the League's social agenda, its attempt to control opium. Opium is a harmful substance; a fact known to many people by the early twentieth century when calls for international efforts to combat opium increased. One of the missions of the League of Nations was to control and suppress opium trafficking and smoking. The organization made progress over the next two decades.

This issue is examined for two major reasons. First, the problem of opium was closely associated with East Asia. The majority of those who smoked opium were Chinese, and even in the inter-war period many of the latter did not realize that opium smoking was addictive and harmful. One has to note that opium had been used as a panacea for centuries in many parts in the world. During the Ming Dynasty, smoking opium in groups had been considered a sophisticated method of social intercourse.[1] On the other hand, the governments of China tried to suppress the habit, and it is well known that China and Britain fought wars over the latter's right to import opium freely into the former. With the advancement of modern medicine, the more that people became aware of the problems of addiction, the more opium became an issue that could easily incite a strong nationalistic reaction in East Asia.[2] Second, the United States was tremendously interested in the issue of opium. Although it remained outside the League throughout the latter's entire history, it participated in various conferences and meetings of the Opium Advisory Committee (OAC) of the League of Nations. In addition, as far as this issue is concerned, it contributed much to setting up universally acceptable and fairer standards.

To establish international order by asking member countries to comply with international rules and standards is not an easy task. Some members can be rather reluctant to collaborate, especially when they have to introduce reforms in their own countries and even change their social customs to meet international requirements. Reforms can be painful and may infringe upon the existing interests of the countries' 'establishment'. Some countries may even start criticizing international organizations for intervening in their domestic affairs. Arguments can also arise over international standards. Are they self-evident? Are there universally acceptable international standards in every field? Who is responsible for setting the standards? What happens if the Powers try to impose self-serving interests on international society?

In the inter-war period many countries gained economic profits from opium trafficking and smoking, making the achievement of international agreements on its control very difficult. For example, India had been a major exporter of raw opium since the late eighteenth century and still retained an interest in the 1920s. This fact did not make Britain and India keen to suppress the production of raw opium in order to achieve international control of the drug.

The following questions are examined in this chapter. How did the major players, i.e. the British Empire, the United States, Japan and China, deal with the issue of opium in the inter-war period? How did they interact and negotiate with each other in the international framework of the OAC? What made them comply or ignore international requirements? The first section of the chapter provides a survey of the OAC's origins. The second section looks at the role played by the United States at the OAC, and considers what made the British Empire change its opium policy. The third section examines how two important East Asian countries, China and Japan, responded to rising internationalism in the 1930s.[3]

The establishment of the OAC

International efforts to eradicate opium smoking started at the beginning of the twentieth century. The first international commission was held, arising out of an American initiative, in Shanghai in 1909. The United States took the initiative partly because from its perspective opium control would not harm its interests. For example, when the first US–Japan commercial treaty was signed in 1858, it contained a provision that limited the importation of opium into Japan to a minimal amount (four pounds per year). Thanks in part to this treaty, opium smoking never became a serious problem in Japan. The United States also signed a similar treaty with China in 1880, and did not bring opium into the latter after that date. Following the colonization of the Philippines in 1898, the United States tried to implement more enlightened colonial rule than the European colonial powers, and thus banned opium smoking in the archipelago.[4]

The Shanghai commission of 1909 could not make any binding decisions, so in 1912 a conference was held in The Hague, where an agreement paved the way for The Hague Opium Convention which urged countries to do their best to reduce illicit traffic in narcotics, including both raw and prepared opium. However, The Hague Convention of 1912 failed to solve the problem. Only eight countries, including the United States and Britain, had ratified it by the eve of the First World War.

In August 1918 the United States suggested to Britain that The Hague Convention should be made effective as soon as possible. Consumption of dangerous drugs was becoming a serious problem in the United States, and the country thought that it could be controlled by chapter three of the Convention concerning the control of morphine and cocaine.[5] Presented with the American proposal, the British Foreign Office asked for opinions from the relevant offices. The Board of Trade replied that Germany, a country with an advanced pharmaceutical industry, should ratify The Hague Convention. The British government then suggested to the United States that the question of suppressing illegal trade in habit-forming drugs should be presented at the Paris Peace Conference.[6] It seems that the major aim of Britain at this stage was to control not opium but other dangerous drugs, and to weaken the mighty German pharmaceutical industry.

On 15 April 1919 the British Delegation to the Paris Peace Conference proposed that Germany should agree to ratify The Hague Convention and enact the legislation required for that purpose. In response, Robert Lansing, the American Secretary of State, proposed that not only Germany but also the allied powers should take the same action. He argued again on 17 April that general ratification would be the simplest method by which The Hague Convention could be activated. Although Sir Robert Borden, the Prime Minister of Canada who represented the British Empire on the day, was not keen on Lansing's idea, the French and Italian representatives supported it. As a result, it was agreed on 19 April that ratification of the Versailles Peace Treaty should, in the case of the countries which had not yet ratified The Hague Convention, be deemed equivalent to ratification.[7] In addition, Article 23(c) of the Covenant of the League of Nations stipulated that the contracting parties should entrust the League with the general supervision of the execution of agreements concerning the traffic in opium and other dangerous drugs. The Hague Opium Convention of 1912 finally became effective and the opium issue went out of the control of the British policy-makers.

Japan signed the Treaty of Versailles and became one of the founding members of the League of Nations. However, it should be remembered that Japanese foreign policy makers considered President Wilson's idealism to be mere lip service. The record of a meeting held by the *Gaikō Chōsakai* [the Advisory Council on Foreign Relations] on 8 December 1918 clearly conveys a sense of the atmosphere that prevailed among Japanese leaders. On that day Makino Nobuaki, a leading diplomat and former foreign minister who would be dispatched to the Paris Peace Conference, stated that:

> Although Japan has always claimed that its stance is fair and just, and that it adheres to the policies of the open door, non-intervention into China, and Sino-Japanese friendship, its actual policies have been inconsistent with what it has claimed, with the result that the powers have come to regard Japan as untrustworthy.[8]

His statement reflected the opinion of some members of the Foreign Ministry who attempted to cope with the post-war situation by changing the direction of Japan's foreign policy. This, however, was not acceptable to the people who were at the centre of Japan's foreign policy-making. Itō Miyoji, one of the privy councillors, demanded that Makino should explain why he thought Japan was regarded as unreliable. Both Itō and another senior politician, Inukai Tsuyoshi, strongly insisted that it was necessary for Japan to possess more territory. Following their remarks, Terauchi Masatake, the Prime Minister from 1916 to 1918, claimed that Japan had never been unfair and unjust.[9] The *Gaikō Chōsakai* thus did not endorse Makino's opinion. Being far away from the major battlefields of the Great War, the Japanese senior politicians did not grasp how earnestly the Europeans sought peace. They prevented Japan from realistically facing the changes in international society.[10]

Japan's conservative leaders were firmly convinced that it would be impossible to establish the League of Nations. They also suspected that any such organization would turn out to be a white-men's club and that Japan might not be treated equally because of race. The Japanese delegates to the Conference were instructed to make efforts to postpone the establishment of the League for as long as possible. Once the League was established, however, it was impossible and unprofitable for Japan to remain isolated.[11] Therefore, Japan participated in the League, had a seat on the Council, and paid her share of annual expenses. Still, even rational-minded politicians such as Shidehara Kijūrō continued to have great misgivings about the League.[12]

The Beijing government did not sign the Treaty of Versailles that allowed Japan to inherit Germany's interests in the Shandong Peninsula, but by signing the Treaty of Saint-Germain, China still joined the League and did so more willingly than Japan. Although the Chinese were disappointed with American non-participation in the League, they believed that an international society based on the League would be more useful for seeking assistance to revise the existing situation in China than bilateral negotiations with the Great Powers.[13] The Beijing government insisted that its financial contribution to the League should be almost as much as Japan and Britain, although it could not actually fulfil its promise and pay its share of expenses. This was because the financial basis of the Beijing government was very weak.[14]

Let us now return to the opium issue at the League. The League's Council formally established the OAC in 1920. OAC meetings were held initially on an ad hoc basis, and later annually. Britain, France, the Netherlands, Portugal, Japan, China, Siam and India were the initial participants in the meetings. All the eight members of the OAC had been involved with opium problems in some way or other. Britain, France, the Netherlands, Portugal and Japan had territories under their rule where opium smoking was widespread. Neither China nor Siam was a colonial power, but they had opium problems of their own. Another member, India, had been a major exporter of raw opium. In the mid-nineteenth century the government of India had raised about 15 per cent of its revenue from opium. This figure had decreased to 7 per cent by the time Britain signed an agreement with China in 1907.[15] The goal set in the agreement was that, if China succeeded in suppressing poppy cultivation, the export of Indian opium to China would cease in ten years. The Sino-British agreements of 1907 and 1911 reduced the dependence of India's public finance on opium further and in the 1920s the export of opium provided the central government of India with about £2 million per year, which constituted about 2 per cent of its total revenue. Under very difficult financial circumstances since the Great War, the government of India was reluctant to give up this reliable source of revenue. The representatives of Britain and India, Sir Malcolm Delevingne and Sir John Campbell, thus insisted that the illegal trafficking of opium and other dangerous drugs should be suppressed, but expressed no interest in addressing the issue of poppy cultivation and opium production in India. India still continued its export of raw opium to places such as Southeast Asia and Taiwan.[16]

At the first OAC meetings the British and Indian representatives severely criticized both Japan and China over the issue of trafficking. Japan had been presented with the problem of opium smoking ever since the colonization of Taiwan in 1895. Among the territories Japan had colonized, the situation in the Guangdong Leased Territory was considered particularly dubious. Although a form of monopoly was adopted there in 1906, the monopoly right was awarded to Chinese merchants. The colonial authorities were indifferent to opium smoking by the Chinese populace there – except as a source of revenue. What was worse, some criminals in the Japanese Empire came to be involved in the smuggling of dangerous drugs. Criminal networks of Japanese, of Chinese in Taiwan and on the continent, and Koreans formed in the 1920s.[17] Meanwhile, in China, despite the tremendous efforts of the Qing government to suppress poppy cultivation in its last days, chaos spread after the revolution in 1911 and domestic opium production and trafficking revived. In the 1920s it was suspected that a substantial amount of opium was being produced in the country.

The British and Indian reproach of Japan in the OAC provoked a nationalistic reaction from the Japanese representatives, especially because the standards and rules Delevingne and Campbell applied seemed to them unfair and unjust. For example, one of the Japanese delegates, Sugimura Yōtarō, commented as follows, 'Although it cannot be said that no Japanese were engaged in the smuggling, this aspect of the problem has been exaggerated too much in the past OAC.' Why, he asked, should India be allowed to continue exporting raw opium? He considered that not only opium smoking but also opium eating should be banned in the future.[18]

China also found the decisions made at the OAC difficult to accept. For example, in December 1925 the American representative to the Geneva International Opium Conference informed Sir Austen Chamberlain, the British Foreign Secretary, of the words of Dr Alfred Sze, the Chinese minister to the United States and representative to the conference, who had stated, 'The Delegate for Japan and I understand one another's minds. We both belong to the East and not to the West. Our training was in the teachings of Confucianism and not of Christianity.'[19] It was extremely unusual in the inter-war period for a person such as Sze to say that his ideas were similar to those of Japanese. Thus, neither Japan nor China could regard as fair and just the standards and rules regarding opium that the British were trying to impose on international society.

The role of the United States

The United States, although outside the League, was tremendously interested in the issue of opium. American voters would have been outraged if they had heard that their government had decided to ignore the existence of the OAC.[20] Meanwhile, the League was worried that if the United States were to deal with the issue separately, the work of the OAC would be considerably impeded. Receiving the League's invitation in 1922, the United States finally began sending delegations continuously from the fourth OAC held that year. This was two years after the OAC had been established. As far as the opium issue was concerned, the United States was to contribute much to the making of fairer international rules.

At the fifth OAC meeting held from May to June 1923, it was decided to convene an international opium conference at Geneva in 1924–25. Non-League-members including the United States were also invited to the Geneva Opium Conference. The point that the United States subsequently made at the OAC meetings and the Geneva Opium Conference was that not only illegal trafficking but also the cultivation of poppies and the production of raw opium should be stopped in order to solve the problem. This was obviously a more universally acceptable and fairer standard than the stance of Britain and India, which concentrated merely on the control and suppression of illegal trafficking.

The position of the British Empire at Geneva turned out to be awkward, but the loud criticism voiced by the United States finally forced it to reconsider its opium policy. In 1926 the government of India declared that it would stop the export of opium, except for medical and scientific purposes, in about ten years. Meanwhile the Colonial Office ordered the Straits Settlements, whose public purse relied heavily on opium, to start efforts to make its finances independent of revenue collected from the sale of narcotics. More than 40 per cent of the total revenue of the Straits Settlements was gained from opium even as late as in the mid-1920s.[21]

Unlike Britain, Japan was not criticized at the Geneva Opium Conference, so it was satisfied with the outcome. Both the United States and China praised Japan's opium policy in Taiwan. However, this complacency did not produce any good results. Although it was true that Japan was not the only source of the problems, its record concerning opium and other dangerous drugs could hardly be considered satisfactory. Tremendous energy should have been put into the control of illegal trafficking, but unfortunately Japan in the late 1920s made very little effort. The control remained extremely loose. What was worse, Japan aimed to develop its pharmaceutical industry further. Japan aspired to become one of the leading pharmaceutical countries and export medicines legally to non-manufacturing countries. It did not place any upper limit on the production of drugs. In other words, it saw the issue of opium and other dangerous drugs only from an economic viewpoint, and paid only limited attention to humanitarian ideals.

In the meantime, the situation in China fell into further chaos. Within four months of the ending of the Geneva Opium Conference, the May Thirtieth Incident broke out in Shanghai, which developed into a full-scale anti-British move-ment. British trade with China was paralysed for sixteen months. The Northern Expedition started in July 1926, which forced Britain to think seriously about defending its vested interests in Shanghai. It even sought ways to rely on the assistance of the Japanese Imperial Army.[22] Mired in instability, for some years China could not submit annual reports on opium to the OAC. The OAC was thus left uninformed about the situation in China.[23]

The Guomindang (GMD) established a government in Nanjing in 1928. From 1929 the League of Nations planned technical co-operation with China. However, the co-operation was not achieved in the field of the control of opium smoking and trafficking. The OAC still could not uncover the real situation in China. Although the League set up a commission of inquiry into the opium situ-ation in East and South-East Asia, and the commission visited several countries and territories in the region in 1929–30, it could not visit China. Britain, which had proposed the establishment of the commission, did not insist on its investi-gating the situation in China. Britain wanted to avoid any possibility of provok-ing any further anti-British sentiment in China.[24] China also did not participate in the International Opium Conference held at Bangkok in 1931.[25]

Developments after the Manchurian Crisis

A sea change took place in East Asia after the Manchurian Crisis. International society strongly criticized Japan's military invasion of the north-eastern prov-inces of China, and in 1933 Japan withdrew from the League of Nations.[26] The arguments at the OAC now began to reflect the growing rivalries in East Asia. It does seem that China felt it necessary to be accepted in international society as a responsible member and acquire its support to fend off Japan's aggression, while the reproach from international society was concentrated on Japan.

In May 1933, at the sixteenth meeting of the OAC, China proposed that a sub-committee should be established to investigate the real situation behind the illegal trafficking of habit-forming drugs in all parts of China, including the north-eastern provinces under Japanese occupation, where a monopoly of opium had been introduced.[27] The result of this investigation, however, was disappoint-ing to China. It was found that China was itself becoming a source of supply for the illicit traffic in narcotic drugs, as well as being a destination for illicit exports from other countries.[28]

At the eighteenth OAC meeting held in May 1934, even S.J. Fuller, the American representative to the OAC and formerly a keen supporter of China, criticized the Chinese lack of effort in suppressing the opium trade and the habit of opium smoking. He noted that the area of poppy cultivation included some of the largest provinces in China, such as Yunnan and Sichuan. While the average annual production of raw opium in the world apart from China was about 1,770 tons, the total production of China in 1930 was estimated at 12,000 tons. Fuller expressed the desire that the Chinese government should endeavour to enforce the existing laws, and the OAC was in general agreement with this opinion.[29]

The critical remarks made by the United States seem to have been one reason why the Nanjing government finally began to control opium and other dangerous drugs in the country. China had to cope with Japanese aggression, and support from international society, and especially from the United States, was indispensable if this was to be resisted. At the nineteenth OAC meeting in 1934, the Chinese representative declared that China would adopt a method of gradual restriction of poppy cultivation and the use of opium with a view to abolish them within six years.[30] In order to achieve this aim, China pronounced it necessary to establish a government monopoly. Many participants of the OAC praised China's decision, although the United States had grave misgivings about the possibility of China's relying on the revenue raised from the monopoly.[31]

When the twentieth OAC meeting opened on 20 May 1935, Japan's withdrawal from the League was already official. However, the British representative proposed that the Council should take steps to ensure the continued representation of Japan on the OAC. This was because Japanese nationals so often played a part in the illicit traffic that it was considered very important to retain the co-operation of the Japanese representative. The OAC agreed with the proposal. The Chinese representative, while supporting the proposal, made a reservation on the legal question of representation on League Committees of governments that had withdrawn from the League.[32]

At this twentieth meeting China reported on opium and other dangerous drugs as follows: first, it had established a registration system for opium-smokers, and the registration had already been closed; second, smokers were being compelled to undergo withdrawal and the government had founded special hospitals for the treatment of addicts; third, Jiang Jieshi had become the Inspector-General for the suppression of opium; fourth, China had decided to establish a government monopoly of opium.[33] In regard to the latter, it was not alone, for the puppet state of Manchukuo had also started a government monopoly of opium in 1933.

The twenty-first OAC meeting was held from May to June 1936. Fuller reported that American authorities had enlisted the aid of Chinese in every province of China to conduct a survey of the production of raw opium and opium derivatives. Based on the survey, he accused Japanese and Korean traffickers in Manchuria and Jehol [Rehe] of being major sources of narcotics. He also accused the Japanese government of imposing only minimal penalties on the traffickers.[34] The OAC passed a resolution to demand that the Japanese government continue and redouble its efforts and take such actions as might be necessary to provide penalties for the illicit traffic in narcotic drugs and their manufacture wherever Japanese jurisdiction extended.[35]

Thus, in the five years after the outbreak of the Manchurian Incident, the situation had changed completely. China had come to participate in international society more fully. In 1935 it adopted the import certificate system, which the OAC had recommended since the early 1920s, and in 1936 it signed the Geneva Opium agreements of 1925. Its annual reports submitted to the OAC became slightly more accurate.[36] It does seem that China felt it necessary to be a responsible member of the international society in order to cope with the escalating political and military pressure exerted on it by Japan. The OAC in turn unanimously praised China's efforts.[37] Although it was not possible for China to succeed in entirely suppressing poppy cultivation and opium smoking immediately after changing its policies, it was apparently making efforts to co-operate with international society in compliance with international rules. The United States was especially sympathetic to China's stance.

On the other hand, the reproach from international society came to be concentrated on Japan. Japan had withdrawn from the League of Nations, and it did not seem to be interested in complying with international rules. The loose control of opium and other dangerous drugs continued in the Japanese Empire, and the puppet state of Manchukuo started to gain profits from the opium monopoly. The fact that very strict control of opium and other dangerous drugs was possible within Japan made members of the OAC and the League suspect that it was intentionally breaking the rules. Disapproval of Japan became even stronger after the outbreak of the Sino-Japanese War in 1937, and Japan finally withdrew from the OAC in 1939.

Internationalism in East Asia

This chapter examines the development of the international control of opium. It considers the factors that made countries comply with the rules of international society. One significant factor is that the rules and standards themselves should appear fair, just and universal. The OAC of the League of Nations did not realize this aim until the end of the Geneva Opium Conference of 1924–25. Initially the governments of the member countries were reluctant to adopt measures that would reduce economic profit. Japan and China suspected that the British Empire, while criticizing the two countries, was trying to protect its own economic interests. Both of them found it difficult to accept Britain and India as international judges concerning this issue. American participation in the OAC was indispensable in this case. It had not been so greatly involved in the opium trade and thus had little at stake. It therefore could make international standards and rules regarding opium much fairer. It contributed much to enlisting the co-operation of various countries in the cause of combating opium.

Japan had been a reluctant participant in the League of Nations from the beginning. The imposition of internationalism, especially when it was regarded as being based on self-serving standards and rules, could incite nationalistic reaction. Sugimura's stance at the OAC and the Geneva Opium Conference was a typical example of this reaction. It does seem that he considered that Japan was being treated as a scapegoat and that he tried to defend the dignity of his nation.

China, meanwhile, had not tried to enter international society that expanded from Europe to include East Asia in the nineteenth century. The League of Nations was arguably the first international stage on which it participated as an actor. China's goal in the inter-war period was to recover the rights it had lost to the Great Powers since the mid-nineteenth century. It thought that the League would provide a framework that would be more effective than mere bilateral negotiations. China's efforts were supported by the smaller countries in the League, which tended to be sympathetic to its unfortunate situation. In addition, the League began technical co-operation with China after the establishment of the GMD government in Nanjing in 1928. However, as far as opium problems were concerned, China did not co-operate with the League until very late in the game. Recent studies in Chinese history have revealed that part of the problem was that the Nanjing government of the time itself relied on opium revenue.[38]

It was only after the outbreak of the Manchurian Incident and the establishment of the puppet state of Manchukuo that Nanjing began to co-operate with the OAC more fully. By this time, Japan had completely failed to cope with the rising tide of internationalism.[39] Feeling self-righteously that it was being unfairly and unjustly treated, it withdrew from the League of Nations. In the mid-1930s, the GMD government was far keener on international co-operation than Japan. What made China convinced that it had to comply with the international rules was, at least partly, the practical necessity that arose from the regional rivalry between itself and Japan. China needed more support from international society, especially from the United States, to resist Japan. It could not continue to neglect the problem of opium smoking. However, it is not clear whether China considered the international requirements fair and just. Separate research on the period after the demise of the League of Nations is needed to examine how full-hearted China's support for internationalism actually was.

Notes

1 Frank Diköetter, Lars Laaman and Zhou Xun, *Narcotic Culture*, London: Hurst, 2004, pp. 74–88. See also Yangwen Zheng, *The Social Life of Opium in China, 1483–1999*, Cambridge: Cambridge University Press, 2005.
2 Henrietta Harrison, 'Narcotics, nationalism and class in China: the transition from opium to morphine and heroin in early 20th Century Shanxi' (paper presented at Harvard University in January 2004).
3 This chapter is based on the author's *Ahen to Igirisu teikoku: kokusai kisei no takamari 1906–43 nen*, Tokyo: Yamakawa shuppansha, 2005. See also Harumi Goto-Shibata, 'The International Opium Conference of 1924–25 and Japan', *Modern Asian Studies*, 36–4 (2002), pp. 969–91; and ibid., 'Empire on the Cheap: The Control of Opium Smoking in the Straits Settlements, 1925–1939', *Modern Asian Studies*, 40–1 (2006), pp. 59–80.
4 Anne L. Foster, 'Prohibition as Superiority: Policing Opium in South-East Asia, 1898–1925', *International History Review*, XXII-2 (June 2000), p. 272.
5 The National Archives, Kew (TNA) FO371/3176 (146169) Page (American Embassy) to Balfour, no. 1105, 23 August 1918.
6 TNA FO371/3176 (155732) Board of Trade to FO, 11 September 1918, and (197836) Balfour to US Chargé d'Affaires, 10 December 1918.
7 *British Documents on Foreign Affairs,* part 2, series I, vol. 3, documents 12, 14 and 15; and D.H. Miller, *The Drafting of the Covenant*, vol. 1, New York: G.P. Putnam, 1928, pp. 219, 339–42.
8 Kobayashi Tatsuo (ed.), *Suiusō nikki*, Tokyo: Hara shobō, 1966, p. 333. *Gaikō Chōsakai* was constituted in June 1917 to unify discussion of foreign policy, and worked until September 1922.
9 Ibid., pp. 334–42.

10 Many Japanese intellectuals shared distrust of Wilson and the Western powers in this period. See Harumi Goto-Shibata, 'Internationalism and Nationalism: Anti-Western Sentiments in Japan's Foreign Policy Debates', in Naoko Shimazu (ed.), *Nationalisms in Japan*, London: Routledge/Curzon, 2006, pp. 66–84.
11 NHK dokyumento Shōwa shuzai han (ed.), *Berusaiyu no Nisshōki*, Tokyo: Kadokawa shoten, 1986, pp. 210–21.
12 Ryūji Hattori, *Shidehara Kijūrō to 20 seiki no Nippon*, Tokyo: Yūhikaku, 2006.
13 Nishimura Shigeo, '20 seiki zenhan ki Chūgoku to "3 no gaikō kukan"', in Nishimura (ed.), *Chūgoku gaikō to kokuren no seiritsu*, Tokyo: Hōritsu bunkasha, 2004, pp. 5–11.
14 Tang Chi-hua, *Beijing zhengfu yu guoji lianmeng (1919–1928)*, Taipei: Dongda tushu gonsi, 1998, chapter 4. See also his chapter 5, section 2 on the opium question.
15 John F. Richards, 'The Opium Industry in British India', *The Indian Economic and Social History Review*, 39/2&3 (2002), p. 157, chart 2.
16 Goto-Shibata, 'The International Opium Conference and Japan', pp. 972–3.
17 British Foreign Office, *The Opium Trade*, Delaware: Scholarly Resources, 1974, vol. 6, part XXVII, no. 83, enclosure (Eastes to Lampson, 5 December 1930); part XXVIII, no. 1 (Snow to MacKillop, 3 December 1930); and TNA FO371/14768, F2079, Croft (India Office) to Orde, E. & O. 2520/30, 8 April 1930. See also Motohiro Kobayashi, 'Drug Operations by Resident Japanese in Tianjin', in Tim Brook and Bob Tadashi Wakabayashi, *Opium Regimes*, Berkeley: University of California Press, 2000, p. 158; and Robert Maule, 'British Policy Discussions on the Opium Question in the Federated Shan States, 1937–1948', *Journal of Southeast Asian Studies*, 33/2 (2002), pp. 216–19.
18 *Nippon Gaikō Bunsho*, 1925, vol. 1, no. 118, fuki 2; and Japanese Foreign Ministry Archives, 2.4.2.30, vol. 8, Sugimura to Shidehara, no. 156, 21 July 1924.
19 TNA FO371/10330, F4187, Bishop Brent to Chamberlain, 11 December 1924.
20 Warren F. Kuehl and Lynne K. Dunn, *Keeping the Covenant*, Kent: The Kent State University Press, 1997, pp. 127–8.
21 See Goto-Shibata, 'Empire on the Cheap'.
22 Harumi Goto-Shibata, *Japan and Britain in Shanghai, 1925–31*, Basingstoke: Macmillan, 1995, chaps 2–3.
23 League of Nations documents (hereafter, LNd), C. 521.M. 179. 1927. XI [OC 686(I)], Report, OAC to the Council, 10th session, 28 September to 8 October 1927, pp. 4, 7; and LNd, A.7.1928. XI, Report, OAC, 11th Session, 12 to 26 April 1928, p. 6.
24 TNA FO371/13254, F4237, Delevingne to Mounsey, 7 August 1928 no.SO.418 (524,525/12); F4799, Strang minute (from Consul London), no. 102 (R)LN), 5 September 1928; FO371/13255, F5280 Lampson to Chamberlain, no. 1035, 24 September 1928; and F6276, FO minute (draft letter to Delevingne and Grindle), 14 November 1928.
25 FO371/15527, F2333, Delevingne to Orde, no.SO.234 541,021/12, 28 April 1931; F2652, Delevingne to Orde, no.SO.290, 13 May 1931; F2668, Patteson (Geneva) to Henderson, no. 28 (LN), 15 May 1931; F4264, Delevingne to Orde, no.SO.456, 3 August 1931.
26 See, for example, Ian Nish, *Japan's Struggle with Internationalism: Japan, China and the League of Nations 1931–1933*, London: Kegan Paul, 1993.
27 LNd, C.385.M.193.1933.XI [OC.1494 (1)], OAC report to the Council, 16th Session, 15–31 May 1933, p. 20.
28 LNd, C.642.M.305.1933.XI [OC.1507 (1)], OAC report to the Council, 17th session, 30 October to 9 November 1933, Appendix III.
29 LNd, C.317.M.142.1934.XI, extract from the Minutes of the 18th session, pp. 2–7. See also Edward R. Slack, *Opium, State, and Society: China's Narco-Economy and the Guomindang, 1924–1937*, Honolulu: University of Hawaii Press, 2001, and Zhou Yongming, *Anti-Drug Crusades in Twentieth-Century China*, Lanham: Rowman & Littlefield, 1999, chaps 4–5.

30 LNd, C.530.M.241.1934.XI [O.C. 1581 (1)], OAC report to the Council, 19th session, 15 to 28 November 1934, pp. 3–4.
31 LNd, C.33.M.14.1935.XI, OAC, Minutes of the 19th session, pp. 55, 57–58, 65, 67–8.
32 TNA FO371/19370, F3298, from LN, No. C.224/1935/XI (86th session of the Council. Extract from final minutes of the 2nd meeting held on 22 May, Geneva); F4923, Coles to Makins, unnumbered, 26 July 1935.
33 LNd, C.253.M.125.1935.XI [OC.1609 (1)], OAC report to the Council, 20th session, 20 May to 5 June 1935, p. 6.
34 LNd, C.290.M.176.1936.XI, OAC, Minutes of the 21st session, pp. 63, 66. Ishii Itarō, who was the Consul-General in Shanghai for four years from September 1932, also noted that the penalty was too light. Ishii Itarō, *Gaikōkan no isshō*, Tokyo: Yomiuri shinbunsha, 1959, p. 50.
35 LNd, C.278.M.168.1936.XI [OC.1656 (1)], OAC report to the Council, 21st session, 18 May to 5 June 1936, pp. 7–9.
36 *Foreign Relations of the United States*, 1935, vol. III, p. 744, Acting Secretary of State to Johnson, 1 August 1935; Johnson to Secretary of State, 9 August 1935; TNA FO371/19366, F6085, 21 September 1935, from LN, C.L.132.1935XI; LNd, C. 278.M.168.1936.XI [OC.1656 (1)], OAC report to the Council, 21st session, 18 May to 5 June 1936, pp. 7–9; LNd, C.L.203.1937, XI, annex, p. 4.
37 Slack, *Opium, State, and Society*, pp. 112, 146.
38 Ibid., pp. 109, 156; and Zhou, *Anti-Drug Crusades in Twentieth-Century China*, pp. 74, 80–1.
39 See Nish, *Japan's Struggle with Internationalism*.

5 Internationalism in East Asia

The naval armaments limitation system, 1922–39

Joseph A. Maiolo

In late August 1939 the Admiralty in London contemplated the fate of the naval treaties should war with Germany come. Some officials argued that it might be beneficial to retain parts of the system of naval arms control introduced at Washington in 1922, and refined at London in 1930, and then again in 1936. A consensus emerged, 'Even with the greatest exercise of ingenuity', the Admiralty concluded, 'so little could be saved that the only practical course would be to denounce the [Naval] Treaties in toto.'[1] In September 1939 the British government formally denounced the naval treaties, and so ended seventeen years of the management of warship construction through international agreements.

During the Cold War, the history of the naval treaty system was often told by political scientists as a cautionary tale to highlight the potential benefits of arms control to regulate superpower rivalry, as well as the hazards of trusting totalitarian states to adhere to arms agreements. Echoing the more pessimistic political scientists, historians of the American and British navies often damned the treaties as an exercise in naïve inter-war idealism – forced upon hard-nosed admirals by misguided politicians – that did nothing more than obstruct the growth of their navies in the run up to the Second World War.[2] Both of these interpretations of the history of naval arms limitation obscure what made the naval armaments treaties possible in the first place, namely shared interests and common understandings among naval elites about the nature of warfare at sea.

This chapter will first set out the common interests and understandings, and second explain why the naval treaty system ultimately broke down. Given the theme of this volume, this chapter will focus exclusively on the Royal Navy and the Imperial Japanese Navy, even though the history of naval arms limitation encompasses much more than the Anglo-Japanese naval relationship. Nonetheless, the behaviour of both navies – particularly the ideas, policies and strategies of their leading decision-makers – exemplifies the larger themes that this chapter will explore.

Usually one does not think of admirals, whose occupation is to plan, prepare and wage wars at sea, as instinctive internationalists. Naval elites during the inter-war years were distinctly nationalist. Their views of the liberal international order established with the foundation of the League of Nations in 1919, and buttressed by the Kellogg–Briand Pact of 1928 (the treaty for the 'renunciation of war as an instrument of policy'), ranged from the sceptical to the downright hostile.

Even so, admirals shared something that cut across national and cultural boundaries – a form of naval internationalism. As professionals they had much in common in what they held to be true 'sea-power', and what they thought future war at sea would and should be. It was this common starting point – or, to put it another way, common grammar of sea power – that made the inter-war treaty system a workable possibility in the first place. The word 'system' is used here to denote something more than a number of actors locked in a competition for power through strategies of 'self-help'. It is used here much in the same way that Paul Schroeder employs it in his *The Transformation of European Politics, 1763–1848*. Schroeder defined an international system as a set of 'understandings, assumptions, learned skills and responses, rules, norms, procedures that agents acquire and use in pursuing their individual divergent aims within the framework of a shared practice'.[3]

What has been labelled the 'common grammar of sea power' resembles the vision of national strength popularised by Admiral Alfred Thayer Mahan in his *The Influence of Seapower upon History, 1660–1783* (1890). Broadly speaking, adherents of this view – both in and out of uniform – agreed that naval supremacy was a pre-requisite for national greatness; that the instrument of naval supremacy was the battle fleet composed of the most powerful units – capital ships; and that the prime object of the battle fleet was to annihilate the opponent's navy in order to 'command the sea'.[4] Of course there were dissenters to this orthodoxy: men who saw the submarine or the airplane as the ultimate weapons in sea warfare. But one looks in vain to locate such men in the top echelons of decision-making in the inter-war period. Not only did the top-ranking naval elites worldwide share this basic understanding of how navies should function as instruments of national power, but they also held common assumptions about how to calculate fleet strengths relative to potential enemies and how to predict tactical outcomes based on these fleet strengths.

In the era of the all-big-gun capital ship, naval planners calculated the result of hypothetical fleet engagements with algebraic formulas or models. The celebrated British engineer Frederick W. Lanchester conceived the most important formula for this type of mathematical forecasting, the so-called N^2 Law. The N^2 Law demonstrated that an advantage in concentrated aggregate firepower conferred upon a larger battlefleet an expanding, cumulative advantage. So, for example, in a sea battle between two fleets composed of ships of equal combat effectiveness – one composed of ten and the other of seven battleships – the relatively small advantage in numbers and firepower of the first fleet translates, according to the N^2 Law, into a crushing outcome. With each round of concentrated fire between the two opposing fleets, the two forces suffer losses, but the smaller fleet shrinks faster and its firepower diminishes much more rapidly than the larger force. The battle therefore ends with the fleet of ten suffering only three ships sunk, while the smaller fleet of seven ships is annihilated.[5]

Mahanian precepts and the N^2 Law made the Washington Treaty's 5–5–3-battleship tonnage ratio comprehensible to its signatories and a basis for agreement. Symbolically, the ratios described the balance in terms of Anglo-American equality and Japanese inferiority; in substantive terms the picture was more complex because treaty equality or inferiority did not necessarily mean matériel equality or inferiority. Put simply, naval officers knew that algebra did not determine performance in war. 'We should have lost the battle of Trafalgar on a Staff Appreciation', one senior British admiral liked to remind his colleagues, 'since our fleet was inferior to the French.'[6]

One reason why, for instance, the Japanese delegation to Washington was prepared to accept an inferior ratio was that the treaty also restricted the construction of advance American bases in the Pacific for its fleet – thus limiting the actual fighting power the Americans could bring to bear in the western Pacific.[7] Naval officers also took great comfort in less tangible factors to calculate the naval balance. Historians often single out Japanese naval officers as 'irrational' for placing too great a faith in 'the Japanese fighting spirit' to compensate for inferiority in matériel terms, but this type of thinking was widespread among the fighting men of the period, including British admirals. In 1938 Admiral Tom Phillips, who in December 1941 would command the *Prince of Wales* and the *Repulse* on their ill-fated mission to intercept the Japanese invasion force destined for Singapore, feared that algebraic models used in war games taught young British officers to think that victory came solely through the accumulation of matériel superiority; 'it is not the gun or torpedo which really counts', he liked to stress, 'but the man behind it'.[8]

Although they were certainly a precondition for the naval treaty treaties, these shared understandings of what constituted sea power and common ways of thinking about tactical outcomes were not enough to build a stable system for the management of international naval rivalries. As we know, several weighty factors brought about the Washington treaties – war weariness, fear of arms races, recession, parsimonious electorates, the civil–military balance, and so on. For Britain, historians have stressed the importance placed on friendly relations with the Americans, and the wish of the Dominion governments to eliminate friction between London and Washington. The United States was, after all, potentially the world's strongest great power with the world's greatest industrial and financial capacity. Indeed, when the Cabinet turned to the American claim for parity at sea, ministers contemplated an Anglo-American naval race with genuine horror: 'We should be up against the greatest resources in the world', some ministers feared.[9] The same was true for the Admiralty. The Royal Navy knew that it could not win an arms race against a US Navy and government determined to be 'second to none'. A preventative war with the Americans while Britain retained naval supremacy was an alternative; however, the one Cabinet committee that examined this absurd scenario found that 'operations would result in a stalemate in which neither side could obtain decisive victory'.[10]

Britain's acceptance of the 5:5 ratio was an acknowledgement of this fact. However, as John Ferris has argued, while London's formal concession of treaty parity may have led to a loss of pride and prestige, it was also a cunning diplomatic ploy. In 1916 and 1918 the US Navy had put into place a huge building programme that would have given them preponderance in modern warships.[11] By accepting treaty equality the Americans abandoned most of their 1916 and 1918 construction programmes, while Britain retained overall matériel superiority – albeit in ships built mostly before and during the 1914–18 war.[12] But the diplomatic ploy worked in averting an Anglo-American naval race. In fact, much to the chagrin of US naval officers, the ploy worked all too well. Until 1934 Congress consistently refused to spend what was needed to build the US Navy even up to treaty strength.[13]

There is another story to be told here. Historians have in this tale of Anglo-American compromise overlooked the powerful common interest between London and Tokyo in preventing the United States from turning over its overwhelming industrial and financial resources to the construction of warships. As early as February 1919, just as his counterparts in London were coming to the same conclusion, the Japanese Navy Minister, Admiral Katō Tomosaburō, explained that: 'Even if we should try to compete with the United States, it is a foregone conclusion that we are simply not up to it.'[14] In 1920–21 research papers prepared by the Navy Ministry calculated that a 70 per cent battleship ratio was essential to the empire's maritime security – but time and again these papers also argued that a naval race would dramatically reduce Japan's naval strength vis-à-vis its principal hypothetical enemy – the United States Navy.[15] At Washington, both British and Japanese admirals made similar concessions to prevent their mutual nightmare – an American bid for global naval supremacy. They arrived at a similar – if not openly coordinated – solution to the same problem: British admirals conceded naval parity to appease the Americans; Japanese officers settled for a 60 per cent battleship tonnage ratio to forestall a naval race. It is in this context that Admiral Katō Tomosaburō's claim that 'Anglo-American coercion is a fantasy [that] has never occurred to us delegates in Washington', should be interpreted.[16] Rather than London siding with Washington against Tokyo, Britain and Japan responded to American preponderance in the same manner – with prudent diplomacy. As we know, however, it was the myth that the 60 per cent ratio was foisted upon Japan by Anglo-American coercion, and that the Washington and London naval treaties were framed to 'choke off the newly rising Empire of Japan', that ultimately took hold in the Imperial Japanese navy.[17]

As indicated at the beginning of this chapter, the use of the word 'system' denotes more than simply shared understandings and assumptions among naval elites; it also suggests a shared set of 'rules, norms, learned skills and responses procedures that agents acquire and use in pursuing their individual divergent aims …'. From the audacious diplomacy of Charles Hughes, the American Secretary of State, both Japanese and British admirals learned that delegations needed to be well prepared before naval arms conferences convened. Hughes opened the first public session of the Washington Conference by announcing his well-worked out proposals for huge naval cuts. This dramatic exercise in 'open diplomacy' caught both the other delegations by surprise, putting pressure on them to make substantial concessions. As Tadashi Kuramatsu has shown, it was precisely this lesson that helped to ensure that the 1927 Geneva Conference was a spectacular failure. The British Admiralty rejected preliminary talks with the other naval Powers to pave the way for an agreement during the conference; the Japanese navy reacted in a similar fashion: the Navy Ministry and Naval Staff hammered out – with some difficulty – concrete negotiating instructions in advance of talks.[18]

The lesson that one needed to arrive at the bargaining table with detailed plans was reinforced by the universal expectation that naval force levels would continue to be legitimised through international treaties. This created a powerful incentive to participate in the system, even for states that had been excluded from the Washington Conference, such as Germany and Russia, but also encouraged perverse behaviours. One example was the Japanese navy's mistaken assumption that existing strength, which had been used at Washington to calculate battleship ratios, would provide the basis for calculation at all future naval armaments conferences. The Japanese navy therefore strove to lay down as much cruiser tonnage as possible in order to assert its claim to a 70 per cent ratio in that category.[19] The Royal Navy, employing the reverse strategy, kept obsolete ships in service as disposable bargaining chips for future naval armaments negotiations. Another consequence of the learning process was that navies began to see the naval treaties as powerful tools or – perhaps to be more precise – weapons in civil–military politics.

For example, American admirals enthusiastically embraced naval limitation by tonnage ratios because it provided at least some protection for the warship-building budget against penny-pinching legislators.[20] Prime Minister Hamaguchi's use of the 1930 London Naval Treaty as a tool to reconcile differences within the navy over cruiser strength sparked the 'infringement of supreme command' crisis; and that crisis ended with the ascendancy of the Naval Staff and those officers who saw a 70 per cent ratio as an absolute minimum for Japanese security.[21] In Britain, the 1930 Treaty played a comparable role: Prime Minister Ramsay Mac-Donald used agreement with the Americans on cruiser parity to reverse the Royal Navy's nearly unbroken record of success during the 1920s in securing large sums for cruiser construction.[22]

Critics of arms control often point out that, while the Washington Conference resolved differences over capital ship construction, naval rivalry was simply diverted to competition in auxiliary vessels, especially heavy cruisers armed with 8-inch guns. Arms control fails, so the sceptical case runs, because antagonists, locked in the security dilemma, will always find alternative ways to compete.

While this case has some merit, it places too much emphasis on the fact that competition continued rather than on the more significant point – that competition was managed and contained. First, it is important to note that disputes over cruisers, especially Anglo-American ones, were bitter precisely because, in contrast to battleships, visions of future war differed most sharply over the use of these vessels. British officers called for large numbers of light 6-inch cruisers to protect Britain's seaborne trade and to enforce a global blockade; American and Japanese officers preferred the heavy 8-inch gun cruisers because their thinking was dominated by one big battle in the Pacific fought between their main fleets. Heavy cruisers were designed to support the main fleet.[23] Regrettably for the British, heavy 8-inch gun cruisers were also ideal for breaking blockades and waging trade war against the British Empire. Again, what is striking about this dispute is the way in which all sides attempted to work within the framework of shared practice established at Washington. Methods to translate and balance divergent strategic interests and different force structures were put forward. The Americans devised the 'yardstick', and the British came up with the 'ton-mileage' formula.[24] Neither worked – and to return to the metaphor of a 'common grammar of sea power', a way to conjugate this troublesome verb simply could not be found – but the point here is that the attempt to do so shows that something more than a clash of naked self-interest was at work.

Of course it would be a mistake to put too rosy a gloss on the cruiser dispute. The 1930 London Treaty was the beginning of the end. The common under-standings and shared interests that had made Washington possible were still present but in diminished form. By 1930 the fear of monumental American naval building programmes was far more of a political than an immediate strategic concern. True, the US Congress had passed the 'Fifteen Cruiser Bill' in 1929, which projected a heavy cruiser fleet of twenty-three by 1935, but actual US naval construction had consistently failed to keep pace with authorised targets. By the early 1930s, US naval building programmes were about keeping ship-yards in business and skilled workers employed, rather than building up the fleet to a predominant position.[25] From 1922 to 1928, in contrast, the Royal Navy had laid down three times as many ships than the US Navy including cruisers. In terms of his bargaining position Admiral Madden, the First Sea Lord, was the victim of this earlier record of success. The only way to appease Washington was to scrap nearly half the British cruisers in order to reduce their number to parity with the Americans.[26] Diplomatically, for Japanese admirals, an Anglo-American compromise was the problem. Strategically, the aim was a 70 per cent ratio against the United States, not Britain, but the danger of an Anglo-American naval arms race to Japan's relative strategic position was still present. In March 1927 Admiral Nomura Kichisaburō pointed out that 'in view of the general situ-ation, a 5–5–3 ratio could be accepted in order to stop unlimited expansion of the American and British fleets'. In the following year the Navy's 'Research Committee on Arms Limitation' reaffirmed Nomura's conclusion.[27] In the event, the Japanese navy did relatively well out of the 1930 Naval Treaty. Overall, the Japanese ratio for auxiliaries – cruisers, destroyers and submarines – was 69.75 per cent. However, in heavy cruisers, the treaty ratio was only 60 per cent.[28]

Ultimately, the explanation of why the naval limitation broke down cannot be found within the workings of the system itself. The larger confrontation between the status quo and the revisionist Powers, which characterised the international system of the 1930s as a whole, made itself felt in the politics of naval armaments.[29] What is fascinating is the way in which the Japanese and British navies behaved after 1930 within the framework of the naval limitation system. In striking contrast to the early 1920s, both British and Japanese admirals were prepared to disregard the potential objections and responses of the US Navy to their naval expansion plans.

One of the consequences of the 1930 London Treaty was to shift the civil–military balance in Tokyo, and within the navy itself, in favour of the so-called 'fleet faction'. To tell the story of this phase of Japanese naval policy, scholars have often focused on Admiral Katō Kanji, whose career spanned the Washington negotiations as well as the post of Chief of the Naval Staff, as an exemplar of the 'fleet faction'. He has been portrayed as a 'narrow-minded' nationalist, bent on sabotaging naval arms talks, despite the disaster this would entail for Japan; while Ian Gow has recently argued that he was a sophisticated realist, who grasped the power political purposes behind 'externally imposed naval limitation'.[30] There is something to both of these views, but neither one fully captures the interaction of structure and agency that shaped Katō's policies. The only way to see this interaction is to look at his policies through the lens of 'symbolic politics'. Students of symbolic politics suggest that agents are often concerned with certain political outcomes because of what they will signal, in important psychological ways, about the relative status of various agents within a social system. Despite the fact that agents prefer to frame issues in purely instrumental terms, they value the status rewards in and of themselves.[31] To apply this analysis to Admiral Katō and other like-minded officers, we need to interpret the increasing importance they attached to the 70 per cent ratio in both instrumental and symbolic terms. True enough, the 70 per cent ratio emerged from conventional calculations of relative strengths; and Admiral Katō was right to argue that the US Navy desired a Japanese force ratio of 60 per cent to ensure that its plan for a trans-Pacific offensive succeeded.[32] Yet, paradoxically, Admiral Katō was prepared to accept an inferior ratio if it was the end result of a naval race, 'It would be better to accept even an inferior strength in proportion to freely decided autonomous national power than a constraint of 70 per cent.'[33] The inferior tonnage ratio was important precisely because of what it signalled about the Japanese navy's relative status within the naval limitation system, as well as Japan's status within the international system overall. As Admiral Katō put it himself in February 1930, 'The real issue is no longer our naval power per se but our national prestige and credibility.'[34]

By the mid-1930s the desire to achieve at the Second London Naval Conference the symbolic goal of equality of status eclipsed the previously acknowledged strategic benefits Japan derived from naval limitation, in particular the advantage of capping the US Navy well below its potential strength. As Navy Minister Ōsumi told the Five Ministers Conference in October 1933, 'if the United States should take a strong stand in opposition to our fundamental policy [on naval armaments], we must resolutely repel it, and with this in view we must proceed to complete our [naval] preparedness'.[35] The systemic explanation advanced here of Japanese naval policy is reinforced by the navy's decision of

August 1934 to construct in secret four super-battleships.[36] Within the context of
the grammar of sea power, the super-battleship strategy made sense: the Japanese navy could make a technological leap forward in the most instrumentally
and symbolically significant warship category. 'In one bound [we can] raise our
[capital ship] strength,' wrote one staff officer, 'from the present 60% of the US
strength to a position of absolute supremacy.'[37] As the mention of 'absolute
supremacy' reveals, this goal had enormous status value.

As we know, the Royal Navy did not have a fleet faction. There were remarks
about 'sharing the rule of the waves' with the 'Yanks', but no semi-organised
bureaucratic opposition to the naval armaments treaties or parity with the Americans. Differences between British and Japanese decision-making norms played
a part here, but more importantly in the 1920s a consensus emerged that naval
diplomacy served Britain's interests by reinforcing the status quo. If Admiral
Katō Kanji is an exemplar of the Japanese fleet faction, Admiral Chatfield, the
First Sea Lord from 1933–39, is the embodiment of Admiralty policy in the
1930s. Like Katō, Chatfield's career also took him from Washington to the top
ranks of his profession.

When Admiral Chatfield became First Sea Lord in 1933, he launched an
ambitious programme to reshape the naval treaty system to achieve a number of
goals. These included reinforcing the rules for conformity in warship design and
transparency in warship construction. Reinforcing conformity with standardised
gun calibres and tonnages was important because it would reduce or stabilise the
cost of warships, making the fleet less burdensome on the British public purse,
and reduce the potential for an arms race while Britain's warship industries were
recovering from the effects of the Depression. Although Britain still possessed
the world's largest capacity for warship construction in the early 1930s, that
capacity was only sufficient to replace the existing fleet – fleet expansion would
have to wait until the early 1940s. Conformity to agreed warship standards
would therefore help to ensure that no other navy could steal a march by building in secret qualitatively superior ships – what the Japanese navy was in fact
doing with the super-battleships – while the Royal Navy built up its fleet and
industrial capacity. As Admiral Chatfield explained, 'the greatest accomplish-
ment of the Washington Treaty was not in limiting the numbers or total tonnages
but in stopping the principle of going one better'.[38] Here the relationship between
the instrumental and the symbolic in British naval policy converged. In 1922 the
British defused an American bid for a navy 'second to none' by conceding
equality in the treaty. In the years that followed, British admirals and diplomats
became convinced, with good reason, that the United States legislators would
never vote enough money to build a fleet 'second to none'. During naval talks in
1934–35, therefore, the British proposed to the Americans that tonnage ratios be
replaced by the requirement that the powers publish annual ten-year warship
building plans. If the US wanted a bigger navy than Britain's, then so be it. But
recent history had shown that they would not. By ignoring rankings and ratios,
British admirals believed that the global naval balance would ultimately settle
down to a natural order with the Royal Navy on top, followed by the United

States and then Japan, and then all the other powers.[39] In Admiralty policy, the instrumental had eclipsed the symbolic.

In March 1936 Britain, France and the United States signed the second London Naval Treaty. It represented a fleeting victory for British diplomacy. It contained the new rules for conformity and transparency that the Admiralty had wanted. Despite the end of the Washington tonnage ratios, the Japanese government refused to sign the 1936 London Naval Treaty, and the Japanese navy pressed ahead with its expansion plans, thereby cementing the close Anglo-American cooperation that many Japanese naval officers believed had worked against them in 1922.

In the end, however, British and Japanese policies were both characterised by much more hubris than rational calculations of the strategic realities. The determination of the Japanese navy to achieve naval supremacy in the western Pacific could not overcome the enormous disparity in national resources between Japan and its principle naval foe, the United States. This gap in financial and industrial power is the main reason why intelligence officers in Washington and London tended to read more bluff than resolution into the Japanese's navy's claim to parity with the US Navy and Royal Navy in the 1930s. As we know, they miscalculated. But so did the Imperial Japanese navy. The super-battleship strategy was based on a flawed premise – that technology itself was static, and that the future belonged to the big-gun ships.[40] The British miscalculated too. The whole purpose behind British naval armaments diplomacy in the 1930s was to cover the period of Britain's relative industrial weakness owing to the effects of the Depression. By the mid-1940s, so the Admiralty planned, not only would the old fleet that had served the British Empire in the 1920s have been completely rebuilt or modernised, but also the Royal Navy would be in a position to outbuild any challenges from Imperial Japan, Nazi Germany and Fascist Italy. As we know, the naval arms race began to accelerate well before then, and war came far too soon for the Admiralty to realise its long-term ambitions of achieving global naval supremacy through diplomacy. While the case of the Japanese navy underscores the limits of mere will and determination to overcome a strategic predicament, the case of the Royal Navy underscores the limits of diplomacy to do the same.

Perhaps this final point is best illustrated by turning to the one key player left out of the Washington system – the Soviet Union. In 1935, in response to the growing threat from Japan in the Far East, Stalin ordered a massive expansion of the Red Fleet within ten years, targeted specifically at Japan's navy. In order to obtain the technology required to build this titanic fleet, he offered to sign a naval treaty with the British – despite the fact that his naval building programme trampled over the treaty's rules for conformity and transparency.[41] Stalin and his officials predicted that the whole naval treaty system – and with it Britain's naval supremacy – would collapse long before Soviet duplicity was exposed. They were right. With war against Germany coming, Britain denounced the naval treaties in 1939. In another illustration of his foresight, Stalin correctly predicted in 1931 that if Japan's bid for armaments supremacy failed then Japan would feel

78   *J.A. Maiolo*

'caught in a trap', between the militarised United States, the revolutionised China and the fast-growing Soviet Union.[42] Nothing could have been more prophetic about Japan's fate a decade later.

Notes

1 The National Archives, Kew (TNA), ADM1/10524 Head of M Branch note, 24 August 1939.
2 See John Maurer, 'Arms Control and the Washington Conference', in Erik. Goldstein and John Maurer (eds), *The Washington Conference, 1921–22: Naval Rivalry, East Asian Stability and the Road to Pearl Harbor*, London: Frank Cass, 1993, for a more current political science perspective.
3 Paul Schroeder, *The Transformation of European Politics, 1763–1848*, Oxford: Oxford University Press, 1994, p.xii.
4 As many scholars have pointed out, Mahan's ideas were more sophisticated and his interpreters more varied than is commonly assumed. On Mahan, see Jon T. Sumida, *Inventing Grand Strategy and Teaching Command*, Baltimore: The Woodrow Wilson Center Press, 1997. On the British Admiralty's interpretation of naval grand strategy, see Joseph A. Maiolo, *The Royal Navy and Nazi Germany, 1933–1939*, Basingstoke: Macmillan, 1998; on Japan, see David C. Evans and Mark R. Peattie, *Kaigun: Strategy, Tactics and Technology in the Imperial Japanese Navy, 1887–1941*, Annapolis: Naval Institute Press, 1997, pp. 135–41.
5 Evans and Peattie, *Kaigun*, pp. 141–4; W.P. Hughes, *Fleet Tactics: Theory and Practice*, Annapolis: Naval Institute Press, 1987; John W.R. Lepingwell, 'The Laws of Combat? Lanchester Reexamined', *International Security*, 12/1 (1987), pp. 89–134; and Thomas F. Homer-Dixon, 'A Common Misapplication of the Lanchester Square Law: A Research Note', *International Security*, 12/1 (1987), pp. 135–9.
6 TNA CAB 2/8 348th Committee of Imperial Defence meeting, 24 February 1939.
7 Japanese war planners had intelligence that American war plans estimated that a 10:6 battleship superiority was required for American victory. See Sadao Asada, 'Japanese Admirals and the Politics of Naval Limitation: Kato Tomosaburo vs. Kato Kanji', in G. Jordan (ed.), *Naval Warfare in the Twentieth Century*, London: Croom Helm, 1978, p. 148.
8 TNA ADM1/9466 PD01625 Phillips (Director of Plans) minute, 25 March 1938.
9 Paul M. Kennedy, *The Rise and Fall of British Naval Mastery*, London: Allen Lane, 1983, p. 277.
10 John Ferris, 'The Last Decade of British Maritime Supremacy, 1919–1929', in K. Neilson and G. Kennedy (eds), *Far Flung Lines: Studies in Imperial Defence in Honour of Donald Mackenzie Schurman*, London: Frank Cass, 1996, p. 130.
11 George W. Baer, *One Hundred Years of Sea Power: The US Navy, 1890–1990*, Stanford: Stanford University Press, 1994, pp. 59–63.
12 John Ferris, 'The Symbol and the Substance of Seapower: Great Britain, the United States and the One-Power Standard, 1919–1921', in B.J.C. McKercher (ed.), *Anglo-American Relations in the 1920s: The Struggle for Supremacy*, Basingstoke: Macmillan, 1990.
13 Dean C. Allard, 'Naval Rearmament, 1930–1941: An American Perspective', *Revue Internationale D'Histoire Militaire* 73 (1991), pp. 35–54.
14 Sadao Asada, 'From Washington to London: The Imperial Japanese Navy and the Politics of Naval Limitation, 1921–1930', in Goldstein and Maurer (eds), *The Washington Conference*, p. 152; and Ian Nish, *Japanese Foreign Policy in the Interwar Period*, New York: Praeger, 2002, p. 129.
15 Ian Gow, *Military Intervention in Pre-war Japanese Politics: Admiral Kato Kanji and the Washington System*, London: Hurst, 2003, pp. 79–80, 83–6.

16 Tadashi Kuramatsu, 'Britain, Japan and Inter-war Naval Limitation 1921–1936', in I. Gow and Y. Hirama, *A History of Anglo-Japanese Relations 1600–2000*, Vol. 3, Basingstoke: Palgrave, 2003, p. 129.
17 S. Toyama, 'The Outline of the Armament Expansion of the Imperial Japanese Navy During the Years 1930–41', *Revue Internationale D'Histoire Militaire* 73 (1991), p. 62.
18 Tadashi Kuramatsu, 'The Geneva Naval Conference of 1927: The British Preparation for the Conference, December 1926 to June 1927', *Journal of Strategic Studies* (1996), 104–21; and ibid., 'Japan and the Geneva Naval Conference of 1927: Preparation for the Conference, February to June 1927', in *The Navy in Interwar Japan*, STICERD paper, LSE, 1996.
19 Kuramatsu, 'Britain, Japan and Inter-war Naval Limitation', p. 129.
20 Allard, 'An American Perspective', pp. 35–6.
21 See Asada, 'From Washington to London'; and Gow, *Military Intervention*, 173–254; and Takashi Ito, 'Conflicts and Coalitions in Japan: Political Groups and the London Naval Conference', in S. Groennings *et al.* (eds), *The Study of Coalition Behaviour: Theoretical Perspectives and Cases from Four Continents*, New York: Holt, Reinhart & Winston, 1970.
22 Ferris, 'The Last Decade'; and Orest M. Babij, 'The Second Labour Government and British Maritime Security, 1929–1931', *Diplomacy & Statecraft* (1995), pp. 645–71.
23 Ferris, 'The Last Decade', pp. 137–9.
24 Christopher M. Bell, 'Thinking the Unthinkable: British and American Naval Strategies for an Anglo-American War, 1918–1931', *International History Review*, 19/3 (1997), pp. 757–809; C. Hall, *Britain, America and Arms Control, 1921–1937*, London: Macmillan, 1987; and R.H. Levine, 'The politics of American naval rearmament, 1930–1938' (PhD dissertation, Harvard University, 1972)
25 Interestingly enough, US naval officers split into two categories: those officers who supported the 1930 London agreement because it at least limited the growth of the Japanese and the British fleets; and those who felt that the Congress would authorise construction to keep pace with US rivals: see Allard, 'An American Perspective', pp. 35–6.
26 Ferris, 'The Last Decade', p. 152.
27 Kuramatsu, 'Britain, Japan and Inter-war Naval Limitation', n.25, p. 137; Gow, *Military Intervention*, pp. 175, 181; and Asada, 'From Washington to London', pp. 169–71.
28 Asada, 'From Washington to London', p. 178.
29 See Maiolo, *Royal Navy and Nazi Germany*; and Stephen E. Pelz, *Race to Pearl Harbor: The Failure of the Second London Conference and the Onset of World War II*, Cambridge, MA: Harvard University Press, 1984.
30 Asada is the chief proponent of the first view; see Gow, *Military Intervention*, p. 317.
31 Robert Ellickson, *Order Without Law: How Neighbors Settle Disputes*, Cambridge, MA: Harvard University Press, 1994, pp. 116–20.
32 William R. Braisted, 'On the American Red and Red-Orange Plans, 1919–1939', in G. Jordan (ed.), *Naval Warfare in the Twentieth Century*, pp. 167–85.
33 Gow, *Military Intervention*, p. 195. Also see Kato Kanji, 'Fundamentals of Disarmament', *Contemporary Japan*, 1936, pp. 487–95.
34 Asada, 'From Washington to London', p. 175. Obviously the object of a 70 per cent ratio also had symbolic importance within the context of Japanese civil–military relations.
35 Sadao Asada, 'The Japanese Navy and the United States', in D. Borg and S. Okamoto (eds), *Pearl Harbor as History*, New York: Columbia University Press, 1973, p. 240.
36 Evans and Peattie, *Kaigun*, p. 295.
37 Asada, 'The Japanese Navy and the United States', pp. 239–40.
38 TNA CAB29/148 NCM(35)23, 30 October 1934.

39 This paragraph is a summary of chapter 1 of *The Royal Navy and Nazi Germany*.
40 Mark R. Peattie, 'Japanese Naval Construction, 1919–1941', in P.P. O'Brien (ed.), *Technology and Naval Combat in the Twentieth Century and Beyond*, London: Frank Cass, 2001, pp. 93–108.
41 Jürgen Rohwer and Mikhail Monakov, 'The Soviet Union's Ocean-Going Fleet, 1935–36', *International History Review*, xviii (4) (1996), pp. 757–1008; and ibid., *Stalin's Ocean-Going Fleet: Soviet Naval Strategy and Shipbuilding Programmes, 1935–1953*, London: Frank Cass, 2001; Milan L. Hauner, 'Stalin's Big-Fleet Program', *Naval War College Review*, lvii (2) (2004), pp. 78–120.
42 Stalin to Voroshilov, 27 November 1931, RGASPI (Russian State Archive for Socio-Political History) f.74, op. 2, d.38 ll., pp. 52–3.

6   Japan and pan-Asianism

Masataka Matsuura

In recent years a number of scholars have emphasized the possibility of coopera-tion and conciliation between Japan and Britain during the 1930s in order to maintain their mutually beneficial commercial relationship.[1] To be sure, a number of pro-British political and financial officials, such as Ikeda Shigeki and Yoshida Shigeru, did advocate compromise with Britain and argued that the Jap-anese economy was dependent on the stability of an international financial and Asian commercial order in which Britain played a central role.[2] But, as we know, reconciliation did not materialize and the two countries went to war. Why? From a Japanese perspective, though it is clear that many efforts were made to avoid war in Japan, contemporary political and economic conditions made the success of those efforts extremely unlikely. This chapter takes a viewpoint entirely dif-ferent from the one I have taken in the past. Rather than thinking about this period from the perspective of those Anglophiles in political and financial circles who were trying to avoid war, it explains why the two countries went to war from a political and economic historical viewpoint. In particular it focuses on one of the primary reasons that made peace improbable, namely the rise of pan-Asianism, which brought about significant changes in 1930s Japan, a transforma-tion that led the country towards a southern advance and the so-called 'Greater East Asia War'.

Earlier scholarship has tended to approach the subject of pan-Asianism from the perspective of intellectual history and has often attempted to trace continui-ties between the Asianism which appeared in the second half of the nineteenth century, and the fascism and militarism of the 1930s and 1940s. Such work has largely ignored the relationship of ideas with the political and economic context of the times. In addition, many empirical studies have described in detail the events that led to the 'Greater East Asia War' from the standpoint of diplomatic and military history. Most of these studies are based on pluralistic models or bureaucratic politics and analyse political processes through the decisions of rational actors. However, few of these studies have concretely and empirically examined the meaning and the influence that ideology exercised on contempor-ary politics and foreign relations. There is almost no research that seriously con-siders why an illogical ideology that proclaimed a 'holy war' against the 'devilish Americans and British' gained ascendancy and contributed to its leaders' irrational decision to launch a war that Japan had no chance, economically or militarily, of winning. If such studies exist, they are usually only in the form of making an ahistorical connection between the American anti-Japanese immigration restrictions of 1924 and the attack on Pearl Harbor in 1941.

It is well known that the Shōwa emperor claimed in the introduction to his postwar monologues that the remote cause of the 'Greater East Asia War' was racial discrimination in the form of the rejection of the Japanese proposal for racial equality at Versailles and American anti-Japanese immigration restrictions.[3] Although many Japanese may have shared such sentiments with the emperor, the connection between these attitudes and the invasion of Malaya and the attack on Pearl Harbor requires a huge historical leap. Pan-Asianism bridges this gap. John Dower has pointed out that government authorities deployed pan-Asianism to mobilize the population during the Pacific War.[4] Pan-Asianism, however, was also an ideology that was used to mobilize people well before December 1941. It gradually accumulated in people's consciousness after the First World War and continued to develop in the 1930s so that it greatly contributed to the formulation of policy. In short, war did not only make pan-Asianism, but pan-Asianism also made war.

There were both continuities and ruptures between nineteenth-century Asianism and 1930s pan-Asianism. The former was in many ways a defensive reaction against the Western imperial aggression but the latter is more complex.[5] Previous history studies have not sufficiently explicated these connections and discontinuities. During the inter-war period, through changes in international relations, such as anti-Japanese immigration policies, the unification of China by Jiang Jieshi, the Manchurian Incident and creation of Manchukuo, and Japan's departure from the League of Nations, and changes in the international commercial structure such as the Takahashi financial measures that allowed Japan to escape the Great Depression and the commercial frictions between Japan and Britain brought on by the economic downturn, pan-Asianism underwent a drastic evolution.

The post-First World War 'shocks'

At the close of the First World War Japanese leaders believed that their country had become a 'first-class' power. Japan had achieved revision of the unequal treaties in 1895 and in 1919 it became a standing member of the League of Nations. Under the Washington Treaty system, Japan's alliance with Britain ended. With the establishment of the League and the influence of Wilsonianism, the immediate postwar period presented Japanese leaders with the opportunity to choose what path to take. The journalist Ishibashi Tanzan called for 'small-Japanism' – for the renunciation of interests in Manchuria, independence for colonial Korea and Taiwan, the repudiation of economic privileges in China and peaceful coexistence with Asia. But the government led by Prime Minister Hara Takashi opted to keep in harmony with the big powers, maintain the mandate system, and continue Japan's march towards becoming a major imperial power.

The rejection of the government's proposed racial equality clause at the Paris Peace Conference came as a tremendous shock and caused Japanese to realize that their country had not been completely accepted as one of the major powers.

In the early 1920s the shock was heightened when American anti-Japanese immigration policies sparked protests in Japan. This anti-American movement became connected with other campaigns pressing for wider political participation and equality such as that by the three-party movement to protect constitutional government (*goken sanpa undō*), the labour movement, and the Suiheisha movement, and were bolstered by groups such as chambers of commerce, newspapers, Buddhist groups, and reservists associations.[6] Anger over American racial discrimination continued to boil into the 1930s, as evidenced by a declaration from the Asia League Association (*Ajia renmei kyōkai*) on the 'Thirteenth Anniversary of our National Disgrace' on 1 July 1936.[7]

The immigration issue led to a reaffirmation among many Japanese that Japan was an Asian country of coloured people and to a widespread expectation that a pan-Asian alliance could improve relations with China in the wake of the Twenty-One Demands.[8] At about this time there were moves to formally create a pan-Asian organization. In August 1926 the first All-Asian Race Conference (*Ajia minzoku kaigi*) opened in Nagasaki. It was led by Iwasaki Isao, the chief secretary of the Seiyūkai Party, and Chinese such as Huang Gong-su, a member of the Chinese national legislature from Jiangxi province. This meeting was of historic importance, as signalled by a Home Ministry Affairs police report which noted, 'This is the first time that an organization concerned with foreign relations and of a non-governmental nature has met in our country.'[9]

Most of the conference participants were Japanese and there were few attendees from other countries. The most prominent were Rash Behari Bose, an Indian political exile, the legislator Huang and his Chinese associates, and a few representatives from the Philippines and the Korean peninsula. There was but one Japanese Diet member attending, Imazato Juntarō, a Seiyūkai politician from Nagasaki. There were several reasons for the absence of high-ranking Japanese public officials. The movement's most enthusiastic supporter, Yokota Sennosuke, had recently passed away and Seiyūkai chief-secretary Iwasaki had been imprisoned on bribery charges. Other powerful figures such as Gotō Shimpei and Tanaka Giichi distanced themselves from the movement, fearing criticism from Britain and the ruling Kenseikai party, led by the pro-British Prime Minister Katō Takaaki. Ministry of Foreign Affairs officials also discouraged other prominent politicians from participating in the meeting.

The meeting underscored the difficulties involved in defining 'Asians', to say nothing of unifying them. Chinese calls for the elimination of Japanese privileges acquired by the Twenty-One Demands competed with the Japanese emphasis on reconceptualizing Chinese–Japanese relations in the framework of a 'yellow Asian brotherhood' united to resist the white Western powers. Liu Huajui, a Chinese participant, for example, declared, 'I am confident that China is the birthplace of culture and has the power to rule the entire world. Asia, in particular, is the center of culture, and China is the greatest country within Asia. ...

Asians stand at the center of the world, and everybody knows that China is the center of Asia.'[10] The tensions evident at the meeting were expressed outside of Nagasaki as well. A Chinese pamphlet entitled *The Asian Continent* distributed in Kobe at the time accused Japan of using the Nagasaki gathering as a way to justify its invasion of other countries and lambasted Japanese rule of Korea, Taiwan and the Ryukyus. The pamphlet claimed that because 'Japan is an island country isolated by the ocean, and it bears no relationship to the continent', it was not qualified even to participate in a gathering of Asian countries. Japan was only doing so, they asserted, to advance its invasion of the continent. Instead, they insisted, the unification of the Asia continent was a principle of the Chinese state.[11]

After the Nagasaki meeting organizers scheduled a second meeting in Shanghai for the following year in 1927, but it was called off because of intensified friction between China and Japan. A further meeting did not take place for another eight years. During this era of party cabinets pan-Asianism, which derived its energy from the rejection of the racial equality clause and the anti-Japanese immigration legislation, was forced into hiding. This marginalization was particularly severe during the cabinets controlled by the Kenseikai and Minseitō, which put great emphasis on maintaining good relations with Britain. It is thus impossible to draw a straight line between the rejection of the racial equality clause and anti-Japanese immigration laws and the 'Greater East Asia War' some twenty years later. Yet one cannot deny that these shocks contributed to hostilities on a sub-conscious level.

If nothing else, the first All-Asian Race Conference was symbolic and full of irony. The tone of meeting was organized to criticize Western governments for their racist policies, yet its venue, Nagasaki, had been the sole window to the outside world during the archipelago's two centuries of relative isolation from much of the Western world. Japanese organizers hoped that criticism of the West would unify Asia, but some Chinese used the event to condemn Japan and its policies.

In thinking about the emergence of pan-Asianism during the 1930s, it is useful to do so in the context of three trends: first, the progress toward the unification of China under Jiang Jieshi's leadership, the reorganization of commercial relations under Finance Minister Takahashi, and the 'Taiwan factor'; second, the economic frictions created by Takahashi's attempts to overcome the world depression and the 'India factor'; and third, Chinese attempts to create a modern state and the aid it received from Western countries.

The unification of China and the 'Taiwan factor'

China had served as the principal imperial model for Japan from the time of the Qin (221–206 BC) and Han (202 BC–AD 220) dynasties. Until the modern era, Japan and other Asian countries understood the international order from the perspective of 'small Chinas'. The Chinese imperial model differed from the Western national and imperial model in that, within the former, nation-states did not maintain clear boundaries. China was regarded as the 'civilized centre' on account of its tremendous economic and cultural resources and prestige, and countries on the 'barbarian periphery' paid their respect to China's virtue in the form of tribute and cultural emulation. As a result, Chinese merchants, who handled the payment of tributary goods, fulfilled an important role in supporting the empire.[12] As Japan entered the modern era, the Chinese imperial model was losing its appeal because of the decline of the Qing dynasty. Severe political fissures ruptured China, and Japan delivered another devastating blow to the Chinese imperial system with its victory over the Qing in 1895. Despite the decline of the Qing, the trading networks and commercial capacity of Chinese merchants remained unrivalled in Asia, and Japanese businessmen were largely unable to compete effectively.[13] The Western imperial powers, too, had long maintained a parasitic reliance on Chinese merchants centred in Shanghai and used this relationship to turn China into a semi-colony.[14]

When Jiang Jieshi established a government in Nanjing and called for the unification of China in 1927, Japanese leaders felt a profound sense of crisis. In response, the Japanese government dispatched troops to the Shandong concession and, fearing a resurgence of Chinese identity in Taiwan, officials launched a full-fledged census registration and began to court Taiwanese merchants and their mainland Chinese partners. Since the mid-nineteenth century Taiwanese merchants had freely traded with the mainland coastal provinces of Fujian and Guangdong, where many of them had originated, and, since the beginning of Japanese colonial rule, had taken advantage of Chinese merchant networks and their own status as Japanese subjects to create a vast commercial network that extended across East and Southeast Asia. Therefore, Taiwanese merchants were indispensable to the Japanese attempt to control Asian trade.[15] Recent scholarship has revealed that Sun Yat-sen and his successor, Jiang, attempted to recreate a Chinese empire like that of the Qin and Han, as well as build a modern nation-state, in the wake of the Qing collapse.[16] This was highlighted by Sun's famous 'Greater East Asianism' talk in Kobe, which imagined the recreation of the traditional Chinese imperial model of a tribute trading system with a civilized centre and barbarian periphery. Since the Meiji period Japanese nationalism, which was grounded in *kokugaku*, regarded the resurgence of a Chinese empire as a threat. Japanese pan-Asianists feared that the new Chinese state might become an empire and extend its territorial authority to match the extensive reach of Chinese merchants. It was for this precise reason that Asianist activist Tōyama Mitsuru, who had supported Sun, turned against Jiang's drive to unify China.

In August 1933 Matsui Iwane, who two years later became the president of the Greater Asia Society, was appointed commander of the army in Taiwan. He soon launched a campaign to bolster support for pan-Asianism and organize the National Defence League in Taiwan. Around this time Finance Minister Takahashi Korekiyo implemented Keynesian economic policies that led to industrialization throughout the empire and increased demand for products from Japan. With unrivalled speed Japan was thus able to escape from the Great Depression.

The economic growth of Korea and Taiwan was particularly impressive. To Matsui and Ugaki Kazushige, the governor-general of Korea, the impressive economic performance of the Japanese Empire was a source of national pride, and served to strengthen their conviction that Japanese colonial management was vastly superior to that of the Western imperial powers.

Matsui's pan-Asian policies were closely linked to this economic strategy. Matsui teamed with other members of the Greater Asia Society, such as Wachi Takaji, a Canton official, and Taketō Mineji, a director of the South China Bank, to use Taiwanese and Chinese merchants to tempt the provinces of Fujian, Guangdong, and Guangxi away from the Chinese Republic. They attempted to create an independent economic sphere that was composed of the Japanese Empire and the provinces carved out of China. For example, they envisioned Manchuria producing soybeans, which could be used for fertilizer, Korea as a base for chemical fertilizers, Taiwan providing sugar and other agricultural products, and the coastal provinces contributing mineral resources, paper, tea, and porcelain. Manchuria's economy was once closely tied to that of central China, but after the Manchuria Incident its economy became linked with Japan, Taiwan, and the south-eastern provinces of China. The Manchurian Incident caused a rise in anti-Japanese sentiments and many Chinese merchants refused to conduct commercial relations with Japan, but Taiwanese and others quickly enlarged their trading activities. From 1932 to 1938 exports from Manchuria to Taiwan grew tenfold and doubled in the other direction.[17] Matsui and Wachi sought to strengthen connections between the empire and the southern provinces, which were already a stronghold of anti-Jiang sentiment, even within the Guomindang (GMD), and to reach out to Chinese merchants as well.

Ironically, the symbol of this strategy became 'Greater Asianism', the slogan proclaimed by Sun Yat-sen, the founder of the Chinese Republic. Matsui and other leaders of the Greater Asia Society used this slogan to appeal to anti-Jiang GMD members in the south and to further 'Japanese–Chinese goodwill'. They were opposed to the unification of China as envisioned by Chiang, and hoped to combine Southeast Asia with Manchuria, Mongolia, northern and southern China, Xinjiang, and Tibet to create an 'Asia for the Asians' with Japan as its leader. They wanted to drive Western capital out of Asia, and to extend the influence of pan-Asianism into such areas as the Philippines, where the influence of Chinese merchants was rather weak and Japanese settlers had done rather well.[18] Matsui, for example, proposed that Japan push southward and drive out Britain, which had concentrated its interests in South China.

In summary, the issues that contributed most to shaping 1930s Japanese pan-Asianism included the drive to unify China, the related fear of a resurgence of Chinese power, and the reorganization of Asian commercial and economic relations after the Manchurian Incident. As a result, events in the Japanese colony of Taiwan and the activities of Taiwanese and Chinese merchants figured importantly in the attempt by Japanese leaders to create an 'oceanic empire' to complement Japan's 'continental empire'.

Finance Minister Takahashi's economic policies, commercial frictions, and the 'India Factor'

Why was the role of Indian exiles as important as that of Taiwanese in the spread of pan-Asianist ideas in Japan? First, many Japanese from before the modern era regarded India as one of the three major Asian countries (*sangoku*), as captured in the phrase, 'Honchō, Shindan, Tenjiku' (Japan, China, India). It is apparent that India was thought to be part of Asia even before the arrival of the Western powers. Second, by the 1930s commerce, which had a direct impact on people's standard of living, and culture, centred on Buddhism, became the principal pillars supporting a pan-Asianism that came to be regarded as a 'counter-civilization' opposed to Western imperialism. After the onset of the depression Japanese companies flooded India and other British colonies in Asia with low-priced light industrial goods in an effort to compensate for their troubles in the Chinese market brought about by the Manchuria Incident. Because the incident and the subsequent anti-Japanese movement alienated many Chinese merchants, Japanese businesses became dependent on Indian merchants as trading partners in Asia. Through this process, an increasing number of Japanese came to regard Indian merchants as warriors in Japan's anti-British trade war. At the same time, some Japanese envisioned Buddhism as the most important common cultural identity that bound Japan to 'Asia' from which it was seeking to drive out the Western imperialists. Because the ideology of modern Japan's empire (*kokutai*) lacked a universal religious core, Buddhism, which originally emerged in India and spread northward to Tibet, China, and Korea, as well as to Southeast Asia, became a culture symbol of 'Asian' civilization.[19] It did not matter whether Indians and Chinese were actually Buddhists believers or not. Finally, India was the jewel of the British Empire that stretched across Asia and Africa and the symbol of the Western encroachment into Asia.

Indian merchants, like Chinese and Taiwanese merchants, actively engaged in commercial activities in the Western powers' Asian empires. Even before the end of the First World War, Japanese cotton products flooded the Indian market, driving out the British textile industry and overwhelming domestic production.[20] When Finance Minister Takahashi abandoned the gold standard, the value of the yen fell drastically and cheap, light-manufactured Japanese products poured into India and the British colonies in Southeast Asia and Africa. The redirection of goods to these areas resulted in part because of the boycott of Japanese goods in China after the Manchurian Incident. Merchants who were less inclined to be hostile to Japan, such as Indians, Taiwanese, and some Chinese, played a key role in opening these new channels for Japanese goods.[21] As a result, the number of Indians who came to Japan increased dramatically. In particular, Kobe, a major Japanese port focused on Asia, became a favoured location for Indians. Its Indian population increased by approximately six times from 1918 to 1938. The expansion of trade with India led to an increase in the influence of Indian political refugees living in Japan, and the inclusion of anti-British, pro-independence rhetoric in the language of Japanese pan-Asianism.

Among the Indian immigrants were a number of prominent Indian exiles. For example, R.B. Bose, the exile who participated in the 1926 All-Asian Race Conference, had been involved in the attempted assassination of the Viceroy, Lord Hardinge, and in the Lahore rebellion. Raja Mehendra Pratap, an Indian prince who had acquired Afghani citizenship and became an independence activist, also sought political asylum in Japan. In addition, A.M. Sahay and others, following the direction of Nehru to establish independence movements overseas, set up commercial offices in Japan. Assisted by Japanese right-wing organizations and student groups, led by Tōyoma and his right-wing colleague Ōkawa Shūmei, these activists disseminated news about Britain's brutal rule and exploitation of India and solicited help for the anti-British independence movement. Support for the movement in Japan grew especially after the civil disobedience marches against the salt tax along the Ganges River in 1930. Money was funnelled through Indian clubs in Kobe and gradually more Japanese became aware of Indian complaints. However, members of the establishment – such as Foreign Ministry bureaucrats, police officials, and the ruling Kenseitō and Minseitō party politicians – viewed the Indian independence movement unfavourably. Even the British intelligence officers who kept Indian activists under surveillance thought that Japanese society was friendlier towards Britain than towards the Indians.[22] The Japanese government's priority was on maintaining good relations with Britain in order to optimize the benefits of cooperation among the imperial powers. Bose, too, complained on the pages of the *Voice of India,* a publication of the Nationalist Group's Japanese Branch, that the Japanese were uninterested in Indian political affairs.[23] However, after Britain announced that it would scrap the Japan–India Commercial Pact in April 1933 Japanese support for the Indian activities suddenly began to flourish.

As soon as Britain clamped down on trade from Japan, members of the Osaka business community identified Britain as Japan's primary enemy in Asia, and suggested that because its Achilles heel was India, pan-Asianists ought to support the independence movement.[24] Tsuda Shingo, the president of the leading textile firm Kanebō, and Greater Asia Society members promoted this line of thinking. The exiled Indians took no time to react to this opportunity. They interpreted the commercial friction between Britain and Japan as another example of the British persecuting Asians, and in activities throughout Japan charged that the Lytton Commission's investigation of the Manchuria Incident and boycott of Japanese goods in China were evidence of Britain's oppressing Japan.

Several groups became a new sounding board and source of financial support for the Indians. The Osaka and Kobe chambers of commerce, which represented light industry and shipping businesses competing against British companies, Buddhist officials and newspaper journalists, particularly in Kobe and Kyoto, offered their help. Two prominent examples were Kobayashi Gidō, a Jōdoshū Buddhist official at the Gokuraku Temple in Kobe, and Igawa Jōkei, a priest and professor at Nishiyama Buddhist College. In September 1931 just as economic tension between Japan and Britain began to rise, dissatisfied with the Tokyo-based Japan–India Society, which promoted friendship between Japan and Britain, Sahay created the Kansai Japan–India Society with the help of the Kobe Chamber of Commerce, the Kobe Buddhist Association, and Kobe Commercial College. Two years later in October 1933, with assistance from the Kyoto Industrial Association, the Kyoto Buddhist Forum, and Buddhist colleges such as Ryūkoku and Ōtani in Kyoto, Sahay established a branch of the society in Kyoto. With Japanese backing, the Indian activists launched their anti-British campaign. They delivered fiery speeches to large crowds at meetings that were publicized by various newspapers, organized by Kokumin Dōmei political renegades who had left the Minseitō party, and supported by textile manufacturers in Osaka and Nagoya. Pratap spent his time participating in these events and travelling across Manchuria, China and throughout Asia to raise a volunteer army to free India from British rule. As a result of these activities, an image of the Western imperialist, as represented by the British in India, conquering and ruthlessly exploiting Asia, permeated nearly every corner of Japan and pan-Asian thought began to coalesce. A subtle but important shift in the attitude of Foreign Ministry officials towards the Indian activists is apparent in the language of their official memoranda. The Indians were transformed from 'an Indian under surveillance' and 'an Indian that we should be careful of' to 'an Indian patriot' and 'an Indian revolutionary'.

Ex-patriot Indians in Japan, such as Bose and Sahay, struggled with the contradiction that they were relying on Imperial Japan to free India from the British Empire. After all, their host country had colonized Korea and Taiwan and was waging an aggressive war against China. These concerns were particularly severe for Sahay, who was familiar with anti-Japanese sentiments in India, and who was closely aligned with the Congress Party, whose leaders, Nehru and Gandhi, were critical of Japan for its invasion of China. In the end, however, Sahay made Indian independence his top priority and hoped that the war with China would not weaken Japan, that it would upset British machinations in China, that the Japanese and Chinese would overcome their differences, and that reconciliation would lead to an Asian unity strong enough to combat British imperialism.[25]

Buddhist aid for the Indian independence movement was not limited to Kobayashi and Igawa, but was also supported by a number of high-ranking priests and temple officials in Kyoto and elsewhere, whose influence on their parishioners should not be underestimated. As suggested by his slogan, 'Great Asia is strung together like beads on a Buddhist rosary', Kobayashi stressed that Buddhism must play an important unifying role in the defence of Asian nations and in the cultural revival of Asian culture by reaching out to the various peoples of Asia.[26] Later, at the request of the army, Kobayashi assisted Subhas Chandra Bose in organizing Indian activists and an Indian national army with the goal of bringing about the destruction of the British Empire.[27] It was not only Jōdoshū Buddhists who supported Indian independence fighters and backed pan-Asianism, though. Many prominent Buddhist leaders of other sects, such as Ōnishi Ryōkei, Ōtani Kozui, and Ōtani Sonyū, did so as well.[28] They envisioned links between Tibetan

Buddhism, Islam, and Hinduism to combat Western imperialism. A few Christian and Shinto believers also supported pan-Asianism. An examination of pan-Asianism is incomplete without a consideration of the influence of religion. Japanese used religious networks as a tool to combat Western imperialism, which claimed to represent the universal values of civilization. The close relationship between pan-Asianism and religious groups such as Buddhist sects is undeniable.

After Prime Minister Tōjō called for Indian independence in a speech in May 1942 a few months after the fall of Singapore, several large parties were held in honour of Resh Behari Bose in Japan before his departure to join an army of Indians based in Southeast Asia, which hoped to drive out the British from the subcontinent. In addition to private right-wing radicals and army officers who backed Bose in Tokyo, textile company executives and shipping company officials, university officials, top Buddhist priests, chamber of commerce leaders, and regional politicians in Kyoto, Osaka, and Kobe lent their support to Bose.[29] Anti-British sentiments after the outbreak of the China War were most intense in the Kansai (greater Kyoto, Osaka, Kobe) area, and Buddhist officials and commercial and manufacturing business leaders, especially in the textile and shipping industries, provided the strongest support for pan-Asianism in the region. Why did commerce and religion, which are both characterized by cooperative action based on harmony and expansionism fuelled by competition, become bound together in support of pan-Asianism, and why was this particularly so in Kansai? The explanation for the close relationship between Buddhism and business, and the vibrancy of pan-Asianism, in Kansai is fairly simple: Osaka and Kobe had strong commercial ties with Asia; neighbouring Kyoto and Nara were the home of many Buddhist temples, many Kansai textile and general trading company leaders were Ōmi merchants (business people who hailed from the Ōmi region of adjacent Shiga prefecture); and Ōmi merchants were overwhelmingly members of the Jōdo shinshū, Jōdoshū, and Tendaishū sects.[30] Furthermore, Kansai hosts many famous Shinto shrines, Ise, Kashihara, Ikuta, and Minatogawa, which are strongly associated with Japanese nationalism. Many people in Kansai became intensely interested in politics and advocates of pan-Asianism after commercial frictions flared after the onset of the world-wide depression, and business ties between Ōmi and Indian merchants contributed to a rise in such attitudes.

Sahay and Bose often met with Greater Asia Society thinkers and newspaper writers to describe their philosophy and activities. These exchanges seem to have deepened hostility towards Britain for a number of Japanese. Mutō Teiichi, for example, a well-known military analyst at the time, as well as an editorialist for the Osaka *Asahi* newspaper and member of the Greater Asia Society, came away from his meeting with Sahay an avowed anti-British ideologue. In the introduction to his *Kōei sekai sensō* (the world-wide war against Britain), a diatribe published just after the outbreak of the China War with a large first print run of 30,000 copies, Mutō declared, 'I am taking aim at the British empire with this book. ... He (the British Empire) is seeking a war against Japan. This is not simply a "Japanese–British War," though, but a "world-wide war against Japan" which is of a much worse nature. ... The Japan–China incident being played out in China now is no other than a "Japanese–British War".'[31] In another book, Mutō repeated his assertion that the Sino-Japanese War was actually a war between Britain and Japan, noting, 'The basis for Japan striking China is that this is actually a holy war to save China from the clutches of a white invasion.'[32] As their relationship with Indian activists deepened, Japanese journalists, like Mutō, served as important mouthpieces to spread the pan-Asianist ideas and anti-British hostility. They alleged, for example, that Britain was manipulating China to make war on Japan.

To Japanese leaders, the British imperial model had served as an alternative to the Chinese imperial model since the Meiji Restoration. While British imperialism was based on the premises of equality between sovereign states that were 'civilized' and 'modern' (which meant they were based on Western laws, administration, financial systems, and culture), it had been shown to be a model that justified white rule over Asian and other coloured peoples. It used war and the threat of military might to obtain unequal treaties, secure key ports, create concessions and colonial settlements, and then gradually move up rivers and railroads into the interior, and gain political and economic control of territory. Based on this model, Western countries had gained control over the resources and economies of many Asian countries, and obtained new capital and markets. Modern Japan had emulated this model with great fervour, using the export of light industrial goods to accumulate capital and taking advantage of the Asian 'treaty port' system to secure territorial concessions, until it collided with Britain during the world-wide depression. Perhaps it should come as little surprise that the Japanese were angered by the Lytton Commission, which found Japan guilty of aggression during the Manchurian Incident, and saw the commission's conclusions as a sham.

Japan became a 'continental empire' through the establishment of Manchukuo. The next conference of the All-Asian Race Conference, whose meetings had been suspended since the Shanghai conference was cancelled, took place in Dalian in Manchukuo in 1934. After seizing Dalian from Russia, Japan made use of it to develop its trade in Asia through so-called 'Dalianism'.[33] The Manchurian Incident and commercial frictions in India, however, gradually changed the primary enemy of the pan-Asianists from the USSR to Britain, and presented Japan with an opportunity to become an 'oceanic empire'. The Dalian meeting focused on the British Empire, and afterwards work was undertaken to organize Japan, Taiwan, South China, and Southeast Asia into a Japanese 'oceanic empire' with Dalian as one of its hub ports.[34] Japanese leaders established Manchukuo as one of Japan's colonial bases and began the economic reorganization of the entire empire and the industrialization of the country's colonies. Japanese pan-Asianists sought to create an alternative co-existence, co-prosperity empire, which differed from the Chinese and British models that had not implemented industrialization and education in their realms.[35] As Japan overcame the depression, Japanese pride in their empire deepened and confidence in their ability to rule colonies grew, as evidenced by the words of Ugaki Kazushige, the governor-general of Korea, Matsui Iwane, the commander of the army in Taiwan, and Takahashi Kamekichi, a popular private economist. Matsui, in particular, boasted of Japanese accomplishments. He expressed satisfaction that Japan had been able to shift its foreign exports, much of which went from Osaka, to Southeast Asia and India and away from China because of the anti-Japanese boycott staged in the wake of the Manchurian Incident. At the end of his tenure as governor-general, he stated that the Taiwanese were indebted to and ought to be thankful to Japan for protecting them from the depression and for generously blessing them with economic benefits. In Taiwan, Matsui encouraged members of the Greater Asia Society to promote pan-Asianism.[36] This strategy was the pride of pan-Asianists, who believed Japan could become a 'super-empire'. For this reason, in 1935 Japanese authorities began to use the word *tennō* instead of 'emperor' and to only use the 'Greater Japanese Empire' (*Dai Nippon teikoku*) to refer to Japan in all diplomatic exchanges to communicate the idea that their ruler was the world's only sovereign of a super-empire. 'Co-existence, co-prosperity' was intended to lead to different colonial relations than those that existed within the Western empires. In summary, the conditions that contributed to and shaped the rise of pan-Asianism during the 1930s were the reorganization of the world economic system because of the global depression, and alliances between exiled Indian, Buddhists, and industrial capitalists.

Japanese opposition to British aid to China

As a result of the rise of the Japanese Empire, which sought to overcome the Chinese and British imperial models, these two opponents appeared to pan-Asianists to come together to defend their interests against Japan. Britain and China were seen as mutually dependent on each other. British imperial rule relied on the Chinese commercial network, and the creation of a unified China seemed to depend on British economic assistance.[37] Chinese currency reform, carried out on the advice of Sir Frederick Leith-Ross in 1935, became a symbol of this mutual dependency. Many Japanese observers believed the reforms put the core of Chinese financial matters under the control of Britain.[38] In addition, many Japanese pan-Asianists and newspapers perceived Jiang's borrowing for the construction of railways in Guangdong and elsewhere in south China, and the creation of iron works companies as a defeat for Japanese interests in the commercial war with Britain in China. General Matsui tried to persuade leaders in south China to cooperate with Japan against Jiang in February and March 1936, but his attempt failed. After the south Chinese leader Hu Hanmin died in May 1936, Jiang's government quickly toppled Hu's allies. The Xi'an Incident in December led to a rise in anti-Japanese sentiments throughout China. As a result, many Japanese believed that Britain was sowing anti-Japanese sentiments throughout China and furthering its own policies even as it continued to export raw materials to Japan.

Just as these sentiments were coming to the surface, an all-out war with China broke out in July 1937. Matsui, the former commander of the army in Taiwan and pan-Asianist, returned to active duty and was dispatched to direct the fighting in China. Matsui thought the war in China was an excellent opportunity to apply the principles of the Greater Asia Society. When he departed for Shanghai to assume his post, he claimed that the true nature of the war between Japan and China was an 'Asian family fight'. Japan, as the older brother, was beating up its proud younger brother, China, not because of hate, but because this was the only way that it could bring it to reflect on its actions.[39] Matsui believed that the way to bring about real goodwill between Japan and China was to cause the Chinese to regret their actions by driving the British and other Western capital out and toppling the Jiang regime, which depended on British aid. He felt that Japan's real enemy was Britain and advocated advancing southward to attack Nanjing, Guangzhou, and Hankou, which were centres of the alliance between China and Britain. The first Konoe cabinet, which initially leaned toward Britain, had Matsui recalled, but when the cabinet failed to resolve the war it was no longer able to constrain pan-Asianism.[40]

On 3 November 1938 Prime Minister Konoe declared a 'New Order in East Asia', and from this time Japan's China war policy became guided by pan-Asianist principles. It was perhaps especially apt that Konoe became a spokesman for pan-Asianism, because he was the son of and ideological successor to Konoe Atsumaro, a nineteenth-century spokesman for Japanese Asianism. In a speech delivered at the Nihon Club on 18 January 1939 Kurihara Shō, the East Asian Bureau Chief at the Foreign Ministry and director of the Greater Asia Society, declared that the war in China, which 'until now had been a semi-colony of the powers', was a battle between Japan and the Comintern, as well as Britain, France, and the United States. Sahay and his fellow Indian exiles probably felt like they were reaping the fruits of their activities when they learned of such statements.[41] The Konoe cabinet's pan-Asianist policies were modelled on those promoted by the Greater Asia Society. Nakayama Masaru, a director of the Society, drafted three central Konoe policies, including the East Asia New Order.[42] Colonel Kagesa Sadaaki, a behind-the-scenes engineer in the creation of the Wang Jingwei government, was also a member. Japanese government officials hoped that Chinese in south China and in Southeast Asia would support the Wang regime and be sympathetic to Japanese aims. The Greater Asia Society was also deeply involved in the Tianjin blockade, the attempt to shut down the Burma Road, and in anti-British demonstrations within Japan and in its colonies. Fearing the collapse of British power in Asia, the United States decided to impose economic sanctions against Japan.[43] As a result, Japan embarked on a path to war with the country it most wanted to avoid.

Conclusion

The final point to make in this chapter is that the Greater Asia Society was not a government entity, but what we today would call a non-governmental organization. The members of the Society created a network that did not operate as an institutionalized government organization; but the Society utilized and exercised influence on military, bureaucratic, political, and economic circles, as high-lighted by the work of Matsui, Wachi, and Taketō. This chapter has only detailed a few aspects of the group's activities. Other examples include the endeavours of Suzuki Teiichi and Hōsei University Professor Nakatani Takeyo, who were both officials in the Asia Development Board (Kōain) and officers of the Society. They spearheaded propaganda, cultural, and pacification campaigns in occupied China by founding Society branches in Tianjin and Shanghai, cooperating with Sahay and other members of the Indian National Congress in China, and collab-orating with the Wang government to promote anti-British sentiment and pan-Asians ideas. As historian Prasenjit Duara has pointed out, Japanese attempts to placate the Chinese met with a degree of success.[44]

However, it must be emphasized that these non-governmental organizations, such as the Greater Asia Society and Buddhist groups, created connections with Chinese and Indian exiles and, in doing so, co-opted the arguments and energy of these groups and used them to support the aims of Japanese pan-Asianism throughout the empire. Pan-Asianism was an ideology that competed with the British Empire for the cooperation of Chinese and Indian merchants, and the Japanese war for pan-Asianism, that is, the 'Greater East Asia War', brought about the downfall of the British Empire, and, ultimately, the Japanese Empire. After the establishment of Manchukuo, Japan sought to control the Asian com-mercial network run by Chinese and Indian merchants and to become an 'oceanic empire' and advance southward.

Supporters of pan-Asianism promoted the ideology through speeches, text-books, radio broadcasts, and newspapers and magazine articles throughout Asia and gradually many average members of the population became sympathetic to the mentality. For example, in a teaching manual published in 1941, Murakawa Kengo, professor emeritus in Western history with a speciality in ancient Greek history at Tokyo Imperial University, who also served as the vice-chair of the Greater Asia Society, wrote that the purpose for studying Western history was to learn of the wars, oppression, and exploitation prosecuted by the West and to rectify them:

> Whites used science and culture as a weapon to conquer much of the world and have achieved global supremacy. We cannot deny that Western culture has made great contributions to the improvement and progress of human life, but we must not overlook the fact that the welfare of all humans has not flourished. Rather we should understand that many conquered humans cry out as the result of their oppression and exploitation in the shadows of white people's vitality and prosperity.... Now that over four full years have elapsed since the outbreak of the China Incident, and our great, unrivalled army has been engaged in a holy war on the continent, their might shining throughout the whole world, it is time for us to begin the great work of establishing the Greater East Asia Co-Prosperity Sphere. As long as the emperor's country moves forward to accomplish its magnificent mission, it is inevitable that there will be friction with the strong white powers that seek

to guarantee their supposed superiority, so it is imperative for us to prepare for difficulties far more severe than those we face today. Our nation's goal of establishing the East Asia Co-Prosperity Sphere, more than anything else, is the first step in accomplishing our mission to bring true peace to the world. We, at this moment, must follow the grandeur of our ancestors and our recent development, believe in our nation's potential, and harden our determination to fulfil this mission to overcome every kind of hardship and ensure the prosperity of the imperial throne.[45]

Previously, Murakawa claimed that all of Japan's modern wars – the Sino-Japanese, Russo-Japanese, the Manchurian Incident, and the China War – were the result of friction and rivalry between Japan and either the white powers, who were intent on maintaining or extending their worldwide hegemony, or the Chinese, who were acting as proxies for the white races.[46] Murakawa's writings, which depended on his status as an emeritus professor of Western history in the college of humanities at the foremost university in the country, and on his so-called understanding of history, probably had a substantial impact on the formation of a pan-Asianist historical consciousness among teachers and students. Yano Jin'ichi, professor emeritus in Asia history at Kyoto Imperial University, who also served as vice-chair of the Greater Asia Society, probably had a similar influence. In this manner, the Greater Asia Society spread the message of pan-Asianism throughout Japan.

In February 1940, Minseitō politician Saitō Takao delivered what became a famous anti-military speech. He plainly criticized the efforts of the Konoe cabinet's attempts to resolve the China war through policies based on pan-Asianism, disparaged the Wang government, and railed against those who 'hid behind rhetoric that glorified holy war, made light of the sufferings of the people, and deployed vague expressions such as so-called international justice, moral diplomacy, and "co-existence, co-prosperity"'. Saitō's speech pointed out that pan-Asianism was the mentality of Japan at that time. His words, however, did not lead to any debate on these issues, but to his expulsion from the Diet and to the formation of the League of Diet Members Supporting the Prosecution of the Holy War, which sang the praises of Konoe's 'New Order'. Soon the Japanese government formed the Tripartite Pact with Nazi Germany and Fascist Italy, and moved closer to war with Britain and the United States.

It is imperative that we consider the relationship between ideology and the political and economic context, and not simply rely on an analysis of systematic political processes in order to understand accurately Japanese politics during the 1930s and any period. On the path toward and in the expansion of the Pacific War, we must understand the degree to which pan-Asianism influenced political events.

Notes

This chapter was translated by Aaron Skabelund.

1 See, for example, the work of Sugihara Kaoru, Akita Shigeru, Kagotani Naoto, and Kibata Yōichi, in Akita Shigeru and Kagotani Naoto (eds), *1930 nendai no Ajia kokusai chitsujo*, Hiroshima: Keisuisha, 2002.

2 Masataka Matsuura, *Nicchū sensōki ni okeru keizai to seiji* (Economics and Politics during the Sino-Japanese War), Tokyo: Tokyo daigaku shuppankai, 1995; and ibid., *Zaikai no seiji keizai shi*, Tokyo: Tokyo daigaku shuppankai, 2002.

3 Terasaki Hidenari and Mariko Terasaki-Miller (eds), *Shōwa tennō dokuhakuroku – Terasaki Hidenari, go-yō gakari nikki*, Tokyo: Bungei shunjū, 1991, pp. 20–1. The English version of the monologues, which was created in preparation for the Tokyo Trials, naturally deleted these comments. Higashino Makoto, *NHK supesharu serekushon – Shōwa tennō futatsu no dokuhakuroku*, Tokyo: Nihon hōsō kyōkai, 1998, p. 130.

4 John Dower, *War Without Mercy: Race and Power in the Pacific War*, New York: Pantheon, 1986.

5 Some prominent figures of nineteenth-century Asianism included Honda Toshiaki, Satō Nobuhiro, Katsu Kaishū, who called for an alliance among Japan, China, and Korea, Tarui Tōkichi who endorsed the merger of Japan and Korea, Konoe Atsumaro who promoted an alliance between Japan and China, and Miyazaki Tōten, Okakura Tenshin, and Tōyama Mitsuru of the Black Dragon Society.

6 See, for example, Kodama Masaaki, 'Amerika 1924 nen imin hō no seiritsu ni taisuru imin ken no dōkō', in Miwa Kimitada (ed.), *Nichibei kiki no kigen to hainichi imin hō*, Tokyo: Ronzasha, 1997; and Miwa Kimitada, '1924 hai-Nichi imin hō no seiritsu to beika boikotto', in Hosoya Chihiro (ed.), *Taiheiyō, Ajia ken no kokusai keizai funsō shi*, Tokyo: Tokyo daigaku shuppankai, 1983.

7 Gaimushō gaikō shiryōkan archive, Tokyo, *Kakkoku imin hō ki narabi ni seisaku kankei zakken. Beikoku no bu [zokuryō chi o fukumu]*, Vol. 6, J.1.1.0.X1-U1, Yasui (Osaka) to Ushio, Arita, Terauchi, Nagano, Nagata, and prefectural governors, 'Ajia renmei kyōkai no beikoku hainichi imin teppai kigan undo ni kansuru ken', 2 July 1936.

8 See, for example, 'Shinajin no tainichi kansō kōka', *Jiji shinpō*, 13 May 1924.

9 Gaimushō gaikō shiryōkan archive, Tokyo, *Minzoku mondai kankei ikken, Ajia minzoku mondai*, Vol. 2, Naimushō keiho kyoku hoan ka, 'Taishō 15 nen 10 gatsu, zen Ajia minzoku kaigi tenmatsu'.

10 *Minzoku mondai kankei ikken, Ajia minzoku mondai*, Vol. 1, pp. 539–41.

11 *Minzoku mondai kankei ikken, Ajia minzoku mondai*, Vols 1 and 2, Yamagata (Hyogo) to Hamaguchi, Shidehara, designated prefectural officials, and Yukizawa, 'Ajia minzoku taikai ni kansuru hantai gekibun haifu no ken', 5 and 6 August 1926.

12 Hamashita Takeshi, Ronald Toby, Arano Yasunori and others have all shed light on the Chinese imperial model. For a more recent analysis, see Kawashima Shin, *Kindai Chūgoku gaikō no keisei*, Nagoya: Nagoya daigaku shuppankai, 2004.

13 Kagotani Naoto, *Ajia kokusai tsūshō chitsujo to kindai Nihon*, Nagoya: Nagoya daigaku shuppankai, 2000.

14 Motono Eiichi, *Dentō Chūgoku shōgyō chitsujo no hōkai*, Nagoya: Nagoya daigaku shuppankai, 2004.

15 Lin Man-houng, 'Nihon shokuminchi ki Taiwan no zai-Manshū bōeki sokushin to sono shakaiteki igi', in Akita and Kagotani (eds), *1930 nendai no Ajia kokusai chitsujo*.

16 Wang Ke, ' "Teikoku" to "minzoku" ', in Yamamoto Yūzō (ed.), *Teikoku no kenkyū*, Nagoya: Nagoya daigaku shuppankai, 2004.

17 Lin, 'Nihon shokuminchi'.

18 The Philippines, an American colony, were excluded from the anti-Japanese immigration regulations.

19 Watanabe Hiroshi, ' "Oshie" to Inbō – "Kokutai" no ichi-kigen', in Watanabe Hiroshi and Boku Chūshaku (eds), *Kankoku Nihon "Seiyō"* (Nikkan Kyōdō Kenkyū Sōsho, vol. 11), Tokyo: Keiō Gijuku Daigaku Shuppan, 2005.
20 Nishikawa Hiroshi, *Nihon teikokushugi to mengyō*, Tokyo: Mineruva, 1987, chap. 5.
21 Kagotani, *Ajia kokusai tsūshō chitsujo to kindai Nihon*.
22 The National Archives, Kew (TNA), FO371/14755 Tilley (Tokyo) to Henderson, 10 May 1930 and ibid., 13 October 1930.
23 TNA FO371/14755 Snow to Henderson, 5 November 1930.
24 Snow to Simon, 23 June 1933, in A. Trotter *et al.* (eds), *British Documents on Foreign Affairs, Part II, Series E Asia, 1914–1939*, Washington, DC: University Publications of America, 1992, vol. 12, pp. 274–5.
25 Masataka Matsuura, 'Han-Ajiashugi ni okeru "Indo yōin" ', in Ishida Ken (ed.), *Teikoku no bōchō*, Tokyo: Tokyo daigaku shuppankai, 2007.
26 Kobayashi Gidō, 'Nenju de tsunage dai-Ajia', *Kachō* (December 1939).
27 Kobayashi, *Raimu ibunshū*, Kobe: Higashi gokuryakuji, 1982.
28 For more about the contribution of Zen priests to the war effort, see Brian Victoria, *Zen at War*, New York: Weatherhill, 1997.
29 R.B. Bose Papers, Daitō Bunka Daigaku, Saitama, Notebook VI 1942; and Nakajima Takeshi, *Nakamuraya no Bose*, Tokyo: Hakusuisha, 2005, pp. 286–8.
30 Itsuki Hiroyuki, *Tariki*, Tokyo: Kōdansha, 2000, pp. 168–9; Arimoto Masao, *Shinshū no shūkyō shakai shi*, Tokyo: Yoshikawa Kōbunkan, 1995; Ogura Eiichirō, *Ōmishōnin no keifu*, Tokyo: Nihon Keizai shinbunsha, 1980; Serikawa Hiromichi, *Nihon no kindaika to shūkyō rinri*, Tokyo: Taga shuppan, 1997.
31 Mutō Teiichi, *Kōei sekai sensō*, Tokyo: Shimizu shoten, 1937, pp. 1–4.
32 Mutō, *Bakushin*, Tokyo: Modan Nihon-sha, 1938, pp. 62–7.
33 Kitaoka Shin'ichi, *Nihon rikugun to tairiku seisaku*, Tokyo: Tokyo daigaku shuppankai, 1978, pp. 34–42.
34 It was symbolic that the Yamato Hotel, across the street from the British consulate, hosted the Dalian meeting. A.M. Nair, *Shirarezaru Indo dokuritsu tousō*, Tokyo: Fūtousha, 1983, p. 139.
35 Hori Kazuo, 'Shokuminchi teikoku Nihon no keizai kōzō', *Nihon-shi kenkyū*, vol. 62 (2001); ibid., 'Nihon teikoku bōchō to shokuminchi kōgyōka', in Akita and Kagotani (eds), *1930 nendai no Ajia kokusai chitsujo*, and ibid., 'Nihon teikoku to shokuminchi kankei no rekishiteki igi', in Hori Kazuo and Nakamura Tetsu (eds), *Nihon shihonshugi to Chōsen, Taiwan*, Kyoto: Kyoto daigaku gakujutsu shuppankai, 2004.
36 Masataka Matsuura, 'Takahashi Zaiseika no teikoku keizai saihensei to taiseikan yūi kyōsō', in Banno Junji *et al.* (eds), *Kensei no seijigaku*, Tokyo: Tokyo daigaku shuppankai, 2005.
37 Furuta Kazuko, *Shanhai nettowāku to kindai higashi Ajia*, Tokyo: Tokyo daigaku shuppankai, 2000.
38 See, for example, Suma Yakichirō, *Suma Yakichirō gaikō hiroku*, Tokyo: Sōgensha, 1988, pp. 76–8.
39 Maruyama Masao, 'Gunkoku shihaisha no seishin keitai', *Maruyama Masao shū*, Vol. 4, Tokyo: Iwanami shoten, 1995.
40 Masataka Matsuura, 'Nicchū sens ha naze nanka shita ka', *Hokudai hōgaku ronshū*, Vol. 59/1 (2006).
41 Gaimushō gaikō shiryōkan archive, Tokyo, *Eikoku naisei kankei zassan, zokuryō kankei, Indo no bu, hanei undo kankei*, A.6.6.0.1–1–2–1, Shimizu (Wakayama) to Kido, Arita, and Director-General of Prefectures in Kinki region, prosecutors in the Wakayama regional courts, 'Eikoku datō Indo dokuritsu kōenkai kaisai jōkyō ni kansuru ken', 14 April 1934.
42 Nakayama Masaru, *Nakayama Masaru senshū*, Tokyo: Nakayama Masaru senshū kankō iinkai, 1982; ibid., *Shina ron to zuihitsu*, Tokyo: Tōkō shoin, 1940; Nakatani Takeyo, *Shōwa dōran ki no kaisō*, Tokyo: Tairyūsha, 1989, pp. 672–3.

43 Hosoya Chihiro, 'Taiheiyō sensō toha nichi-ei sensō de ha nakatta ka', *Gaikō shiryōkan shiryō* 10 (November 1979).
44 Prasenjit Duara, 'The Discourse of Civilization and Pan-Asianism', *Journal of World History,* 12/1 (2001), pp. 99–130.
45 Murakawa Kengo, *Seiyōshi kyōtei (chūgakkō yō)*, Tokyo: Chūtōgakkō Kyōkasho Kabushiki Gaisha, 1941.
46 Murakawa Kengo, 'Kōa gendōryoku toshite no Nihon', in Satō Shizen (ed.), *Kōa Taikan*, Nagoya: Shin Aichi shinbunsha, 1940.

7 Bombing, Japanese pan-Asianism and Chinese nationalism

Hans van de Ven

An aspect of the Sino-Japanese War of 1937–45 that has received little attention is the Japanese bombing of Chinese cities. Recent Chinese scholarship on the war has concentrated on the fighting of Nationalist ground forces especially in the first years of the war, in part to redress the suggestion of a previous generation of historians that the Nationalists made no sustained effort to resist the Japanese invasion. The Nanjing Massacre, the Japanese use of chemical weapons, and the exploitation of comfort women have also emerged as significant – and emotionally charged – topics over the last two decades that continue to have serious contemporary political significance for Sino-Japanese relations. These topics have overshadowed bombing, which in reality was a major aspect of the fighting and which featured prominently in the early reporting of the war.

This chapter uses the case of Canton to examine the economic and social effects of bombing. The Canton case suggests that, if, as is well known, the Japanese were never able to consolidate their rule in China's rural areas, the carnage caused by bombing also rendered it impossible for them to establish control over cities, let alone turn them into centres of prosperity exemplifying the benefits that would come from Japanese rule. It also examines the Japanese bombing of Shanghai during the first months of the war. This generated a wave of negative publicity for Japan portraying it as a militarist and barbaric country violating basic principles of civilized conduct. On the other hand, if only years before China was widely described as mired in civil warfare, wracked by famine, and ruled by an oppressive and corrupt elite, China became hailed as a plucky if still young nation fighting for civilization. Bombing helped to give rise to significant changes in perceptions of China and Japan.

The chapter begins with an analysis of Japanese pan-Asianism, which needs to be taken more seriously than has been done, at least as the rhetoric that the Japanese chose to deploy to give meaning to their actions. Based on the idea that Asian cultures were bound by a set of core cultural values and shared a common destiny, it posited that Japan's task was to eliminate Western imperialism from Asia. Both the social and economic havoc that Japanese bombing caused, as well as the changes in perception of China and Japan that it helped foster, undermined Japanese pan-Asian aspirations and strengthened respect for Chinese nationalism.

Japanese pan-Asianism

Masataka Matsuura makes the case that 'war did not make pan-Asianism, but pan-Asianism made war'.[1] Whether pan-Asianism was held as deeply or popularly as Matsuura suggested is a question for further research. But it was clearly influential in the Japanese army and figured prominently in rhetorical justifications of its actions in China. It also was an essential element in the ideological framework on which the Japanese hoped to build new social, political, and cultural configurations in China.

Japanese pan-Asianism was in part a response to the rejection of Japan's proposal to include a statement about racial equality in the Versailles Peace Treaty. That would have had enormous consequences for the white Dominions of Britain as well as for the United States. Western criticism of Japan's occupation of Manchuria in 1931–32 was seen as hypocritical in Japan, and precipitated its withdrawal from the League of Nations. If Fukuzawa Yukichi had advocated that Japan should 'escape from Asia' and become modern and civilized by adopting Western models, developments such as these convinced many Japanese that the West would never accept it as an equal and that its future lay in liberating Asia from Western imperialism and leading an Asian revival.[2]

A principal proponent of Japanese pan-Asianism was General Matsui Iwane, who led Japan's forces as they assaulted Shanghai in the summer and autumn of 1937. Halett Abend, a *New York Times* journalist in China, interviewed Matsui in 1935 in Shanghai when Matsui was on his way back to Japan from a Greater Asia Society speaking tour through East and Southeast Asia. If Abend later would become a proponent of American support for China, in 1935 he still had sympathy for the Japanese, like many other Westerners in China who believed that Japan was needed to maintain some sort of order in a country that seemed bent on tearing itself apart in civil wars. In 1935, Abend and Matsui spent a long day talking about the future, ironically enough in the Shanghai Club frequented by the local foreign establishment. Abend later wrote that Matsui had told him that 'the white man's culture is alien and unadaptable for the Oriental' and that it was Japan's 'divinely appointed mission' to reconstruct the Orient and restore Asia's 'lost freedom and power'.[3]

In a 1938 interview with H.G.W. Woodhead, the editor of *The China Yearbook*, Matsui discussed Japan's mission in China. He again talked about Japan's destiny, stating that 'the growth and development of our own country make it inevitable that Japan should expand in China'.[4] Ending Chinese nationalism, which he saw as an infantile and misguided movement and which took the form of boycotts of Japanese products, was a major aim of Japan's war in China, according to Matsui. In his conversation, Matsui also outlined a project to build up a Chinese government sympathetic to Japan. He told Woodhead that this would necessitate a take-over of the Chinese Maritime Customs Service (CMCS) on which central revenues depended heavily. The CMCS, founded in 1854, was a Chinese bureaucracy but staffed at its upper level by mostly British foreigners. Matsui then rejected cooperation with the British and revealed to Woodhead that he had wanted to enter the Shanghai International Concession to seize the CMCS headquarters and so secure a revenue source for a Japan-friendly Chinese regime. That would have led to serious problems with the European Powers and the US. Only the diplomatic difficulties resulting from the 12 December attacks on the USS *Panay* and HMS *Bee* had convinced him to stay his hand.

The dismissal of Chinese nationalism as puerile featured in Japan's rejection of an invitation to participate in the November 1937 Brussels Conference of the signatories of the 1922 Nine Power Treaty to discuss events in China. Japan defended its decision, explaining that 'not only does [Japan] not harbour any ill will against the people of China nor cherish territorial ambitions, but on the contrary is eagerly seeking both the material and spiritual progress of the Chinese people'.[5] It described Chinese boycott movements – a diplomatic weapon of the weak and observed more in the breach than in reality – as provocations justifying 'measures of self-defence'. According to Japan, 'the key to the solution of the current dispute lies in the Nanking Government's realization of its mistaken ways' and the best thing that Western countries could do was 'to cause the Nanking Government to reflect'. Given the destruction that Japan inflicted on China, such language only made sense if one accepted the premises of Japanese pan-Asianism, including its view of Chinese nationalism as the fallacious folly of an immature people.

Japanese pan-Asianism also featured in a pamphlet issued by the Press Section of the Army Ministry on the anniversary of the outbreak of the fighting. It argued that during the previous year, Japanese armies had conducted a holy war that had begun to forge a new pan-Asian reality:

> From the first, both in North and Central China, the crusade for the overthrow of the anti-Japanese administration and the revival and reconstruction of East Asia has steadily progressed, and recently the important town of Hsuchow [Xuzhou] has been captured. The Rising Sun Flag is waving over an extensive domain in which manifold traces of the war remain, but the day of East Asia's revival is brightly dawning. Since the beginning of our Empire's history, it has never embarked on a holy war of such magnitude, nor until today has its world significance been so great.... The object of the holy war is to make China reflect and for no other reason is she being chastised.[6]

It is easy to reject such statements as mere rhetoric, advanced to justify Japan's invasion of China. However, rhetoric is itself not without significance. But in addition, pan-Asianism probably had deeper resonance and greater possibilities than is usually allowed. As Prasenjit Duara has pointed out, it was not just Japanese diplomatic pique at the rejection of its Versailles proposals or the League's criticism of its occupation of Manchuria that gave rise to Japanese pan-Asianism.[7] It also drew on the rejection of the Enlightenment ideal of a world governed rationally by secular bureaucracies that had emerged in the late nineteenth century. Cultural uniqueness and ethnic identity gained force at the turn of the century in political discourse and state construction projects.

The emergence of Shintoism in Japan was paralleled in China by Kang Youwei's efforts to give a new meaning to Confucianism. In the 1890s Kang defined Confucianism as the unique cultural tradition of China and he proposed that it should become a state religion. After the 1911–12 revolution, the first president of the Republic, Yuan Shikai, attempted to shore up his beleaguered regime by re-instituting worship of Confucius and agreeing to the mandatory inclusion of the Confucian Classics in the educational curriculum. As C.A. Bayly has noted, the diffused and syncretistic religious traditions of Asia in the course of the nineteenth century developed strong centres of authority, developed new rituals, and focused on specific texts to assert an essence that influenced and shaped nationalist projects.[8]

The idea that Asians shared a unique cultural identity was not just a Japanese idea. Following the First World War, Rabindranath Tagore, the first Asian writer to be accorded the Nobel Prize for literature, wrote about Asian culture as stressing harmony with nature, social solidarity, and pacifism. He advanced Asian values as ones able to redeem the West's materialism, aggressiveness, and its will to dominate and whose destructive potential the First World War had revealed. These ideas found a substantial following in the West.

Japanese pan-Asianism rejected the stress on Oriental pacifism in such interpretations, which was seen as implying the continued subordination of Asia to the West. Ōkawa Shūmei argued that military action strengthened a civilization and maintained that it was the task of Japan to defeat militarily Western corruption and decadence.[9] When Tagore visited China, he was welcomed by a wave of criticism. Thus, although considerable support existed for the idea of a shared Asian culture that could be contrasted to that of the West, profound disagreement existed about what that shared identity was and who in fact represented it. This too formed an obstacle for the realization of the Japanese interpretation of pan-Asianism.

Nonetheless, a number of significant figures sought to make use of Japanese pan-Asianism, without necessarily subscribing to Japanese leadership. Matsui's Greater Asia Society supported Indians fighting against British domination, including Rash Behari Bose, long exiled in Japan and the founder of the Indian National Army in 1942 who hoped to liberate India from the British with the help of the Japanese. In Burma, Aung San formed the Burma Independence Army after the Japanese occupied Bangkok in Thailand. Aung San continued to work with the Japanese even when they forced him to rename his army the Burma Defence Force and limited his freedom of action.

In China there was Wang Jingwei. Throughout much of the 1930s Wang had been the number two in the Nationalist Government and had advocated a policy of accommodation with Japan, in part because he did not believe that China had the military resources to resist Japan. Following the fall of Wuhan in November 1938 Wang parted ways with Jiang Jieshi and began direct negotiations with the Japanese, first in Hanoi and later in Shanghai. Lengthy discussions culminated in the establishment of a new national government under Wang in March 1940, which continued to exist for the next five years.

A different way of indicating the significance of pan-Asianism was that Japan's attack on China ran counter to an alternative construction of the fighting based on anti-communism. German diplomatic personnel rejected Japanese claims that its operations in China served anti-communism by 'creating strategic clarity'.[10] The German ambassador to China, Oskar Trautmann, a collector of early Chinese bronzes, argued that Japan could not succeed in China and would be drawn into a damaging quagmire, 'the result will be a clear strengthening of Russia and consequently of Bolshevism'.[11]

Canton ravaged

At the outbreak of hostilities, according to the British military attaché in China, the Chinese air force consisted of 900 serviceable aircraft of which only 202 were fully equipped. Of these seventeen were heavy bombers, twenty-four light bombers, eighteen attack bombers, and seventy-five fighters. Drastic shortages of petrol and oil as well as bombs radically curtailed the effectiveness of the few planes that China actually could put up in the air.[12] Although, as Mark Peattie has argued, it took the far superior Japanese air units some time and surprisingly heavy losses to establish air supremacy, the Chinese air force nonetheless was unable to conduct a sustained campaign against its foe. This made it impossible for Chinese forces defending Shanghai to be supplied or relieved during daylight.[13]

Japanese bombing initially focused on railroads, bridges, and railroad stations as well as anything that could be construed as a military installation, including oil dumps, urban water works, electric plants, harbour facilities, and military hospitals. The paragraphs below rely on internal twice-weekly reports produced by the staff of the Canton Custom House of the CMCS. Led by foreigners, the Custom House continued to function in the British concession on Shameen Island until shortly after the outbreak of the Pacific War in December 1941. The reports, called *Current Events and Rumours*, relied on staff contacts within Chinese society as well as local publications. They were sent, probably via Hong Kong, to the Inspectorate General in Shanghai, which like the Canton Custom House continued to function in Shanghai's International Settlement until the outbreak of the Pacific War. The reports constitute a significant source of local information produced by well-informed observers. The following describes how Canton initially managed to cope reasonably well with Japan's bombing raids in the first months of the war, but then was destroyed by the campaign of terror bombing begun in February 1938. After their occupation of the city in October 1938, the Japanese found that the damage they had inflicted was so intensive that they were not able to restore order, let alone revive Canton's usual prosperity.

The first significant Japanese air raid on Canton occurred on 21 September when two Japanese aircraft carriers entered Guangdong waters. At 6:40am, two flights of fifteen bombers descended on the city to attack airfields. Raids continued during the days and nights over the next week, but while bombs caused hundreds of houses to be destroyed, at least one thousand people to lose their lives, and refugees to stream out of the city, 'the railway tracks were quickly repaired and the whole line functioned as usual'.[14] In October, 'despite the furious attacks, all important bridges are unharmed, and, after the damaged tracks have been repaired, these lines are functioning as normal'.[15] One reason that success came slowly was the effectiveness of Chinese anti-aircraft guns that protected the city as well as its main bridges. As late as February 1938, according to one report, 'hostile planes succeeded in penetrating the city' but 'were instantly greeted by heavy a-a [anti-aircraft] guns and machine gun fire. They were finally forced to retreat, causing no great damage.'[16]

The city initially coped well with Japanese bombing. To keep Canton running, the authorities took measures to secure essential supplies such as salt (used as a spice but also as a preservative, the only one available to most people), food, and water. Because the Japanese had attacked the waterworks, 'the Police Authorities have encouraged the people to open as many wells as possible'.[17] Taxes on salt were reduced or waived,[18] the brewing of alcohol proscribed, and farmers were issued with small loans, tools, and seeds for food grains that could replace rice such as potatoes.[19] 'A sum of $3 million has been loaned to farmers. It is hoped that the annual shortage of ten million piculs (a picul is about sixty kilograms) will be cut in half.'[20] In May 1938 *Current Events* noted 'although all sorts of rumours have created panic in the city, the price [of rice] has nonetheless not risen'.[21]

In December 1937 an Emergency Food Commission was set up with the aim of building up a reserve of six months' supply of grains.[22] Guangdong was a chronic food deficit area which depended on imports from overseas, including Thailand and Burma. Because the Japanese blockaded the coast, which incidentally threw half a million fishermen out of work because the Japanese burned and sank their junks,[23] the Canton authorities had to secure supplies from China's inland provinces, especially areas such as Jiangxi, Hunan, and Hubei, which were traditional food surplus areas. Wholesale dealers were put under pressure, a monopoly was dissolved, and a new company formed to import rice from Hunan,[24] while an arrangement was also made with the Guangxi authorities to bring in rice from that province.[25] Rice merchants from Guangdong, Hunan, Guangxi, and Jiangxi were brought together to coordinate the supply of rice to Guangdong.[26] By February 1938 Canton's 600 or so rice dealers had stored 50,000 bags of rice, enough for several months.[27]

Another measure that proved important to keep the city operating was to compel businesses to stay open. Initially a curfew had been enforced strictly, but was soon relaxed: 'After the second alarm has been sounded, vehicles and pedestrians are allowed to go on their way until an aerial battle actually takes place above the city', and electricity was not cut off until midnight.[28] In late October 1937 *Current Events* reported that 'cinema theatres and restaurants are now thronged with customers, the whole city looks as prosperous as usual, and the panic prevailing a month ago has gone'.[29] Bombing seems to have only increased popular support for the war. On 30 December, despite an air raid warning, a large parade took place and 'over 100,000 assembled at the Sun Yatsen Auditorium' to express support for continued resistance.[30] In April 1938 a mass lantern procession celebrated Chinese tactical victories in north China.[31]

The campaign of urban terror bombing that the Japanese began in the spring of 1938 against Canton was part of Japan's increasingly desperate effort to break the Nationalist will to fight and so bring the war to an end. Although the Japanese were able to occupy the Beiping-Tianjin area quickly, Jiang Jieshi dragged them into a war of attrition by opening a second battlefield at Shanghai in August 1937. After taking that city in November and Nanjing, the Nationalist capital, the following month, the Chinese Nationalists did not surrender. In the spring of 1938 perhaps a million forces participated in the Battle of Xuzhou on the north China plains. The Japanese prevailed once more, but their hope to take Wuhan on the Yangzi River in central China was frustrated by Jiang's decision to break the dykes of the Yellow River at Huayuankou on 1 June 1938, which drowned the Japanese forces in water and mud. It also forced them to wait for the levels of the Yangzi River to rise during the summer to undertake an arduous infantry advance with naval support along the north and south sides of the Yangzi River. When Wuhan finally fell in October 1938, the Japanese had committed a far higher number of forces for a much longer time than they had anticipated, but Chinese resistance continued. Japan was anxious to gain a quick victory in China because they feared a conflict with the Soviet Union, with which they shared a long border around their Manchurian possession. The Japanese bombing campaign against Canton was designed to put further pressure on China with little danger to itself and without the need to deploy substantial naval and ground forces.

Current Events for the long months of the spring and summer of 1938 reported regularly on Japanese air assaults and the devastation they wreaked. On 10 April two incendiary bombs fell on the former Powah Theatre, which had been converted into a factory for making uniforms, killing about 100 and wounding 200, mostly women and girls. On 12 May, 'taking advantage of the moonlight, the Japanese resumed night raids, aiming on railways … two bombs fell on the Tak Ching Road, in the civic centre, and some 30 people were killed'.[32] During the last days of May Japanese air units attacked Wongsha Station and government departments, with the result that 'two thousand civilians were killed or wounded, about 400 houses demolished, and many people rendered homeless, as most bombs fell on residential areas'.[33]

This became virtually a daily routine. The early June 1938 issue of *Current Events* reported that 'in spite of world criticism, the Japanese continued to bomb the city by day and night…. The police urged the old and weak, women and children to evacuate. About eighty per cent of shops are closed. The municipal Health Department and the Police Department are collaborating in disinfecting the areas hit by bombs to prevent epidemics arising from decomposed bodies.'[34] In the month of June, according to *Current Events*, 1,650 people were killed and over 6,000 wounded. Foreign institutions in Canton did not escape. The British St Hilda's School, the American-owned Lingnan University, the French Doumer Hospital, and the New Zealand Missionary Hospital all suffered heavy damage.

The bombing gradually tore Canton apart. During the early days of the war, the Canton Police Bureau ordered an evacuation of 'the old and physically weak', partly to decrease Canton's consumption needs.[35] After the initial air raids subsided in October, shops had re-opened and Canton residents had returned.[36] But in the spring, refugees once again left the city. In May, as Japanese bombing began to destroy more and more houses in residential areas, 'the result has been a renewed exodus of the city'.[37] In June 1938 'the Police Bureau urged the old and weak, women, and children to evacuate' and again most shops in Canton closed their doors.[38] When the Japanese marched into the city, 'a wholesale exodus of people to Fati and Fonchuen' ensued,[39] and 'fires raged for three days and were especially ruinous in the western suburb where about 70 per cent of the shops ... were destroyed'.[40] When, following the fall of the city in October, the Japanese urged Chinese residents to return to the city in December, many found that their houses had been looted.[41] Even if people wanted to return, they could not necessarily do so.

Japanese attempts to restore order and revive the city's economy failed. Despite a good winter crop in 1938, the destruction of the communications network meant that the price of rice rose sharply, while firewood, essential for cooking, also had become expensive.[42] Efforts to convince Canton residents to return to the city backfired. 'It is estimated that, out of 100,000 people returning to the city during the first half of February of 1939, 90% ... are destitute and have no means of living. Many have committed crimes such as thefts and robberies, which have been increasing daily, with the result that the well-to-do dare not return.'[43] Electricity too could not be restored, because 'the electric plant is too heavily damaged'.[44] Only a few government and army offices were supplied with electricity.

The darkness that engulfed the city every night made the restoration of order difficult. In January 1939 the Japanese began a concerted effort to take the arms out of Canton society and deal with banditry. Although looting initially subsided, the Japanese approach of using local Chinese forces to assist them proved unwise: they 'used warrants to go on looting sprees'.[45] Despite a curfew, which harmed the city's retail trade and its night life and so added to its unemployment problems,[46] 'occurrences of robberies and hold-ups in broad daylight have not diminished. It is risky to walk even in the main streets, and foreign as well as Chinese residents have been held up in small alleys and robbed of all money.'[47] The Japanese brought heavy pressure on Canton shop owners and businessmen to resume work. But, according to an April 1939 issue of *Current Events*, 'there would seem to be no immediate prospect of restoring the city to its former prosperity, until the prosperous merchants are encouraged to return and the selling of loot in the open market and other obstacles to trade have been eradicated.... The Japanese have issued prohibitions on the sale of loot, but there are still considerable areas into which patrols seldom venture and where daylight hold-ups are a frequent occurrence.'[48] The Japanese themselves were enthusiastic looters. The American Commissioner of Customs in Canton, Lester Knox Little, reported in January 1940 that for a week he had seen at least one hundred trucks every day loaded with household furniture being taken to docks for enshipment to Japan.[49]

In November 1939 the Japanese decided to recruit the destitute and unemployed into the police force and use them on rehabilitation work, providing them with food and some wages. The results were mixed. 'The public was apprehensive that they might be seized indiscriminately and be made to serve.'[50] In February 1940, *Current Events* reported that 'armed robberies and hold ups in day light became more prevalent'.[51]

By the spring of 1940 farmers had become unwilling to sell their crops because they no longer had faith in any circulating currency. Rice shortages became severe. In May 1940, *Current Events* reported that 'partly due to the exhaustion of existing stocks before the first crop is available, the price of rice has gone through the roof. The painful effects have been felt not only among the poor but also the middle classes.'[52] *Current Events* summed up the general mood, writing 'it is generally believed that unless efforts are made to check a further rise in living costs, riots, intensified burglary, robbery, and social disturbance are bound to occur when the hard pressed people have no alternative but starvation'.[53] Partly because floods wrecked the summer crop in 1940, shortages that year led to panic in the autumn, when the new harvest should have come in: 'rice merchants closed their doors as a precaution against riots'.[54]

Desperation became a routine sight in Canton. In August 1940 the Customs reported that women were being crushed in lines for salt shops and that 'beggars are daily seen dying of starvation, while babies, abandoned by their parents, are often found lying by the roadside. Kidnapping of children is reported prevalent.'[55] In March 1942 'the snatching of edibles from women and children by young ruffians has been seen frequently along the streets'.[56]

The lesson of Canton was clear: to bomb a city to rubble would present the Japanese with enormous problems when they became its rulers. Yet the lure of bombing as a shortcut to victory made that lesson hard to learn. In June 1940 Japanese forces occupied Yichang, the last major city on the Yangzi River before it enters Sichuan Province, which was home to China's wartime capital of Chongqing. The Japanese used Yichang airfields for a massive campaign of terror bombing stretching out over many months, in the hope of pounding the Nationalists into submission. While the campaign exacted huge damage and drove urban populations underground into caves and bomb shelters, it did not break the Chinese will to resist.

Shanghai

The bombing of Canton is less well known than the Japanese air campaign against Shanghai in the early months of the War of Resistance. Because of the presence of a large number of foreign residents and many Western journalists, the Battle of Shanghai was widely covered. Several incidents became famous around the world virtually as they happened as journalists telegraphically flashed photographs and stories to their editors in London, New York, Paris, and elsewhere. On 'Bloody Sunday' (14 August 1937) bombs caused carnage in Nanking Road, the famous shopping street near the Bund, and at the Great World

Amusement Centre in the French concession (see Figures 7.1 and 7.2). Some 120 people died in Nanking Road, while 1,047 did so at the Great World, where shrapnel bombs exploded among crowded refugees and ignited petrol tanks of waiting cars. The bombing of the railroad station crowded with refugees in the Nandao section of Shanghai resulted in one of the most enduring photographic images of the war. It showed a parent-less, charred, and crying baby sitting in

Figure 7.1 Nanking Road bomb (source: originally published in Shanghai, China, in the journal *Oriental Affairs*, 1937).

Figure 7.2 Chapei destroyed (source: originally published in Shanghai, China, in the journal *Oriental Affairs*, 1937).

front of a bombed-out railroad platform. Such images and the reports that Western journalists filed damaged Japan's reputation in the West and contributed to a reassessment of Chinese nationalism.

The bombs that fell on Nanking Road and the Great World were actually dropped by Chinese aircraft. They had targeted the Japanese flagship, the *Idzumo*, provocatively moored near the Japanese consulate in the Hongkew Section, or 'Little Tokyo', of the International Settlement. Yet, most foreigners did not blame the Chinese, but held Japanese intransigence and provocation accountable. The Japanese had refused to remove the *Idzumo*; in contrast to the Chinese, they had declined to promise not to allow their forces to enter the International Settlement or the French Concession; and they had dismissed a suggestion that they make an accommodating gesture in return for Chinese agreement to withdraw Peace Preservation Forces – in reality made up of army regulars – from near the demilitarized zone agreed in 1932.[57]

A series of incidents during the months and years preceding the outbreak of fighting had begun to give rise to a general Western perception of the Japanese as high-handed, provocative, and unreasonable. One involved Japanese accusations that the Chinese had kidnapped a Japanese soldier. Japanese marines 'ran wild in Shanghai's Little Tokio and sandbagged strategic corners and mounted machine guns'.[58] It later became clear that the soldier was a deserter who had feigned his own kidnap to cover his tracks. Before fighting began in Shanghai, but after war had already erupted in north China, the Japanese despatched two officers to the Hongqiao airfield, where they were killed by nervous Chinese guards. The commander of British Forces in Shanghai, Major General Alexander Telfer-Smollet, commented that although 'narrowly legal' the trip 'was obviously unwise in view of the political situation'.[59]

On the night of the Nanking Road and Great World debacles the Chinese Minister of Foreign Affairs visited the British ambassador Hugh Knatchbull-Hugessen, expressed profound regret, offered condolences, promised compensation, and explained that the bombs had been dropped by pilots injured during the attack on the *Idzumo*.[60] British diplomats and officials contrasted the Chinese attitude with that of the Japanese. The Japanese attacked Knatchbull-Hugessen's motorcade on 26 August as he travelled from Nanjing to Shanghai, believing that Jiang Jieshi was in one of the cars. Although the cars flew Union Jacks, one Japanese aircraft strafed the motorcade, while the second bombed it after it had come to a halt. Knatchbull-Hugessen suffered serious chest and spine injuries, from which he would take months to recover.[61] In contrast to Chinese diplomats, the Japanese initially refused to acknowledge responsibility and when the Foreign Secretary, Anthony Eden, demanded a formal apology, punishment of the perpetrators, and a Japanese promise that greater care would be taken in the future, after much pressure the Japanese went no further than replying that 'they may have been the ones who shot and bombed Knatchbull-Hugessen and therefore expressed their regret'.[62] What this incident was to Britain, the Japanese attack on the USS *Panay* on 12 December would be to the US. The Japanese sank this gunboat and strafed sailors who had jumped ship.

The reports of Western journalists attempted to provide evocative accounts of what it was like to be bombed. Abend, the *New York Times* journalist who had interviewed General Matsui, produced one of the more memorable descriptions. When the fighting broke out in Shanghai, he had been stuck in north China, but he reached Shanghai on 22 August after an exhausting journey. The next day he went to buy supplies, including binoculars, at the Wing On Department Store. When his assistant went into the store, he looked up, noticed the silver streak of an air-plane high above, but unconcerned put his head back and lit a cigarette:

> Then it hit. There was a tremendous sickening lurch of the ground, accompanied by a shattering explosion so close that my eardrums and my windpipe seemed to be affected ... the worst part of a bombing experience is that period of utter paralysis which follows the concussion. For as much as four minutes, if the bomb is a big one, nothing moves except swirling and thick dust, and there is no sound except the continued tinkle of falling broken glass and the rumble of crumbling masonry. After about four minutes the wounded begin to moan and shriek and drag themselves away; then come sounds of sirens and ambulances and fire engines, and then the tempo of shocked life picks up with terrifying rapidity.[63]

This description, with its initial stillness and gently falling debris followed by accelerating noise, may have had an impact in Hollywood. Abend talked about his experiences with the movie-maker Cecil B. DeMille in 1942 when DeMille was preparing for 'The Story of Dr Wassell', which starred Gary Cooper and won an Oscar for best effects.[64]

Photographs of and reports about bombing made an impact in the West because of the increasing fears about a new world war and the yet unknown realities of urban bombing. At this time, the Spanish Civil War, lasting from 1936 to 1939, gripped Europe. The two conflicts were linked not only because people read about them in the same newspapers and magazines or watched reports about both in cinema news bulletins, but also because Germany had just concluded a pact with Japan while it fought on Franco's side in the Spanish Civil War. Some journalists travelled straight from Spain to China. They included a new breed of war reporters and photographers, such as the Dutch film maker Joris Ivens, who led the History Today film crew, and Robert Capa. James Bertram dedicated his *North China Front* of 1939 to 'Griff McLaurin, killed in Spain, November 1936'.[65] The images from Shanghai played into the still fresh revulsion with the German bombing of the Basque village of Guernica, which had led to large demonstrations in many European cities and prompted Pablo Picasso to create his famous painting of the same name. It was first exhibited at the Paris Exhibition in July 1937, just when the fighting began in China, and drew enormous crowds.

Even more than the Japanese failure to observe diplomatic niceties, it was the effect of bombing on civil populations that provoked horror around the world. Woodhead's Shanghai magazine, *Oriental Affairs*, noted, 'we have ocular evidence of what it means to bring war in its modern form into a city of over three million inhabitants'. There had been 'an appalling list of civilian casualties' and 'the extensive use of aircraft has shown that even where military objectives are aimed at, the toll on non-combatants must reach alarming proportions'.[66]

J. Gunnar Anderson described the Japanese carpet bombing of Zhabei, a Chinese section of Shanghai north of Suzhou Creek and west of Hongkew, in his *China Fights for the World* of 1938. Anderson was a mining expert who developed an interest in Chinese archaeology; he would become Curator of the Museum of Far Eastern Antiquities in Stockholm. The Zhabei bombing took place when the Battle for Dachang between entrenched Japanese and Chinese forces raged to the north of Shanghai. The Japanese hit Zhabei hard in the hope of forcing a decision in a war zone where determined Chinese resistance had forced them to pour in more and more reinforcements without being able to force a decision. Anderson described the bombing, which he saw from the Park Hotel in the International Settlement, as follows:

> The Japanese bombers joined in the work that night. Air bombs, guns, trench mortars, machine guns, and rifles, every means of destruction this powerfully mechanized enemy had at his disposal was let loose in a rain of explosives, fire and steel over this quarter of the city that had been tortured for months and was now doomed to destruction. When at last night descended upon this day, then and not till then did we see the full extent of this abominable destruction. The flowing wall of fire stretched all the way from north-north-east to west-south-west.... The burning of Chapei [Zhabei] will be reckoned as one of the great fires of the world.[67]

Frank Oliver in *Special Undeclared War*, published in 1939, expressed his revulsion following a Japanese air raid on Nanjing on 25 September in words as astonished as they were despairing:

> In a single day, over 500 civilians were killed and wounded. A diplomat who was present told me: 'A hundred planes came over like flights of geese (I counted 88) and bombs were dropped in almost every section of Nanking within the city walls. Possibly the electric was a military objective, possibly a small water pumping station near me (too damned near) was another. But what about the Central Hospital? It had a big red cross on it. The Hospital was found marked on a map on the body of a Japanese aviator.'[68]

Oriental Affairs recorded 'the growing indignation at the loss of civilian lives during air raids' around the world.[69] Neville Chamberlain, the British Prime Minister, was unequivocal in his condemnation at the Conservative Party conference: 'non-combatants have been killed and mutilated by aerial weapons which, we are told, were aimed at military objectives, but which in no case can be considered instruments of precision. It is a sickening and horrifying spectacle, from which the mind revolts and which in many countries has aroused the strongest feelings of indignation at its inhumanity.'[70] At the Royal Albert Hall in London the Archbishop of Canterbury, the leader of the Church of England, presided over a meeting where a Nanjing professor, Zhang Pengzhong, spoke. The meeting passed a resolution expressing 'horror and emphatic condemnation of the indeterminate attacks upon civilian and non-combatants by Japanese forces'.[71]

Joseph Grew, the American ambassador to Japan, who until Pearl Harbor remained hopeful that internationalism might yet prevail in Japan, described the bombing of Shanghai as 'one of the most horrible episodes in modern times'.[72] Following the raid on Nanjing of 25–26 August, he approached other diplomats, including the German ambassador, about the possibility of a joint approach to Japanese authorities to ask for Japanese observance 'of restraints which considerations of humanity and international comity usually impose on the bombing of the political capital of a country'.[73]

Indicative of what Japanese military tactics implied for the future of Japanese pan-Asianism in Asia itself, a 1937 German diplomatic report from India noted that the Japanese invasion of China had strengthened the British position there. It referred to an article by Professor Gulshan Rai in the *Civil and Military Gazette* that had depicted the Japanese attack on Shanghai in the most ominous terms. It noted that while Indian nationalists would welcome anything weakening the British, most had been appalled. An article in *The Leader* of Allahad concluded 'all right thinking men throughout the civilized world will be with China and against the military gangsters in Japan who are seeking to rob it of its valuable territories and convert it into a vassal state'.[74]

Anthony Eden perhaps summed up best the change in perceptions of Japan when at a later date he stated in the House of Commons that 'The Japanese claim that their forces are animated by the lofty code of chivalry, Bushido, is nauseating hypocrisy.... The House will agree that we can best express our sympathy with the victims by redoubling our efforts to insure his utter and overwhelming defeat.'[75] Japanese bombing, perhaps initially attractive to the Japanese in part because of its distinct 'modern' nature, became a symbol of Japanese brutality, as a cartoon suggested in *The North China Herald* (see Figure 7.3).

Conclusion

Bombing, and especially terror bombing of urban areas, was one element in the Japanese conduct of the war that produced a shift in perception of China and Japan in the West and in other parts of Asia, which would isolate Japan and thereby condemn it to defeat at a time when victory depended on building international alliances. It was against the background of the outrage provoked by Japanese bombing that stories of Chinese heroism and pluck became desirable and began to make sense. The Chinese defence of Shanghai's North Station provided fuel for such an account. Rhoads Farmer, an Australian journalist, wrote in his memoirs that when Chinese troops were preparing to turn the six-storey Administration Building of North Station into a fortress, 'old China hands' had said that 'when the Japanese start, they'll run like rabbits'. But that kind of statement had become distasteful. Farmer went on: 'they did not run, although they lost command of the air

Custodian: "WELL, IT'S A NEW ONE ON ME!"

Figure 7.3 Oriental bombing versus jazzy bombing (source: originally published in Shanghai, China, in the journal *Oriental Affairs*, 1937).

in the first few days of the fighting and were henceforth bombed incessantly'.[76] Similarly, after the Japanese had occupied Zhabei, an isolated 'doomed battalion' defended a building north of Suzhou Creek. It flew the Chinese flag and held out for four days. Farmer reported that 'Shanghai gasped with pleasure' because 'this one flag fractured the picture of Japanese conquest'.[77]

Telfer-Smollet expressed admiration for the heroism of the 'doomed battalion', and abhorrence at the fact that the Japanese would not agree to a British proposal to allow it to withdraw and be disarmed, and then be interned by the British. He himself had made the proposal, which had been sanctioned by Jiang Jieshi. The Japanese had refused, and when a withdrawal was nonetheless attempted 'the Japanese mounted machine guns and searchlights'.[78] In his report, which mostly dealt in a businesslike way with military issue such as the order of command, logistical and supply problems, and the rate of disease (gonorrhoea came first), Telfer-Smollet expressed his horror at other instances of Japanese brutality, including the tying up of naked Chinese prisoners to trees and leaving them for hours without water.[79] He argued that British forces needed to remain in Shanghai, not as nineteenth-century foreigners had argued, because of the cruelty of Chinese legal practices, but because of Japanese barbarity.

The resolution of the Brussels Conference of the signatories of the Nine Power Treaty also indicated the change in Western perceptions of China and Japan. It praised China for abiding by the principles of civilized international cooperation: 'China is engaged in a full and frank discussion of the matter [the Sino-Japanese conflict] with other parties to the Treaty, but Japan refuses to discuss it with them.'[80] With respect to the Japanese claim that it had taken military action pre-emptively in self defence and to end anti-Japanese policies in China, it pointed out 'that there exists no warrant in law for the use of armed force by any country for the purpose of intervening in the internal regime of another country, and the general recognition of such a right would be a permanent cause of conflict'. After the Boxer Rebellion of 1900 China had been condemned for violating the rules of international diplomacy and civilized conduct. In 1900 Japan had joined the Allied Expeditionary Force, and shortly afterwards in 1902 Britain and Japan had concluded the Anglo-Japanese alliance as equal nations for collaboration in bringing stability to East Asia. In 1937, in part as a result of its military conduct, Japan had become the outcast nation.

The American President Franklin Roosevelt put this as follows in his 'quarantine speech' of October 1937:

> ... surely the ninety percent who want to live in peace under law and in accordance with moral standards that have received almost universal acceptance through the centuries, can and must find some way to make their will prevail. It seems unfortunately true that the epidemic of world lawlessness is spreading. When an epidemic of physical disease starts to spread, the community joins in a quarantine of the patient.[81]

These were all words and it would take a long time before they were matched with action. Nonetheless, the changes in perception resulting from Japan's attack on China did help lay the conceptual basis for it's inclusion in the Allied Nations, which would bring with it the end of the Unequal Treaties and the abolition of Western privileges.

Developments and factors other than Japanese bombing contributed to the emergence of a new attitude toward China. The intensifying critique of imperialism both in the United States but also in Europe, the official British accommodation of Chinese nationalism since the late 1920s, the rise of Nazism in Europe, and the writings of Leftist scholars, activists and journalists like Edgar Snow, John Lossing Buck, and R.H. Tawney all prepared the ground. But bombing worked like a cathartic event, clarifying issues and sifting possibilities. It triggered people's most basic fears, in a way that diplomatic incidents or even fighting between standing armies could not, and was an equalizer: what it did to defenceless Chinese people it could also do to oneself.

The wave of sympathy for China did not mean that racial and cultural stereo-typing disappeared never to return. The belief that 'East was East and West was West' continued to have considerable force. Most Western military observers did not take the fighting between China and Japan as providing valuable lessons for Western armies.[82] Partly as a result of Chinese decisions about how to represent themselves, the images of China after the victory of the Chinese Communist Party, including the 'blue ants' of the Great Leap Forward and the Red Guards of the Cultural Revolution, continued to sustain the idea of a Chinese 'Other'.

Yet in 1937 the response to Japanese bombing was to abandon dismissals of China as backward and not yet a nation. Instead, a discourse emerged based on the idea of civilization and a common humanity. A 1939 letter by a British China merchant published in the *Daily Mail* and the *Daily Telegraph* stated:

> ... up to a few years ago, the word 'China' was a mere geographical expression.... In the days of Empire, graft was not only usual but was even recognized. The makers of the Chinese Republic have had a difficult task in metamorphosizing the national character. In this respect the war has been of tremendous assistance to the Government, because the intense antipathy to the Japanese which is universal throughout China has made the Chinese ready to follow a centralized government for the first time.[83]

This change in perception made possible the opportunity for Lei Haizong, one of the most eminent of China's historians, to tell American soldiers in Kunming in 1943 during a lecture on Chinese military history that Chinese history was 'in every way comparable to American history and European history from the Middle Ages – and beyond'.[84] He concluded his lecture by arguing that the mass murder of civilians 'would not cease before the establishment of some form of stable order on a world-wide scale as it was the case with the Warring States of ancient China'.[85]

Notes

1 See Masataka Matsuura, 'Japan and Pan-Asianism' in this volume.
2 Prasenjit Duara, *Sovereignty and Authenticity: Manchukuo and the East Asian Modern*, Lanham: Rowman and Littlefield, 2003, p. 92.
3 Halett Abend, *My Years in China, 1926–1941*, London: The Bodley Head, 1944, pp. 278–9.
4 The National Archives, Kew (TNA), FO676/397 'Mr Woodhead's Interview with General Matsui regarding Anglo-Japanese Relations' (1938).
5 *Oriental Affairs*, November 1937, pp. 272–3.
6 TNA FO676/397 Press Section of the War Office (Japan), 'One Year After the China Incident' (1938).
7 Duara, *Sovereignty and Authenticity*.
8 C.A. Bayly, *The Birth of the Modern World, 1780–1914*, Oxford: Blackwell, 2004, pp. 325–65.
9 Duara, *Sovereignty and Authenticity*, p. 98.

10 TNA GFM33/115 Von Weizsaecker to Tokyo, 28 July 1937. These are German Foreign Ministry documents captured by the Allies at the end of the Second World War.
11 TNA GFM33/191Trautmann to Berlin, 13 September 1937.
12 TNA FO676/327 Air attaché memorandum, 19 July 1937.
13 Mark Peattie, *Sunburst: The Rise of Japanese Naval Air Power, 1901–41*, Annapolis: Naval Institute Press, 2002, pp. 102–28.
14 *Current Events and Rumours*, 1–15 October 1937, in 'Current Events and Rumours, 1937–1938', Second Historical Archives of China, Nanjing [hereafter SHAC], 679/32417.
15 Ibid.
16 *Current Events*, 1–15 February 1938.
17 *Current Events*, 16–30 September 1937.
18 *Current Events*, 1–15 September 1937.
19 *Current Events*, 15–30 December 1937. The measure was not effective.
20 *Current Events*, 6–31 October 1937.
21 *Current Events*, 16–31 May 1938.
22 *Current Events*, 15–30 December 1937
23 *Current Events*, 16–31 October 1937.
24 *Current Events*, 16–31 March 1938
25 Ibid.
26 *Current Events*, 1–15 July 1938.
27 *Current Events*, 1–15 March 1938.
28 *Current Events*, 1–15 October 1937.
29 *Current Events*, 16–31 October 1937.
30 *Current Events*, 15–30 December 1937.
31 *Current Events*, 1–15 April 1938.
32 *Current Events*, 16–31 May 1938.
33 Ibid.
34 *Current Events*, 1–15 June 1938.
35 *Current Events*, 16–31 August 1937.
36 *Current Events*, 1–15 October 1937
37 *Current Events*, 16–31 May 1938.
38 *Current Events*, 1–15 June 1938.
39 *Current Events*, 16–31 October 1938.
40 Ibid.
41 *Current Events*, 1–15 December 1938.
42 *Current Events*, 16–31 December 1938.
43 *Current Events*, 16–28 February 1939. The 1939–40 issues of *Current Events* can be found in SHAC, 679/32418 'Canton Current Events and Rumours'.
44 *Current Events*, 16–31 March 1939.
45 *Current Events*, 16–31 January 1939.
46 *Current Events*, 1–15 December 1939.
47 *Current Events*, 16–31 April 1939.
48 *Current Events*, 1–15 April 1939.
49 SHAC, 679/31476 Maze to Cubbon, 7 January 1940, enclosing Little's report.
50 *Current Events*, 15–30 November 1939.
51 *Current Events*, 1–15 February 1940.
52 *Current Events*, 1–15 May 1940.
53 Ibid.
54 *Current Events*, 1–15 November 1940.
55 *Current Events*, 16–31 August 1940.
56 *Current Events*, 1–15 March 1942. The 1941 and early 1942 issues of *Current Events* can be found in SHAC 679/32419 'Canton Current Events and Rumours'.

57 *Oriental Affairs*, September 1937, 132; and Knatchbull-Hugessen to Halifax, 17 August 1937, in Ann Trotter *et al.* (eds), *British Documents on Foreign Affairs: Reports and Papers from the Foreign Office Confidential Print (BDFA) Part 2, From the First to the Second World War, Series E, Asia, 1914–1939*, II (East Asia), 45 (July 1937–March 1938), pp. 68–9.
58 Rhoads Farmer, *Shanghai Harvest*, London: Museum Press, 1945, pp. 34–5.
59 TNA WO 32/4347 'Despatch by Major General APD Telfer Smollett on the Shanghai Emergency', Part I, p. 9.
60 TNA FO676/328 Knatchbull-Hugessen to FO, 14 August 1937.
61 *BDFA*, Air Attaché and Military Attaché to Halifax, 26 August 1937, p. 81.
62 *BDFA*, Japanese Note, p. 110.
63 Abend, *My Years in China*, p. 258.
64 Ibid.
65 James Bertram, *North China Front*, London: Macmillan, 1939.
66 *Oriental Affairs*, 1937.
67 J. Gunnar Anderson, *China Fights the World*, London: Kegan & Paul, 1938.
68 Frank Oliver, *Special Undeclared War*, London, Jonathan Cape, 1939, p. 145.
69 *Oriental Affairs*, November 1937, p. 254.
70 Ibid., pp. 261–2.
71 Ibid., p. 260.
72 Quoted in Martin Gilbert, *A History of the Twentieth Century, Volume 2: 1933–1951*, London: HarperCollins, 1998, p. 157.
73 TNA GFM33/191 Grew to Dirksen, 31 August 1939.
74 TNA GFM33/2951 'Kalkutta, 26 Juli 1937', in 'Political Relations Germany–China, July 1936–December 1937'.
75 TNA WO 325/4 Eden statement to the House of Commons, 10 March 1942.
76 Farmer, *Shanghai Harvest*, p. 51.
77 Ibid., p. 86.
78 TNA WO 32/4347 Telfer-Smollett Despatch, p. 88.
79 Ibid., p. 53.
80 *Oriental Affairs*, December 1937, p. 341.
81 Quoted in Gilbert, *Twentieth Century*, p. 157.
82 Peattie, *Sunburst*, pp. 102–28.
83 SHAC 679/31476 'F. Maze to J.H. Cubbon', 2 November 1939, enclosing clipping. The letter was by B.C. Westall.
84 Lei Haizong, 'The Warring States (473–221 BC): The Modern Period in Ancient China', War Area Service Corps, Kunming, 1943. See also http://nacrp.cis.sfu.ca/nacrp/rticles/leihazong/leihaizong.html.
85 Ibid.

8 Britain and the origins of the San Francisco system

Tomoki Kuniyoshi

Introduction

The Treaty of Peace with Japan was signed by forty-nine nations in San Francisco on 8 September 1951. The signatories included most of the belligerents in the war against Japan, but the delegation of the Soviet Union, followed by the representatives of Poland and Czechoslovakia, left the conference without signing the treaty. As a result of the peace treaty, Japan regained its sovereignty and returned to an international society where the Cold War was already taking full shape. The Soviet refusal to sign the treaty and the absence of the People's Republic of China (PRC) resulted from tensions between East and West and reflected Japan's alignment with the West. Only hours after the conclusion of the peace treaty, the Japanese Prime Minister, Yoshida Shigeru, signed a security treaty with the United States. The nature of post-war international relations in East Asia, which were greatly determined by the 1951 settlement, has often been described as the 'San Francisco System'.

Given America's ostensibly predominant influence on post-war East Asian international relations, the bulk of earlier works on the Japanese peace settlement have concentrated on the role of the United States.[1] However, since the release in the 1980s of the relevant British documents, the position of Britain has also been examined by authors such as Roger Buckley, Peter Lowe and Kibata Yoichi.[2] Regardless of the divergence in their focus, these authors tended to conclude that Britain played a moderate part in the formation of the peace treaty as the joint draft-sponsor, but only within the framework of a formula which the Americans had drawn up according to their own requirements. Indeed, Britain made many concessions to the Americans, including the exclusion from the peace treaty of any restriction on rearmament.

In contrast, this chapter focuses attention more on the contribution made by Britain to the formation of the San Francisco System, rather than looking at specific peace treaty questions. The term 'San Francisco System' has been commonly used in various monographs, but its definition varies according to authors. For example, Akira Iriye describes the System as a new regime of American–Japanese relations resulting from the San Francisco treaties, under which Japan's economic recovery and prosperity, including its security, were to be closely linked with the emerging American strategy. He further points out, as a new feature of the regional order, the increased economic ties between Japan and Southeast Asia in the absence of any vigorous trade between Japan and mainland China.[3] By shedding more light on the role of Britain, this chapter sees the San Francisco System as reflecting broader East Asian international relations rather than being predominantly determined by US Cold War policies.

For the purposes of subsequent argument, the System is here defined as covering three major elements. First, as a result of the partial peace treaty with the West, Japan's political split with its communist neighbours became decisive. Although Japan normalized its relationship with the USSR in 1956, a political rapprochement between Japan and the PRC was not achieved until the early 1970s. Second, as part of the 1951 settlement, three security arrangements, namely the US–Japan Security Treaty, the security treaty between Australia, New Zealand and the US (ANZUS) and the US–Philippines mutual defence treaty, were formulated. The distinctive feature of the post-war security framework in the Pacific was that no over-riding multilateral arrangement materialized that involved all of America's allies in the region; instead, several 'separate' pacts were concluded with the United States. Thus, Japan depended solely on the bilateral security treaty, never joining any multilateral security arrangement. Third, regardless of its political distance from the PRC, Japan's trade with mainland China continued to evolve after the peace settlement, despite a temporary severance of bilateral relations from 1958 to 1962. These three elements interlocked to form the System, and it can be said that, at least until the early 1970s, Japan's foreign policy was conducted within the framework of the System.

In discussing Britain's involvement in the peace settlement, this chapter mainly explores two questions. First, it examines what objectives Britain developed regarding the peace settlement and what factors affected the unfolding of its aims. Second, it discusses how effective Britain's approach was in influencing American thinking. The chapter thereby attempts to assess how great a part Britain played in the formation of the San Francisco System. The focus here is placed more on the political and security aspects rather than on the economic dimension.

Britain's bid for an early peace

Douglas MacArthur, the Supreme Commander for the Allied Powers, addressed the need for an early peace treaty with Japan to foreign correspondents at a luncheon at the Press Club on 17 March 1947. This was the first time that any senior American policy-maker had formally made a declaration urging a swift end to occupation. Having played a limited role in allied occupation policies, by spring 1947 Britain had developed a strong preference for an early peace treaty and therefore welcomed MacArthur's proposal. Britain's initial motive for seeking a settlement stemmed chiefly from economic concerns. It was keen to push for a full restoration of Japan's trade, particularly with Southeast Asia. Whitehall opined that Japanese consumer goods were urgently needed in

British territories in this region. It was also necessary to secure a share of the Japanese market for the British rather than permitting continuous American predominance.[4]

Spurred on by MacArthur's statement, the British government completed a first examination of peace treaty objectives by mid-1947. Britain's initial aims were to impose numerous restrictions on Japanese activities, aimed at countering any renewed threat.[5] The proposed measures would not only ensure demilitarization but also extend to the economic field.[6] Indeed, the government thought that, given the demilitarization inherent in the peace settlement, the only likely threat to British interests in the near future would be an economic one.[7] It should be noted that in considering any Japanese threat, the Foreign Office had in mind, as its primary security interests, the British territories in Southeast Asia and Hong Kong as well as Australia and New Zealand.[8]

Meanwhile, in April Britain proposed the convening of a Commonwealth conference. This idea arose out of a suggestion by Ernest Bevin, the foreign secretary, that, in view of the likely difficulty in collaborating with the Russians, as seen in the ongoing negotiations over the European settlement, Britain should co-operate with friendly powers, first the Commonwealth and then the United States, in order to achieve a settlement in the West's favour.[9] Moreover, London feared that Washington, provoked by MacArthur, might soon take the initiative and thus felt the need to stake a claim to a seat at the negotiating table before the United States exerted a dominant sway over the peace treaty terms.[10]

But why did Britain need to convene a Commonwealth conference rather than act alone in negotiating with the Americans? First, the Foreign Office believed that it would facilitate peacemaking if the Commonwealth adopted a common stance, which would later be acceptable to the Americans.[11] It took the view that the 'British Group' – i.e. the Commonwealth members and Western European allies, such as France and the Netherlands – should collaborate with the 'United States Group' to compete with the 'Soviet Group'.[12] According to Esler Dening, the assistant under-secretary of state in charge of Far Eastern affairs, the combined American and British blocs would outvote the Soviet bloc in any final peace conference.[13] Second, London was mindful of Australia's growing assertion that it should play a principal part in any Japanese settlement in the light of its involvement in the Pacific War and its continuing military contribution to the occupation. Herbert Evatt, the Australian minister for external affairs, was especially vociferous, even advocating Australia's primacy over Britain in this issue.[14] It was necessary, therefore, for Britain to fall into step with the Commonwealth by placating Australia, the most assertive Pacific dominion, before approaching the Americans.

Despite the Commonwealth initiative, from late 1947 the American government became increasingly hesitant about moving towards an early peace treaty. Contrary to its original anxiety about a possible Commonwealth counter-bloc emerging, the State Department found the outcome of the Canberra Conference 'encouraging', for it discovered that the former's thinking was close to that of the Americans.[15] Nevertheless, the State Department encountered difficulties in drafting a settlement which would both ensure that Japan should not come under the influence of a hostile power, and yet still secure Soviet participation in the peace treaty. Having long advocated peacemaking by the four members of the Council of Foreign Ministers, the Soviets did not accept American-led peacemaking by all eleven powers of the Far Eastern Commission (FEC).[16] On the other hand, Washington regarded the exclusion of the USSR as dangerous, since an economically and politically unstable Japan might be prey to Soviet influence, particularly in view of the future withdrawal of American forces consequent upon any peace treaty.[17]

In terms of the Cold War in Asia, the dilatory American approach caused anxiety in Britain. The Foreign Office believed that the Japanese would resent an indefinite occupation, something which might lead Japan to seek more amicable relations with the USSR, a country openly critical of America's occupation policy.[18] In order to secure Japan's long-term alignment with the West, the occupation needed swiftly to end. The Foreign Office was also concerned that a protracted occupation might prevent the recovery of the Japanese economy. Its anxiety was that continuing low standards of living might make the Japanese sympathetic to communism.[19] The recent successes of the Chinese Communists increased British fears.[20] Thus, Britain needed to persist in its efforts to persuade the United States of the desirability of a rapid settlement.

In order to assist the Americans in breaking the deadlock, the Foreign Office frequently communicated its views to the State Department. It saw the latter's position as very similar to its own in many respects, and thus sought to help the latter win the day in its discussions with the Pentagon by persuading the Americans that the British proposals were feasible. Indeed, in June 1948, when noting that the State Department's view regarding the moderate restoration of the Japanese economy conformed to that of the British, Dening commented that, 'it is up to us to furnish ammunition for them'.[21]

One notable British proposal was the idea that a bilateral security pact between the United States and Japan should be signed at the same time as the peace treaty. Dening drew up this proposal in preparation for his mission to Washington in May–June 1948. The Foreign Office deemed one of the main causes of the stalemate to be the Pentagon's reluctance to withdraw US forces from Japan at a time when relations with Russia were deteriorating.[22] Dening thought that a bilateral pact would ensure a continued American military presence even after the conclusion of the peace treaty, and thereby remove American anxieties that the end of the occupation would necessarily precipitate a withdrawal of its forces.[23] Moreover, he hoped that such an arrangement would provide for Japan's security and thus enable the Americans to proceed even without Soviet participation in the peace treaty.[24] Unlike the Americans, the British had long regarded Soviet participation as inessential.[25]

The proposed bilateral pact also met Britain's own regional defence needs. The Chiefs of Staff took the view that a dominant American presence in Japan would deter any communist attack on Hong Kong.[26] Therefore Britain's main strategic aim soon became that of securing Japan against Soviet influence.

As communist domination of China became imminent, the Chiefs of Staff further concluded that only American military strength in Japan and Okinawa could counter possible aggression against British interests in Southeast Asia.[27] Thus, the security of British interests now rested on the maintenance by the United States of forces in Japan and Okinawa, but more for the purpose of regional protection from the communists than from a resurgent Japan.

These British ideas did not enjoy much success until mid-1949. The State Department's unwillingness to act sprang from fear of a possible threat from Russia. It was not yet confident of the viability of a partial peace treaty which excluded the USSR. It feared that, if the United States started to negotiate without them, the Soviets might propose better terms in order to attract the Japanese.[28] Moreover, anxiety persisted in Washington that such a solution might only provoke the Russians into aggression, since there would be a continued state of war between Japan and the Soviet Union.[29] Also noteworthy is that, unlike the British, the State Department had taken it for granted that American forces should be withdrawn from Japan after the peace settlement, except in the case of Okinawa.[30] This led to doubt about the feasibility of the bilateral security arrangement proposed by the British.[31] The Foreign Office was critical of this naivety on the part of the US government. It was convinced that a continued American presence would deter Soviet aggression, believing that any Russian action would be influenced not by legal questions but purely by power–political considerations.[32]

By September 1949 when the Anglo-American foreign ministers' talks took place in Washington, the State Department's opinion had moved closer to Britain's. Unlike the Department of Defense, the State Department had come to share the view that a prolonged occupation might have an adverse psychological effect on Japan and an increasingly deleterious impact on the programme for the rehabilitation of its economy.[33] An early peace treaty was thus desirable in order to secure Japan's permanent association with the West, particularly now that it seemed clear that China was lost to communism.[34] In response to the State Department's initiative, on 9 June the Joint Chiefs of Staff (JCS) set out the US security essentials for any Japanese settlement. Among these, the most significant development concerned the location of post-peace treaty US bases. The JCS proposed the continued use of Yokosuka as a naval military base. This meant that only the securing of bases both on the adjacent islands, including Okinawa, and on the mainland would meet US desiderata. In order to do so, the JSC went further to suggest that 'the peace treaty should not be such as to preclude bilateral negotiations for base rights in the Japanese main islands'.[35] The State Department realized that the British-proposed bilateral security pact harmonized with these new US requirements.[36] Britain's stance was all the more helpful because, at this point, the State Department felt that the US needed to secure the support of the majority of its allies for its own peace treaty terms in order to attain a multilateral peace treaty, since the Soviet Union would be very unlikely to sign a peace treaty which countenanced American base rights in Japan.[37] In this regard, Washington, to some extent, could count on Britain's acting as a mediator between the Commonwealth and themselves.[38] In this way, Britain's position strengthened the State Department's inclination for an early peace.[39]

This new direction was further encouraged by the fact that, by the end of September 1949, MacArthur had revised his opinions. Whereas previously he had advocated a neutral Japan, at this point he suggested that a bilateral security arrangement should be concluded which would come into force simultaneously with the peace treaty. The State Department welcomed this, concluding that his ideas were coming into line with its own.[40] MacArthur's change of heart was closely connected with British efforts. In early September, Ivor Pink of the British Liaison Mission had explained to MacArthur his government's view on security, including the argument that, following the British example in Egypt, American forces could be retained in Japan without any legal constraint by concluding a bilateral agreement concurrently with the peace treaty. Pink observed that MacArthur seemed to have been impressed by this argument.[41] This certainly seems to have been the case, for, when MacArthur later conveyed his suggestion to Washington, he referred to the example of Egypt to illustrate how the United States might retain its bases in Japan. Moreover, this was a view which W. Walton Butterworth, Assistant Secretary of State for Far Eastern Affairs, State Department, found of interest.[42] The narrowing gap between the State Department and MacArthur was significant for American decision-making in that two of the main policy-makers were now able to collaborate against the Pentagon which still insisted that a peace treaty was premature. Even so, the Pentagon was not won over until John Foster Dulles took the initiative in spring 1950.

Modifying the American-led Settlement

After Dulles, as a consultant to the State Department, assumed leadership of American preparations for the peace treaty in April 1950, intra-governmental consensus-building rapidly proceeded. However, the security issues, in particular the question of Japanese rearmament, still frustrated any final agreement. Washington's requirements at this time included not only the retention of bases in Japan but also the rearming of Japan, given the possible future departure of American forces. Dulles considered that the United States alone would not wish to provide security for an indefinite period, and that Japan should soon share responsibility for its own defence.[43] However, although the Japanese government expressed its acceptance of the American military presence in May 1950, Yoshida seemed to hesitate over Japan's taking any substantial defence contribution, an attitude which increased Washington's concerns.[44] Thus, the Truman administration was in no rush to reach a settlement based simply on the British proposals. In contrast, the British assumed that Japan, once permitted, would eventually attempt to rearm; unlike the Americans, they did not regard the lukewarm attitude of the Japanese government as deep-rooted.[45]

The outbreak of the Korean War in June 1950 did not have any great impact on British peacemaking efforts, but merely strengthened the direction of established policy. This was exemplified by Britain's attitude towards security questions and its desire for an early peace treaty. By early 1950 British ministers had given general approval to limited Japanese army rearmament, so they had already accepted the essential part of the 'reverse course'.[46] In late 1950, Britain came to support a greater scale of rearmament, including the navy and air force.[47] As the war intensified the sense of the imminent military threat to Western interests, the Foreign Office hoped that the development of Japan's own defence capability might release some US forces for use in the European theatre in any future major war.[48] British ministers therefore approved the Chiefs of Staff's increased support for an American–Japanese security treaty as the only practicable scheme which would provide some safeguards against Japan's capability for future aggression.[49] Moreover, once the war broke out, the Foreign Office argued even more strongly than before for an early peace treaty. In British eyes, a further delay was undesirable, as the conflict in Korea made the Japanese increasingly aware of their heightened bargaining position.[50] On the other hand, the Foreign Office recognized that the Japanese, hoping to secure an American security guarantee, were now growing more receptive to the idea of post-war bases. It thus argued that, with Japanese goodwill at its height, the Americans should take the initiative in order to achieve desirable security arrangements.[51]

Britain's position as Commonwealth leader was seriously undermined after Dulles started negotiations with individual FEC powers in September 1950. The United States was now in a better position to perceive the divergence of views within the Commonwealth. Anxiety on the part of the Pacific Commonwealth nations over the American plan not to restrict rearmament especially struck Dulles, and he found the position of Australia and New Zealand, unlike that of the British, to be rigid on this issue.[52] Naturally, Britain did not wish to leave the Americans to reconcile the divergent Commonwealth views, but to resolve them through its own initiative.[53] However, the Commonwealth prime ministers' conference, held in London in early January 1951, did not do much to mitigate the intransigent attitude of the Australian and New Zealand leaders.[54]

In order promptly to obtain a non-restrictive peace treaty, the Americans themselves thus had to persuade the two countries. For this purpose, prior to his visit to Japan in January–February 1951, Dulles and his team drew up a proposal for a Pacific Pact, a multilateral security arrangement with the off-shore Pacific island countries of Japan, the Philippines, Australia, New Zealand and possibly Indonesia. The pact was intended to facilitate Japanese rearmament as part of a multilateral collective defence scheme, in which Japan's forces would be created for international purposes, conforming to the UN charter. Thus, it was designed both to tackle the constitutional restraint on the possession of independent military forces and to overcome regional fears of Japan.[55] Washington did not plan to extend formal membership to include Britain, for it was felt that this might invite other European countries, such as France and the Netherlands, to press their own claims. As a result, an American commitment might then be extended to continental Asia. Furthermore, such an extensive membership might bestow an unfavourable image of imperialism upon the American-led security arrangement.[56]

However, Dulles encountered considerable opposition from the British, when the plan was revealed to them in Tokyo. They were mainly concerned about the composition of the proposed pact. Their exclusion came as a shock, and was considered especially undesirable since it might give the impression that Britain had renounced its responsibilities in the Pacific, causing unquestionably grave repercussions in Hong Kong and Malaya. In addition, as the pact covered only the Pacific island countries, it was feared that it could have detrimental effects on the excluded continental Southeast Asian nations, including Malaya, by encouraging communist aggression in these areas. London also worried that such a multilateral treaty might oblige Australia and New Zealand to provide forces for the security of Japan or the Philippines. This might frustrate the ongoing Commonwealth plan in which both nations were expected to contribute to defence in other vital theatres in the event of war, especially the Middle East. The Chiefs of Staff considered a broader regional security arrangement covering Southeast Asia to be desirable as a long-term goal, but premature at this time.[57] In opposing Dulles's proposal, Britain's preference was for a US–Japan bilateral defence arrangement, together with a simple declaration of American guarantees regarding Australia and New Zealand.[58]

Dulles resented Britain's unyielding objections. In February 1951 he complained to Alvary Gascoigne, the head of the British Liaison Mission, Tokyo, that:

> It is not helpful for the UK merely to indicate that it does not like the idea of such a pact. If, however, the British Government could persuade Australia and New Zealand to come along with our idea of the [peace] treaty, we could drop the idea of a pact at once.[59]

His comment demonstrates that he did not at the time regard Britain's influence on these Pacific nations as effective. Thus, despite British opposition and because he remained unclear about the attitude of Australia and New Zealand, he continued to pin some hopes on the Pacific Pact until his subsequent visit to Canberra. Admittedly, however, his visit to Tokyo weakened Dulles's enthusiasm for Japan's inclusion in the Pacific Pact, owing to his impression that the latter might be able to get round the constitutional question regarding rearmament without the benefit of such a pact.[60]

For the leaders of Australia and New Zealand, a tripartite pact was the best option. In examining the Pacific Pact, both countries' leaders believed that Japan's inclusion was impractical due to likely objections from the general public. The participation of the Philippines was more acceptable to Australia, but New Zealand's Chiefs of Staff were doubtful about its benefits in view of the priority given to Commonwealth defence.[61] Although the tripartite treaty was thus an ideal solution, Percy Spender, the Australian minister for external affairs, in particular, feared that it was dangerous flatly to oppose Dulles's original idea, since this might result in the United States abandoning its efforts to establish a multilateral security arrangement. Spender did not intend to allow the discontent with the Pacific Pact in its present form to spoil this 'last opportunity' of ensuring an American commitment to Australia's security.[62]

So how could the desired tripartite pact be achieved? In answering this question, it is important to mention that Britain's continued efforts and the New Zealand government's anxiety gradually convinced Dulles and his department that Britain was taking a firm grip on the dominions in this matter. Britain's most conspicuous attempt to do so came when Dening stayed in Canberra during the Dulles Mission. His purpose was to prevent Australia and New Zealand from agreeing to the Pacific Pact under pressure from the Americans.[63] He contacted Spender and Frederick Doidge, the New Zealand minister for external affairs, before their meeting with Dulles and reminded them of Britain's position.[64] In the meantime, noting Britain's firm attitude and New Zealand's recent announcement of its reluctance to enter into a security pact that excluded Britain, Washington began to doubt the feasibility of the Pacific-island proposal.[65] Given the evidence of Britain's growing profile in US policy-making, both Spender and Doidge were now in a position to take advantage of Britain's opposition to the Pacific Pact in order to obtain a tripartite arrangement without declaring their own particular objections.

The Canberra talks took place between 15 and 18 February. In the meeting with Dulles, both Spender and Doidge showed keen interest in an American commitment to their countries' security, but at the same time expressed their hesitation over the proposed Pacific Pact, highlighting British opposition, and thereby concealing their own need to oppose it.[66] This was the final blow to Dulles's original idea of the Pacific Pact, and the inclusion of Japan was thus dropped. In doing so, Dulles stated to both leaders that British opposition was 'formidable', so that he could not proceed with the original idea.[67] However, it was only the perceived unity of the Commonwealth under British influence which finally brought Dulles to give up on his original Pacific Pact.

Although Britain succeeded in ensuring the exclusion of Japan from the Pacific Pact, this alone did not wholly meet its wishes. Contrary to the British hope for a simple declaration of American security interests in the region, as a result of the Dulles Mission Australia and New Zealand moved towards a more formal security arrangement with the United States. It was also not in the British interest that Dulles still continued to entertain the possibility of including the Philippines in the proposed security arrangement.[68] However, when Britain later expressed strong opposition to this, the State Department gave way.[69] The American compromise was largely due to the need to hasten the peacemaking process.[70] In the end, the tripartite security arrangement also came to be acceptable to Britain, especially because ministers had finally admitted that there was some force in the Australian and New Zealand argument that America's commitment to their security would facilitate their contribution to Middle Eastern defence rather than undermine it.[71]

As regards the security arrangements with Japan, despite Britain's dissatisfaction, expressed in objections, for example, to the overly prescriptive wording of the US–Japan Security Treaty and the timing of its conclusion, the eventual settlement did conform to its basic military need to secure a permanent American presence in Japan and Okinawa.[72] Yet, since Britain saw the broader regional arrangement as a long-term goal, it did not view the San Francisco settlement as final, but only as a first step towards a more comprehensive solution. Thus, subsequent British efforts were directed towards formally linking the American presence in the region to the defence of Southeast Asia and Hong Kong. As an initial stage, the Chiefs of Staff suggested in late August 1951 that there should be early talks between the British, American and French Chiefs of Staff, in cooperation with representatives of Australia and New Zealand, to discuss the defence problem in Southeast Asia. They wanted these talks to serve as an opportunity to formulate a common tripartite policy for the region.[73] Moreover, an exchange of views between Britain and Australia regarding the broadening of existing security arrangements in the Pacific commenced shortly after the peace settlement.[74] It is also important to note that Dulles and the State Department did not abandon the Pacific Pact as their long-term goal. Dulles deemed that the bilateral security pact with Japan would serve as a transitional arrangement, which could subsequently be developed into a broader multilateral arrangement.[75]

The most critical question in the final phase of the Anglo-American negotiations was *which China* should be invited to sign the peace treaty.[76] Britain's initial position was that the PRC should be present, but the State Department was under huge domestic pressure not to invite the Communist regime, for while Britain had already recognized the PRC America remained hostile, particularly after the Chinese intervened in the Korean War in October 1950. The meetings in London in June 1951 between Dulles and Herbert Morrison, the British foreign secretary, resulted in an agreement that neither regime should be invited. This temporary compromise reflected the need of the United States to secure majority support for the peace treaty which it was sponsoring. Indeed, in April 1951 Dulles had enquired into the possibility of proceeding with a peace treaty without British participation, but this was deemed to be unrealistic.[77] The exclusion of Britain would have further underlined the 'partial' nature of the peace treaty, fanning Japanese public criticism.[78]

The Morrison–Dulles agreement soon became ineffective, for in early 1952 the Japanese government, under pressure from Dulles, started negotiating with the Nationalist regime in Taiwan. One can point here to a British diplomatic failure. However, Britain at least succeeded in excluding the Nationalists from the peace conference. For, in view of the likely impracticability of inviting the PRC, Britain's aim had already been modified to ensure the exclusion of the Nationalists, so that Japan could freely negotiate with either Chinese regime after the San Francisco treaty.[79] Britain's desire was for the United States and Britain to avoid responsibility for cutting off normal contacts between Japan and the Chinese mainland.[80]

In the end American pressure denied Japan such a free hand. However, it can be said that the adamant British stance at the time of the 1951 settlement left the Japanese some perceived room for future rapprochement with the PRC. The San

Francisco peace treaty did not damage the relationship between Beijing and Britain, whose attitude served as a clear encouragement to Tokyo, in particular Yoshida, who had in mind the adoption of a 'two-China' policy.[81] Indeed, Yoshida later hoped that British leverage upon Washington would facilitate his manoeuvres for the development of Japan's relations with the PRC. This approach reached its highpoint with Yoshida's visit to London in autumn 1954.[82] Hence, the differences between the United States and Britain over China laid the foundation for long-lasting international relations in East Asia which were not uniformly hostile to Communist China, and in which Japan was constantly tempted to pursue its 'two-China' policy throughout the 1950s.

Conclusion

Britain's motives regarding the Japanese settlement were ambivalent. While commercial interests urged certain restrictions on Japanese economic performance, Cold War considerations increasingly came to the fore, inclining the British to a more lenient peace treaty and leading them to emphasize the need to secure the American presence in the region. Although fear of renewed Japanese militarism did not completely vanish, attention was soon concentrated, at least at government level, on the Soviet threat. Strongly concerned about the stability of Southeast Asia and Hong Kong, the British government promoted a proper economic and political role for Japan in the region.

Prompted by these objectives, Britain contributed significantly to the formation of the San Francisco System. First, Britain's suggestion for an early peace treaty regardless of Soviet participation and with the concurrent conclusion of a bilateral security pact gradually won the support of the State Department and MacArthur. It can be said that by proposing this particular solution from quite an early date, Britain attempted in substance gradually to drill the United States in how the Western Allies should fight the Cold War in East Asia. Second, Britain decisively influenced the form of the eventual security arrangements in the West Pacific. When Dulles endeavoured to tackle the question of rearmament by means of the Pacific Pact, he eventually discarded it on account of British opposition. Instead, the United States had to conclude three separate arrangements, including the US–Japan bilateral treaty. Third, Britain's stance over Chinese representation at the peace conference did not fatally impair its relations with the PRC. Thus a conduit between the West and China was maintained. Britain's China policy in turn strengthened Japan's principle of separating economics from politics in dealing with the PRC.

For Britain, Commonwealth unity acted as a strong source of power in exerting influence on American thinking, whether in supporting Washington's position or in urging modifications. As a regional power, Britain's capacity for leverage was very restricted, given the limited military forces at its disposal for the Far Eastern theatre, but Commonwealth unity was an important asset that allowed it to exercise greater influence. In particular, its leadership of the Commonwealth was crucial after the United States had decided to proceed without

Soviet participation. In this situation, Washington needed to obtain Commonwealth agreement, since this would suggest international support for an American-led peace settlement. Accordingly, the degree of British influence depended upon how far Washington perceived the 'British Group' to be united. In that sense, its contribution to the collapse of the Pacific Pact was the most successful example of Britain's effective sway.

In conclusion, it can be argued that Britain's significant contribution to the formation of the San Francisco System and its continuing subscription to it made the System more 'stable' than it might otherwise have been. The System continued to come under pressure during the 1950s from various Japanese opposition groups. After the Yoshida era, while the Japanese government pursued the revision of the security treaty and the normalization of its relationship with the Soviet Union largely within the framework of the System, there was simultaneously growing public outcry against the System itself, culminating in the 1960 Security Treaty Crisis. In this climate, Britain continued to endorse the System. When it came to Japan's relationship with the Soviet Union and the PRC, Britain maintained its distance from Japan's position. During the Japan–Soviet normalization negotiations in 1955–56, Britain took a non-interventionist line. It welcomed reduced regional tension through normalization, but only within the System. This was made clear when, despite Japan's hopes for Britain's help, Britain did not respond favourably to the Soviet Union's offer to allow the reversion of the two southernmost Kurile Islands to Japan, which contravened the territorial provisions laid down by the 1951 settlement. Britain wanted to foster regional stability by preserving the status quo in East Asia. In these circumstances, 'a sit-by and watch' policy was the best possible course in order to avoid alienating Japanese opinion.[83] Meanwhile, although Britain's policy towards China created a favourable environment for Japan, it never aided the latter in challenging the System by working with it to expand its trade with mainland China. Yoshida's manoeuvre of 1954, based on the expectation of British leverage on America over China, in the end failed to win British goodwill. Britain did not want its relations with the United States to deteriorate, and the British themselves feared that too great a development of Japan's trade with China might lead to an unfavourable political collaboration between the two.[84] Despite the previous conflict of views with the United States over China, Britain thus supported the San Francisco System as maintaining a politically advantageous status quo, and therefore helped contain Japan within that System. Lastly, the security elements of the System were bolstered by support from Britain. After the Japanese settlement, Britain attempted to obtain an extended American commitment to Southeast Asia on the basis of the existing security arrangements in the Pacific. However, Britain never sanctioned Japan's military association with the multilateral regional security framework, Southeast Asia Treaty Organisation (SEATO), which was signed in 1954, and maintained its preference for the bilateral US–Japan security arrangement.[85]

Notes

1 See, for example, Igarashi Takeshi, *Sengo Nichibei Kankei no Keisei*, Tokyo: Kodan-sya Gakujyutsu Bunko, 1995.
2 See Roger Buckley, *Occupation Diplomacy: Britain, the United States and Japan, 1945–1952*, Cambridge: Cambridge University Press, 1982; Peter Lowe, *Containing the Cold War in East Asia: British Policies towards Japan, China and Korea, 1948–53*, Manchester: Manchester University Press, 1997; Kibata Yoichi, *Teikoku no Tasogare: Reisenka no Igirisu to Ajia*, Tokyo: University of Tokyo Press, 1996. The pioneering work which emphasizes the British role is Hosoya Chihiro's *San Francisco Kowa he no Michi*, Tokyo: Chuo Koronsha, 1984.
3 See Akira Iriye, *The Cold War in Asia: A Historical Introduction*, Englewood Cliffs, NJ: Prentice-Hall, 1974, pp. 182–91.
4 Buckley, *Occupation Diplomacy*, pp. 145–6.
5 The National Archives, Kew (TNA) FO371/63772 F9238/1382/23 FE(O)(47)40 'General United Kingdom Aims in the Settlement with Japan', Foreign Office memorandum, 12 July 1947.
6 TNA FO371/63775 F10373/1382/23 ORC(47)35 'Measures for the Control of Japan' Foreign Office memorandum, 25 July 1947.
7 TNA FO371/63772 F9238/1382/23 FE(O)(47)40 'General United Kingdom Aims in the Settlement with Japan', Foreign Office memorandum, 12 July 1947.
8 TNA FO371/63771 F8617/1382/23 'Territorial, Political and General Clauses of the Treaty of Peace with Japan', Foreign Office memorandum, 26 June 1947.
9 TNA FO371/63767 F2591/1 Bevin (Moscow) to Sargent (FO), 10 April 1947.
10 TNA FO371/767 F2591/1 Sargent to Moscow embassy, 11 April 1947.
11 See TNA FO371/63770 F7903/1382/23 Dening to Bevin, 16 June 1947.
12 TNA FO371/63774 F10125/1382/23 FE(O)(47)46(Revise), 'General Conference of All States at War with Japan', Foreign Office memorandum, 8 August 1947. According to the Foreign Office, the 'United States Group' accommodated the Philippines and the Central and South American countries, while the 'Soviet Group' included the three Eastern European communist regimes.
13 TNA FO371/63776 F10622/1382/G Dening to Clarke (Paris), 28 July 1947.
14 See TNA FO371/63775 F10455/1382/23 Gascoigne to Dening, 1 August 1947.
15 National Archives and Records Administration, United States [hereafter: NARA], RG59 Central Decimal Files of the Department of State [hereafter: DDOS], 740.0011 PW(Peace)/ 9–247 Penfield to Marshall, 2 September 1947. For prior American uneasiness about the Canberra Conference see, for example, NARA, DDOS, 740.0011 PW (Peace)/6–247, Marshall to US Embassy, Canberra, 2 June 1947.
16 Smith (Moscow) to Marshall, 23 July 1947 in *Foreign Relations of the United States* [hereafter: *FRUS*], *1947, vol. VI* (Washington: Governmental Printing Office), pp. 473–4.
17 See Durbrow (Moscow) to Marshall, 2 December 1947, ibid., pp. 583–4.
18 See TNA FO371/69926 F8091/6139/23/G Dening (Washington) to Wright (London), 1 June 1948.
19 See TNA FO371/76213 F15665/1021/23 Foreign Office minute, 18 October 1949.
20 See TNA FO410/101 F1975/1019/23 Gascoigne (Tokyo) to Bevin, 20 January, 1949.
21 TNA FO371/69887 F7999/662/23 Dening minute, 21 June 1948.
22 See TNA FO 371/69887 F6643/662/23/G 'Remarks made in conversation by a US officer in Secretary Royall's office who accompanied the Draper Mission to Japan' attached to Graves (Washington) to MacDermot, 1 May 1948.
23 See TNA FO371/69927 F8770/6139/23/G Dening minute, 24 March 1948.
24 Memorandum of conversation, 2 June 1948 in *FRUS, 1948, vol. VI*, pp. 796–7.
25 See the British Embassy to the Department of State, presented to Borton by Graves on 9 October 1947 in *FRUS, 1947, vol. VI*, pp. 531–2.

26 TNA DEFE6/2 JP(47)80(Final) 'Hong Kong – Permanent Garrison' Joint Planning Staff (JPS) memorandum, 27 June 1947.
27 For the development of the British military staff's view regarding the Far East see TNA DEFE6/6 JP(48)101(Final Revise) 'Far Eastern Strategy and Defence Policy', JPS memorandum, 17 March 1948. See also TNA DEFE6/7 JP(49)124(Final) 'Strategic Implications of the Situation in China', JPS memorandum, 12 January 1949.
28 NARA, DDOS, 740.0011-PW (Peace)/5–649 Fearey to Butterworth, 6 May 1949.
29 NARA, DDOS, 740.0011-PW (Peace)/no decimal number (in Box 3515), 'Russian Rights consequent upon separate Treaty of Peace', State Department Memorandum, 5 December 1949.
30 Kennan report, 25 March 1948, in *FRUS, 1948, vol. VI*, p. 692.
31 NARA, DDOS, 740.0011-PW (Peace)/6–1748 Butterworth to Lovett and Armour, 17 June 1948.
32 See for example TNA FO371/76211 F5773/1021/23 Tomlinson minute, 29 April 1949.
33 See Butterworth to Webb, 19 May 1949 in *FRUS, 1949, vol. VII, part 2*, pp. 752–3.
34 See Sebald to Acheson, 20 August 1949, ibid., pp. 830–40.
35 Report by the Joint Chiefs of Staff, 9 June 1949, ibid., p. 775.
36 See Douglas (London) (forwarding Kennan's message) to Acheson, 13 July 1949, ibid., p. 799.
37 See NARA, DDOS, 740.00119 Control (Japan)/6–2249 Butterworth to Acheson, 22 June 1949.
38 See NARA, DDOS, 740.0011 PW (Peace)/7–1349 Butterworth to Kennan (London), 15 July 1949.
39 See Green memorandum, 29 July 1949 in *FRUS, 1949, vol. VII, part 2*, p. 824.
40 See memorandum of conversation, 21 September 1949, ibid., pp. 862–4. See also memorandum of conversation, 2 November 1949, ibid., pp. 890–4.
41 TNA FO371/76210 F14219/10115/23 Gascoigne to Scarlett, 3 September 1949.
42 Memorandum of conversation, 5 February 1950, in *FRUS, 1950, VI*, pp. 1133–4.
43 See Dulles to Nitze, 20 July 1950, ibid., pp. 1246–8.
44 See Reid to Butterworth, 10 May 1950, ibid., pp. 1194–8 and Dulles Summary Report, 3 July 1950, ibid., pp. 1231–2.
45 See TNA FO410/102 FJ1194/3 Gascoigne to Bevin, 18 September 1950.
46 See Kibata, *Teikoku no Tasogare*, pp. 59–60.
47 TNA CAB128/19 CM(51) 1st Cabinet conclusions, 2 January 1951; TNA CAB129/43 CP(50)318 'Japanese Peace Treaty: Security Aspects', Bevin and Shinwell memorandum, 21 December 1950.
48 See TNA FO371/83889 FJ1194/3 Gascoigne to Bevin, 18 September 1950, and C.P.Scott minute 3 October 1950.
49 TNA CAB128/19 CM(51) 1st Cabinet conclusions, 2 January 1951; TNA CAB129/43 CP(50)318 'Japanese Peace Treaty: Security Aspects', Bevin and Shinwell memorandum, 21 December 1950.
50 TNA FO371/83013 F1022/20 Foreign Office minute, 12 July 1950. See also TNA FO410/102 FJ10111/52 Gascoigne to Attlee, 1 August 1950.
51 TNA FO371/83013 F1022/20 Foreign Office minute, 12 July 1950.
52 See Dulles to MacArthur, 15 November 1947, in *FRUS, 1950, vol. VI*, pp. 1349–52. See also the footnote to Memorandum of Conversation, 22 September 1950, ibid., p. 1307.
53 TNA FO371/83834 F1021/143 Tomlinson (New York) to Shattock, 9 October 1950.
54 See Lowe, *Containing the Cold War in East Asia*, pp. 34–6.
55 For the Pacific Pact, see Dulles to Allison, 11 January 1951, in *FRUS, 1951, vol. VI, part 1*, pp. 790–1.
56 See NARA RG59 Lot Files of the State Department, E-1252 Bureau of Far Eastern

Affairs, Japanese Peace Treaty Files of John Foster Dulles, Subject File, 1946–52 [hereafter: Dulles Lot], Box 10, Folder *Pacific Pact*, Rusk to Dulles, 8 February 1951.

57 For British objections to the Pacific Pact, see TNA FO371/92529 FJ1022/24/G FO to Tokyo no. 169, 30 January 1951, and FO to Tokyo no. 170, 30 January 1951. See also TNA CAB129/44 CP(51)47 'Pacific Defence' Younger memorandum, 9 February 1951.

58 See TNA FO371/92529 FJ1022/24/G FO to Tokyo no. 169, 30 January 1951. For Britain's preference for a looser form of tripartite security arrangement see TNA DO35/2927 (serial number 80) CRO to UK High Commissioners, Canberra and Wellington, 6 February 1951.

59 NARA, Dulles Lot, Box 13, Folder *United Kingdom: Sir Alvary Gascogine*, 'Notes on Conversation between Ambassador Dulles and British Ambassador', 6 February 1951.

60 NARA, Dulles Lot, Box 7, Folder *Japan Trip January–February 1951*, 'Note on Mission Staff Meeting at Ambassador Jarman's Residence on February 14, 1951'.

61 Document 231, 'Report on the Australian–New Zealand Consultations with Dulles at Canberra', 7 March 1951 in Robin Kay (ed.), *Documents on New Zealand External Relations vol. III: The ANZUS Pact and the Treaty of Peace with Japan* (Wellington: Historical Publication Branch, Department of Internal Affairs, 1985) [hereafter: *DNZER*], pp. 631–3. See also document 209, 'Minutes of a meeting of the Chiefs of Staff Committee and Officers of the Department of External Affairs', 6 February 1951, ibid., pp. 566–7.

62 Document 224, 'Note on Discussions between the New Zealand and Australian Ministers of External Affairs', 13 February 1951, ibid., pp. 590–1.

63 TNA DO35/2927 (no. 137) High Commissioner (Canberra) to CRO, 15 February 1951.

64 TNA FO371/92534 FJ1022/139 Williams (Canberra) to CRO, 9 March 1951.

65 See Hiroyuki Umetsu, 'The Birth of ANZUS: America's Attempt to Create a Defence Linkage Between Northeast Asia and the Southwest Pacific', *International Relations of the Asia-Pacific*, 4 (2004) p. 178. For the perceived influence of New Zealand attitudes upon American attitudes, see TNA DO35/2927 (no. 106) CRO to High Commissioners, Australia and New Zealand, 9 February 1951.

66 For the tripartite meeting, see document 226, 'Notes on the Australian–New Zealand–United States Talks in Canberra', 15–17 February 1951, in *DNZER*, pp. 593–613. See also TNA FO371/92534 FJ1022/139 Williams (Canberra) to CRO, 9 March 1951.

67 Document 226 in *DNZER*, p. 604.

68 This unsatisfactory result was partly because of Dening's inability to communicate fully with Dulles due to the former's illness during his stay in Canberra. See TNA DO35/2927 (no. 171) High Commissioner (Canberra) to CRO, 20 February 1951.

69 See Memorandum of Conversation, 5 April 1951, in *FRUS, 1951, vol. VI, part 1*, pp. 186–7.

70 NARA, Dulles Lot, Box 3, Folder *Defense 1951*, Acheson to Marshall, 6 April 1951.

71 See TNA CAB128/19 CM(51) 16th Cabinet conclusions, 1 March 1951; TNA CAB128/19 CM(51) 19th Cabinet conclusions, 12 March 1951.

72 For Britain's criticism of the security treaty see TNA FO371/92611 FJ10345/8 Clutton (Tokyo) to Johnston, 12 September 1951, and Johnston minute, 19 September 1951

73 TNA DEFE4/46 Confidential Annex 'Operational Aspects of the Defence of South-East Asia' to COS(51) 137th meeting, 29 August 1951.

74 TNA DEFE5/35 COS(51)734 'Broadening of Existing Defence Arrangements in the Pacific', Chiefs of Staff memorandum, 10 December 1951.

75 NARA, Dulles Lot, Box 5, Folder *France*, memorandum of conversation, 11 June 1951.

76 On the question of Chinese representation at the peace settlement see Hosoya, *San Francisco kowa he no michi*, pp. 43–8.

77 Dulles Mission Staff meeting minutes, 18 April 1951, in *FRUS, 1951, vol. VI, part 1*, p. 984.
78 For the possible effects on Japan of a peace treaty without Britain, see Dulles Mission Staff meeting minutes, April 17 1951, ibid., pp. 980–1.
79 TNA FO371/92544 FJ1022/312 Johnston minute, 18 April 1951.
80 TNA FO371/92541 FJ1022/288 Tomlinson to Johnston, 16 April 1951.
81 For Yoshida's 'two China' policy, see Chen Zhao-bin, *Sengo Nihon no Chugoku seisaku: 1950 nen dai Higashi Ajia kokusai seiji no bunmyaku*, Tokyo: University of Tokyo Press, 2000, pp. 2–3.
82 See Tanaka Takahiko, 'Anglo-Japanese Relations in the 1950s: Cooperation, Friction and the Search for State Identity', in Ian Nish and Yoichi Kibata (eds), *The History of Anglo-Japanese Relations, 1600–2000: The Political and Diplomatic Dimension, vol. 2: 1931–2000*, Basingstoke: Macmillan, 2000, pp. 205–12.
83 For Britain's stance over the Japan–Soviet normalization talks see Tanaka Takahiko, *Nisso-kokko kaifuku no shiteki kenkyu: sengo nisso kankei no kiten, 1945–1956*, Tokyo: Yuhikaku, 1993, pp. 106–12, 138–44, 184–92, 262–7.
84 See Chen, *Sengo Nihon no Chugoku Seisaku*, pp. 122–30.
85 TNA FO371/111876 D1074/315 Makins (Washington) to FO, 4 August 1954.

9 The Cold War and nationalism in Southeast Asia

British strategy, 1948–60

Peter Lowe

The Labour government headed by Clement Attlee established the basic approach, followed subsequently by the Conservative administrations led by Winston Churchill, Anthony Eden and Harold Macmillan. This approach may be defined as combining recognition of the legitimacy of the aspirations advanced by nationalist movements with an appreciation of the urgency of preventing communism from assuming control of nationalism.[1] Some on the left of the Labour party believed that colonial empires should be liquidated with reasonable speed as a matter of principle; the centre and right of the party, particularly when Labour was in government, responded pragmatically and was influenced by the strength of nationalist movements in the areas concerned and by how vital any specific area might be in the short-term viability of the British economy. Thus, it was understood by Attlee and his principal colleagues that independence must be granted in the Indian sub-continent, Ceylon and Burma, since the alternative would be violence on a large scale, which could not be countered with the resources available.[2] Mistakes were made in the immediate postwar readjustments in underestimating the developing strength of the forces challenging the empire but realism then prevailed. By contrast, there was no suggestion of extending independence to Malaya in the aftermath of the Pacific War. Malaya was an essential dollar-earner: Attlee promised eventual independence in a statement issued in 1949 but with no date stipulated when this would take effect.[3] Ironically the ensuing Conservative governments reached the conclusion that the price to be paid for containing communism successfully in Malaya and ensuring stability was willingness to grant independence at a much earlier date than had been contemplated by the Attlee government.[4] Labour and Conservative administrations were influenced by the major blunders committed by the Netherlands and France in their respective endeavours to reoccupy their colonies in Indonesia and Indo-China.[5] The process of grasping the magnitude of these blunders was compounded by rueful acknowledgement of the invidious British role in assisting the return of the Dutch and the French in 1945–46.[6]

The delicacy of the challenges facing British ministers and officials was accentuated by the centrality of Britain's relationship with the United States. The experience of joint cooperation during the wars in Asia and the Pacific, between December 1941 and August 1945, revealed the friction resulting from the common awareness of expanding American power and Britain's reduced status: Christopher Thorne and Richard Aldrich have demonstrated the ambiguous relations between 'allies of a kind'.[7] American passion for liberating colonial peoples was at its most fervent when Franklin Roosevelt occupied the White House. The deterioration in relations with the Soviet Union, marking the onset of the Cold War, caused Harry Truman to modify anti-colonialism. However, it remained a significant influence in the perceptions and conduct of American politicians and officials, seasoned with the confident belief that the United States could achieve far more than the old European empires.[8] Unhappily American initiatives were frequently distinguished by an absence of subtlety and an over-simplification, which undermined the attainment of the aims cherished in Washington and London.

The start of the communist rebellion in Malaya, in the summer of 1948, marked the growth of a wider British anxiety concerning the defence of Southeast Asia as a region.[9] The continued resistance of the Democratic Republic of Vietnam to the re-imposition of French colonialism underlined the common apprehension that indigenous communist movements, assisted by the Soviet Union and the People's Republic of China, could triumph in the region with fatal consequences for the West in the Cold War.[10] The outbreak of war in Korea in June 1950, stimulated new tension, rendered far graver by Communist China's entrance into the Korean conflict in October–November 1950.[11] In August 1950 Anglo-French discussions addressed the scope of the external and internal threats.[12] Intelligence was exchanged and mutual briefings were given concerning the communist campaigns in Malaya and Indo-China. France desired closer cooperation with Britain and the United States: this should embrace propaganda of a nature calculated to influence the significant Chinese communities in Southeast Asia. The danger of a Chinese invasion via two possible routes was identified: this could be implemented across the northern frontier of Tonkin or/and along the Burma–Siam border. French intelligence indicated that approximately 100,000 Chinese troops were stationed within two days' march of the frontier; the maximum notice of a Chinese invasion was anticipated as two weeks. French forces would act defensively if the Chinese attacked: the French were perturbed at the contingency of a Chinese offensive via Burma and Siam. They estimated that in the dry season (November–April) an infantry force could reach the borders of Indo-China within twenty-one days of crossing the Burma frontier.[13] Further discussions in September 1950 comprised candid exchanges in which the French admitted that the internal and external difficulties in Indo-China were worsening: they advanced what later became celebrated as the 'domino theory' – the whole of Southeast Asia could fall if Indo-China fell. The burden falling on the French army was large and increasing with obvious implications for French commitments in Europe.[14] The United States became heavily involved in meeting the bulk of the cost of the war against communism in Indo-China between 1950 and 1953. In the course of discussions with the US Joint Chiefs of Staff (JCS) and the State Department in August 1952 it was made clear that the United States was extremely reluctant to contemplate a form of regional organisation, including coordination of defence policy in Southeast Asia. The JCS expressed the opinion that the American people would not tolerate another Korean-type situation, leading to the commitment of US forces in Indo-China.[15] Britain and France worked to secure a US commitment and viewed the development of five-power coordination as the most effective means of bolstering Western defence in the region. Anxiety was voiced at the bellicose feelings expressed at senior levels of the US navy towards China. While the British wanted improved planning to combat aggression, they did not relish the prospect of cavalier conduct by American admirals, not dissimilar to the behaviour of General MacArthur in Korea to which they had taken strong exception.[16] It was reported in August 1952 that 'The United States Navy are a law unto themselves, and the influence of Admiral Radford (their C-in-C., in the Pacific), is believed to be very powerful in favour of their "all-out policy against China".'[17]

The rapid decline of the French position in Tonkin, associated with growing concern over Laos, led, reluctantly, to the conclusion that partition in Vietnam might be the least unsatisfactory solution: it 'might salvage more from the general wreck than any other'.[18] The joint intelligence committee (JIC) devoted much time to deliberating on the importance of Indo-China and the dire consequences of its fall. Contingency plans for coping with a Chinese invasion of Southeast Asia were prepared and updated. In January 1953 revised timings for a Chinese invasion were submitted to the JIC: the Malayan frontier could be reached by the two invasion routes within four months and six months instead of the previous estimates, respectively, of five months and seven and a half months.[19] A JIC report in February 1953 warned that experience in Korea had shown that it was dangerous to underestimate the Chinese: they had revealed ingenuity in surmounting logistical difficulties which could well have puzzled well-equipped Western armies. The Chinese army was the biggest in eastern Asia with a total strength of two and a half million: it could deploy 280,000 men in an invasion of Southeast Asia.[20]

The Foreign Office retained a consul-general in post in Hanoi after the Democratic Republic of Vietnam had gained legitimacy at the Geneva conference in 1954. This facilitated limited contact with lower level DRV officials and obtaining of intelligence. The personality of Ho Chi Minh intrigued policy-makers. Ho was probably the only communist leader described in the Foreign Office as possessing considerable charm. Near the end of the year 1953, the JIC reflected on the prospects for encouraging 'Anti-Soviet Communism', building on the precedent of Marshal Tito in Yugoslavia.[21] A revealing JIC memorandum reviewed the history of communist movements, which had broken with Moscow or displayed genuine independence. Yugoslavia was the conspicuous example where Tito had opposed Stalin and resisted Russian endeavours to penetrate the party machinery. Albania and China were identified as potential candidates for severing relations with the Kremlin. Where else might Titoism erupt? The gaze of the JIC alighted on Ho Chi Minh and the prospects were perceived as reasonably positive:

At first sight Ho has many of the attributes of Tito. He is not a Soviet creation in the sense that the leaders of eastern European countries are, and he
has so far fought his own battles. He has, however, received much material
assistance and encouragement from China and the USSR. His prestige is tremendously high in nationalist circles in Indo-China and elsewhere in Asia.
Perhaps most important, there is a deep rooted antagonism in the Associate
States to Chinese penetration. This antagonism might induce Ho Chi Minh,
once established to pursue an independent policy ... If Ho Chi Minh
obtained control of Indo-China and showed signs of pursuing an independent policy, it would be to our interest to show him, as we showed Tito, that
independence from Moscow and Peking would not leave him isolated.[22]

The reference to Ho's high standing in Asia was no doubt influenced by Nehru's
cordiality towards Ho: Nehru was fast emerging as one of the most prominent
nationalist leaders in Asia and he had respected Ho since their first meeting in
the later 1920s.[23] Therefore, a few months before the Geneva conference on
Korea and Indo-China convened, the JIC contemplated a possible solution,
which would exclude Bao Dai or his successors. This was not a development
that would have been favoured by the United States government. The problem
with the path detected by the JIC was that it was too late to achieve such
an outcome: the pressure of events pushed Ho towards China, despite the well-
founded speculation of the JIC that Ho did not relish dependence on Beijing. But
the policies of the Truman and Eisenhower administrations rendered it impossible to achieve the kind of accommodation achieved with Tito's Yugoslavia.

   During the first half of 1954, against a sombre background of the collapse of
French military authority in Indo-China, the JIC assessed the broad trend in
Southeast Asia. Communism was growing in Indonesia and this could assume a
threatening character.[24] Yet it was unlikely that communism would attempt to
seize power in Indonesia but the forces of nationalism could decide to work with
the communists. In Thailand (Siam) communism was not a danger but Thai
leaders were noted for opportunism – hence Thailand's survival as a sovereign
power – and a rise in China's influence could persuade Thai leaders to submit to
Beijing's wishes. Equally China might foster subversion and this could comprise
any of the following: inciting unrest among dissidents and minorities; the Viet-
minh could stimulate trouble in the impoverished north-east of Siam as an extension of the current campaign in Laos.[25] The future of Malaya was described as
complex and the pattern would not become clear until elections were held in
1955. Success for the communists in Indo-China and Thailand would threaten
Malaya: if this occurred, it could impact on the unstable coalition within the
principal political party in Malaya, the United Malays National Organisation
(UMNO). Left-wing elements in UMNO might decide to seek cooperation with
the Malayan Communist Party (MCP). UMNO was challenged from the right by
the Party Negara, now led by its former leader, Dato Onn bin Jaa'far. The political situation was very fluid and forecasting was hazardous.[26] Implicit in the
memorandum was continuing underestimation of Tunku Abdul Rahman, Onn's

successor. The Tunku was thought to lack the requisite skills to be other than a transitional leader. The British revised their opinion in 1955–56, following the sweeping election victory won by UMNO and, then, by the tough stance adopted by the Tunku in his negotiations with the MCP leader, Chin Peng, at Baling in December 1955. Chin Peng's memoirs, supplemented with the records of academic symposiums in which he participated, provide valuable insights into his thinking and into the dilemmas confronting the MCP during the 1950s. He recognised that the original aims and aspirations of the insurrection had been thwarted, probably permanently; however, the struggle could only be terminated on a basis that would permit the MCP to claim that its honour remained intact and that it had not surrendered. While Chin Peng was not successful in attaining his aims, he nevertheless revealed dedication and tenacity while near, or at the top of, the MCP for a prolonged and continuous period. His retrospective accounts assist in explaining how and why the communist insurrection began and why it ended as late as 1989.[27]

Questions concerning the future role of Japan preoccupied officials in Whitehall in the middle to later 1950s. This resulted from a combination of Japanese revival and American determination to cement Japan deeply within the Western defence system. A continuation of British wariness may be identified in official and semi-official correspondence. The chiefs of staff considered the desirability of the chairman of the Japanese joint staff paying an official visit in February 1956. The War Office reported that Lt.-General Hayashi Keizō wished to receive an official invitation, even if his expenses were not met by the British government. It was in Britain's interest that the Japanese defence forces should maintain limited progress 'along the present moderate lines'; it was also desirable that Japanese defence personnel should not rely solely upon the United States for guidance.[28] On the other hand, there were significant counter-arguments including 'the undoubted fact that it will attract wide publicity both here and in Japan and that it will be resented in at least two quarters; namely, in Lancashire where for reasons of trade anything or anybody Japanese is regarded as a menace and among those who were ill-treated while prisoners-of-war or internees in Japanese hands'.[29] The Foreign Office on balance supported allowing the visit to take place but on the basis that 'it should be as unobtrusive as possible and should be strictly confined to the Services'.[30] During the ensuing month the JIC debated a memorandum assessing the future outlook in Japan. It was held that Japan would be dominated by right-wing political forces; Japan's alignment with the West could not be regarded as necessarily persisting: Japanese governments were likely to become more vocal and to demand greater recognition of Japanese interests. The Japanese economy was quite stable but the situation was potentially dangerous and might deteriorate swiftly if Japan could not facilitate imports at a rate adequate to offset population pressure. An economic crisis would provide opportunities for either the extreme left or right to exploit. The United States wished to accelerate Japanese rearmament, so that American resources in Japan could be reduced. The Japanese six-year rearmament plan, scheduled for completion in 1961, envisaged an army of 180,000 men, an air force of 50,000 and a navy of 33,000 with fifteen destroyers and a number of smaller vessels.[31]

The appointment of Kishi Nobusuke as prime minister in 1957 stimulated renewed doubts in Whitehall. Kishi's murky past, plus his interest in rebuilding a Japanese role in Southeast Asia, gave rise to much concern. Arthur de la Mare reported from Washington in May 1957 that he had discussed Japan's position with Jeff Parsons of the State Department: the latter indicated that the Japanese government was not currently very active in its ideas for developing Southeast Asia.[32] Kishi embarked on a tour of the region in the summer of 1957; the Foreign Office was anxious over the political implications of a new Japanese role rather than its economic dimensions, although the former could follow naturally from the latter. Peter Dalton replied to de la Mare, 'Possible American interest in the mobilization of Japanese resources for the economic development of Southeast Asia is, of course, not necessarily the same as the suggestion for setting Japan up as a political leader for the area.'[33] American enthusiasm for supporting Japan could, if it materialised, clash with the Foreign Office's preference for encouraging India: Nehru had succeeded in creating a sense of momentum for Indian policy in Asia and officials in Whitehall had reflected for some time on a future positive Indian initiative in stabilising Cambodia and Laos, as part of a reinvention of the old Indian cultural influence in these countries.[34] Dalton told de la Mare to avoid conveying suspicion of American aims but to report information on plans that might be formulated in the State Department.[35] In July 1957 de la Mare wrote to Dalton that he had spoken to Parsons again and that Parsons stated that Kishi was contemplating the creation of three agencies to deal with Southeast Asia. These were the Asia Development Fund, capitalised at approximately US$500 million; a 'Rediscount Institute', possibly following the precedent of the European Payments Union; and an Asian Trade Fund, which would address seasonal price variations in basic raw materials. Parsons thought that the latter projects would be capitalised at approximately US$100 million. Kishi anticipated that the above bodies would be structured on a multi-party basis and would incorporate all the members of the Colombo Plan prepared to participate. Kishi was impressed, following his tour, with the strong desire of the peoples of Southeast Asia to raise living standards and to frustrate communist designs in the region; equally Kishi felt that they could not achieve better living standards without outside assistance.

De la Mare reported that he had conveyed reservations to Parsons:

I could not help feeling a little apprehensive as to how all this would turn out ... I did not, of course, expect Mr. Kishi's motives to be entirely disinterested but was there really any element of disinterest in them? Was this the old 'Greater East Asia Co-Prosperity Sphere' dusted off and refurbished to make it look more attractive to the Americans? I reminded Parsons of Ogden Nash's little verse about the Japanese with which you are no doubt familiar.[36]

Parsons acknowledged that this was understandable but he felt that memories of Japanese domination between 1942 and 1945 were fading; in addition, Japanese individuals sent to Southeast Asia were carefully selected and did not display the abrasive characteristics of old. In a subsequent conversation, in September 1957, Parsons conceded that Kishi's past career 'left something to be desired' but he had not given grounds for anxiety since he assumed office.[37] It is reasonable to deduce that, while the British government was as determined as the US government to contain and, if possible, to repel communism, there was no desire to see this accomplished through encouraging Japanese ambitions. The British approach was the product of the Japanese contribution to demolishing the British empire in 1942, of atrocities inflicted on allied prisoners-of-war, and of economic competition perceived as unfair.[38]

The Colombo Plan was the most imaginative proposal devised to remedy the social and economic difficulties faced by the peoples of South and Southeast Asia. Foreign Office officials liked to point out that it was essentially a concept, rather than a plan. Ernest Bevin provided impetus for its launch at a Commonwealth conference held in Colombo in January 1950; Bevin believed that poverty, degradation and their concomitants must be addressed urgently in order to undermine support for communism. Despite grave ill-health, Bevin travelled to Colombo and emphasised that Britain would extend full support to the developments resulting from implementation of the Colombo concept.[39] It was widely welcomed in the newly independent states in South and Southeast Asia, since it promised aid in stimulating growth without the attachment of political strings. The Chancellor of the Exchequer, Hugh Gaitskell, told the House of Commons on 28 November 1950 that 'this great and imaginative programme' would be supported to the full extent permitted by British resources.[40] Britain and other Commonwealth countries would draw on accumulated sterling balances and it was anticipated that Britain could contribute over £300 million in the period 1951–57. Much discussion with individual countries was required; the position of non-Commonwealth states wishing to participate would be viewed sympathetically. The delicate state of the British economy precluded undue generosity, hence the qualifying clause in Gaitskell's statement. This provoked grumbles during the early to middle 1950s that Britain should be contributing more but the Treasury kept a tight grip on the financial levers, as the domestic economy in the United Kingdom recovered gradually. Unsurprisingly Britain looked to the United States to involve itself and to provide a large proportion of aid: this was the economic equivalent of the political–military role which Britain desired the United States to fulfil in Southeast Asia. For precisely this reason the Truman administration responded cautiously to the proclamation of the Colombo Plan: the United States had sufficient commitments internationally, even before the outbreak of the Korean War compounded the pressure.

The Foreign Office informed the embassy in Washington, in January 1951, that the Treasury was anxious to ensure full cooperation from wealthier countries: the Chancellor had privately urged this upon representatives of the United

States, Canada, Australia and New Zealand. The reaction of the United States was vital:

> The greatest danger as we see it is that the United States administration will give the Plan too low a priority among the intimidating list of commitments that now face them, and that their contribution towards it will seem manifestly inadequate to the recipient countries. If this should happen, it is only too probable that the hopes engendered by the plan will wither overnight with disastrous consequences both economic and political.[41]

The Foreign Office stressed the importance of deploying judicious diplomacy in Washington, so as to ensure a positive American response but without the latter assuming a bullying role towards the Commonwealth. The Treasury took the opportunity to reiterate the vital importance of supporting the states of Southeast Asia when a member of the American embassy called in January 1951; he was informed that the United States must act resolutely and not convey the impression that it had written off Southeast Asia.[42] The United States was persuaded of the necessity to endorse the Plan unequivocally and the Truman administration moved in the desired direction. This was complementary to its financial commitment in Indo-China. In this context C.G. Harris of the Foreign Office minuted, sardonically, on 16 May 1952, that Britain's lack of funds was a considerable handicap – 'While the French may fear the American Greeks bringing gifts, they will have even less use for the penniless and only vaguely potentially gift-bearing British ones.'[43] British diplomats worked to encourage the involvement of Vietnam, Cambodia and Laos in deliberations over the Plan and revealed exasperation at predictable French attempts to circumscribe the supposed 'independence' of the Associate States.

The question of the participation of France and the Netherlands was contentious because of the bitter struggles within their Asian colonies to secure independence. Britain did not wish to alienate India or other Southeast Asian states and it was clear that the Indian authorities were not in favour of French and Dutch membership.[44] Britain itself reacted negatively to American support for Japanese membership of the Plan. A brief prepared for Lord Reading, minister of state in the Foreign Office, at the beginning of 1952 stated that there would be some political advantages in admitting Japan but it would not be desirable economically because Japan could not contribute finance and could become a competitor for the limited funds available. It might be feasible to admit Japan at a later stage but not in the near future.[45] In addition, Australia and New Zealand were not sympathetic to Japanese admission and the colonial administration in Malaya was also opposed.[46] The 'Commonwealth bloc' was one factor inhibiting the United States. B.A.B. Burrows wrote from Washington, in June 1952, that differences within the Truman administration had been significant: some regarded British colonialism as a problem when attempting to convince countries in Southeast Asia to support the Plan, while others saw the Commonwealth as an encouraging body. Also some doubted the viability of the development plans submitted by individual states. Suspicions of British motives within Congress complicated the situation: some within Congress perceived the Colombo Plan as a cunning British scheme to commit the United States to propping up the Commonwealth.[47] The State Department was sympathetic on the whole but it would take some time for the United States to support the Plan with real vigour.

During the middle and later 1950s, the Colombo Plan gained wider recognition and acceptance in South and Southeast Asia. Japan joined, as the process of gradual reconciliation took effect. A Foreign Office memorandum concluded, in August 1961, that the Plan had been 'enduringly and surprisingly successful largely because it had developed empirically': it had met urgent needs but had not imposed onerous obligations. However, excessive pressure should not be exerted on the structure and the limitations to what could be achieved in the short to medium term must be grasped. The familiar restatement of the restrictions resulting from the weakness of the British economy appeared: it was impossible for Britain to increase its total overseas expenditure, although greater flexibility in British expenditure within the confines of the Plan was desirable.[48]

In terms of significant organisations functioning in Southeast Asia to which Britain contributed, the Southeast Asia Treaty Organisation (SEATO) equalled the Colombo Plan in importance. A Foreign Office memorandum, prepared in May 1954, argued that an association of Southeast Asian states, enjoying the moral support of India, Pakistan and Ceylon, should be developed soon. It was essential to ensure that the new forces of nationalism in the region worked with the West to thwart communist designs: 'Most of the countries of Southeast Asia are almost as suspicious of Western as of Communist intentions, and no form of collective defence organisation that is visibly dominated by the Western Powers (particularly the United States) will be politically viable.'[49] It would be advantageous if a defence treaty could be linked with the Colombo Plan, so that defence and economic aims could be pursued cohesively. At this point Anthony Eden, the Foreign Secretary, commented in the margin: 'No! The essence of the CP is that it is non-political. You would scare off India, Indonesia & Burma.'[50] Membership was envisaged as including the Associate States of Indo-China, Thailand, Ceylon, Pakistan and the Philippines. It was unlikely that India and Indonesia would sign a defence treaty but it was possible that Burma could be persuaded to adhere. The core Western membership would comprise the United States, Britain, Australia and New Zealand. France might be unenthusiastic and it could be preferable for France not to belong, since this would render the new organisation more attractive to Asian states – 'We should, of course, rigidly oppose any suggestion for the inclusion of Formosa, South Korea or Japan.'[51] This statement underlined one fundamental divergence between Britain and the United States. The latter preferred a wider grouping embracing East Asia; however, Britain did not wish to be drawn into further confrontation with China, which would occur if Britain became too involved with Taiwan (Formosa) and South Korea.

Britain's approach to SEATO was also affected by determination not to enter into commitments that could turn out to be too expensive or provocative. The

Treasury loomed ever larger as the 1950s progressed and it was determined to restrict expenditure. Shortly before the Manila conference convened, in September 1954, the Treasury summoned a meeting, attended by representatives from the Foreign Office, Ministry of Defence, Colonial Office, Commonwealth Relations Office and the Board of Trade. It was emphasised that SEATO should not entail heavy economic or military demands. Reassuring responses came from the Foreign Office and the Ministry of Defence: SEATO could require a small military secretariat and an intelligence establishment largely provided by personnel already present in the area. Any military forces to be contributed by the United Kingdom should already be in the region. Hong Kong would be excluded from SEATO because it was important not to give the United States scope to urge inclusion of Taiwan or Japan. The Treasury representatives stressed that SEATO should not duplicate the work of the Colombo Plan; R.A. Butler, the Chancellor of the Exchequer, wanted care to be exercised at Manila, so that Britain did not enter into open-ended commitments.[52] The Treasury continued to keep a watchful eye on the costs incurred in SEATO membership, apart from pressing vigorously for due economy to be observed in the Foreign Office budget.

The key personality in influencing British policy in 1954 was Anthony Eden. He made a partial recovery from his serious health problems and enjoyed a successful year in directing policy. Above all, he demonstrated outstanding leadership and finesse in handling the complex problems pursued at the Geneva conference. While not as restrictive in his attitude towards SEATO as his colleague, R.A. Butler, Eden did not wish to enter into commitments that were extensive. He wanted to attract as many Asian states as possible into membership of SEATO: he wrote to the ambassador in Washington, on 22 May 1954, that negotiations with the communist states were bound to involve concessions 'probably entailing creation of a buffer State on China's southern border'.[53] This would be omitted from SEATO, although the American approach was different – 'The Americans, however, appear to contemplate an organisation that would assist them to reconquer Indo-China. Her Majesty's Government for their part would not be prepared to participate in such a venture.'[54] John Foster Dulles, the American Secretary of State, wished to be explicit that SEATO was committed to opposing communist aggression. During the exchanges with Washington in August 1954, concerning the draft of the Manila treaty, Eden agreed that while it was not easy to define aggression precisely, he could not accept the insertion of the word 'communist' before 'aggression' in the redrafted version of Article IV(1). Eden was equally preoccupied with reassuring Asian opinion that SEATO would not act to repel aggression, for example, against Burma, without consulting the government concerned. Therefore, he preferred to adopt the wording of Article V of the NATO treaty: this was very familiar and Britain had always maintained that it was defensive in character.[55]

The relationship of the Associate States in Indo-China to SEATO was a delicate matter. The Eisenhower administration wished to promote a closer relationship and this was resisted by Eden. He notified the State Department on 27 August 1954 that it had always been his opinion that to consult the Associate

States over their designation under the Manila treaty would conflict with the agreements reached at Geneva. He believed that they should be unilaterally designated. At the same time, aggression directed at any of the Associate States would justify consultation with them on appropriate action.[56] G.G. Fitzmaurice, the senior legal authority in the Foreign Office, minuted that technically the Geneva agreements would not preclude the Associate States from participating in consultations regarding SEATO, provided that they were not parties to the Manila treaty. In essence, it was a political, rather than a legal, matter and he concurred with the view that a statement referring to Cambodia, Laos and Vietnam should be circumspect.[57] The Manila pact was duly signed in September 1954 and SEATO was established in Bangkok with a prominent Thai diplomat and politician, Pote Sarasin, as the first secretary-general. In November 1955 Sir Robert Scott, the commissioner-general in Southeast Asia, reflected on the first year of SEATO, Britain was the sole member opposed to describing SEATO as 'anti-communist'. Scott believed this was correct: to emphasise anti-communism overtly would be to fuel communist propaganda. India, Indonesia and Burma were receptive to neo-colonial allegations. The chief minister of Malaya (still a colony), Tunku Abdul Rahman, argued that it was not desirable for Malaya or Singapore to join an organisation that was vehemently anti-communist. Scott observed: 'Tengku (*sic*) Rahman is about as far from being a fellow traveller or a communist as anyone in these parts. He has good reason to fear this growing influence of the Chinese and what is more has experience of communist tactics in his own country.'[58] Malayan membership of SEATO was highly desirable when independence was granted: it was unlikely that India, Indonesia or Burma would join. Scott recognised that the enthusiasm of American policy-makers for stressing anti-communism might not spring wholly from American obsessions linked with domestic politics but could also arise from anxiety at the tense state of relations between Pakistan and India:

> It has been clear from the outset that one of the Pakistani motives in joining SEATO was to ask for help against India and under cover of SEATO to get military equipment and economic aid, which would be denied to India. At last month's discussions at Honolulu the Pakistani attitude revealed very clearly their preoccupation with India. It may therefore be that the American desire to define the SEATO commitments in terms of anti-communism is prompted by the fear that unless this is done SEATO may be involved in a war between India and Pakistan. This would be a serious risk and something we must all guard against ... But our position can surely be safeguarded otherwise than by turning SEATO into an aggressive anti-communist (i.e. anti-Chinese) alliance.[59]

Scott's assessment was warmly endorsed by his predecessor, Malcolm MacDonald, now serving as high commissioner in New Delhi.[60] Scott reflected further in a subsequent letter to the Foreign Office, sent on 13 December 1955. Britain should work to consolidate SEATO while eschewing dangerous strategies. Australia, Thailand and the Philippines tended to support the United States without expressing significant reservations. The difficulty with this approach was that the Americans sometimes advocated 'unsound' or even 'dangerous' courses of action. The approach should be 'to harmonise our two aims of strong American interest and a healthy SEATO'.[61] So far, attention had focused on the military threat but the civil side of SEATO required consideration: Scott observed that all involved agreed that the chief threat came from subversion and the correct mixture was required to strengthen the non-military contribution.[62] The Foreign Office followed a line of extending moderate encouragement to educational and cultural activities of SEATO in the later 1950s. These included awarding SEATO fellowships to worthy academics; establishing the SEATO Engineering College in Bangkok; providing some financial support for students from SEATO member states to study in British universities and colleges; and to issue a small number of publications. As always, the Treasury mandarins were eagle-eyed on expenditure. A Foreign Office minute recorded, in January 1957, that the Treasury had written two 'threatening letters' concerning escalating costs of SEATO activities.[63] American, Australian and Thai officials regarded the British approach as too negative. Keith Waller of the Australian embassy in Bangkok, expressed strong criticism of the negative British line in discussion with John Lloyd of the commissioner-general's office in Singapore in July 1957. Waller said that the United States, Australia and New Zealand agreed that Britain was not contributing enough to SEATO and that British statements contained excessive carping.[64] In September 1959 the secretary-general, Pote Sarasin, became more outspoken in criticising British views: this partly reflected financial differences but also involved Britain's preference for not seeing SEATO associated more closely with NATO and CENTO.[65]

As regards military strategy, SEATO military planners recommended, in December 1955, that military operations should incorporate the use of both nuclear and non-nuclear weapons. Robert Scott commented that governments must take the vital decisions and not local commanders. However, he agreed that in certain circumstances nuclear weapons should be used:

> I have no doubt that the Staff Planners are right in saying that only if nuclear weapons are used can the threat to the countries of South East Asia be reduced to manageable proportions. Their estimate that it would be necessary to provide 10 divisions to hold a perimeter round Bangkok in the face of conventional attack bears this out. By no stretch of the imagination can one expect that there would be 10 SEATO divisions ready for battle on such a line. But the Planners believe that any aggressive sortie can be strangled at birth, provided nuclear weapons are used against the enemy at the moment we see what they have in mind. The decision to use the bomb (and especially to use it first) must, however, rest with Heads of Governments and not with Military Commanders on the spot and cannot be taken in advance.[66]

The aspect of publicity was very delicate because of its impact on opinion in South and Southeast Asia. The United States was regarded as too assertive and talk of using nuclear weapons would exacerbate matters.

SEATO military advisers decided, in January 1956, that parts of the treaty area could not be defended unless strong SEATO action could be taken. This would involve deployment of air power against selected targets in China and North Vietnam. Nuclear weapons would be required: SEATO members should 'adopt a concept of operations employing atomic and non-atomic munitions'.[67] The menace of communist subversion was growing and the challenge facing Pakistan had grown, which included deteriorating relations with Afghanistan. Overt communist aggression on a large scale was not imminent but war plans to combat such a threat were needed in order to placate the apprehension voiced by the smaller Asian states. Nuclear weapons were a major factor in providing reassurance: 'We consider that it is essential that the future strategy for the defence of the treaty area, in limited war with China and in global war, should be based on the assumption that nuclear weapons would be used by SEATO at the outset. Without this assumption planning is bound to be unrealistic as SEATO cannot hope to produce the forces which would be required.'[68] The military advisers thought that member states should indicate the nature of their contributions to defend the treaty area; this was embarrassing for Britain, which was not prepared to stipulate a contribution until further clarification had been secured.

One year later defence planners revisited these issues. A brief prepared in Whitehall underlined the necessity of considering nuclear counter-action in the course of fulfilling the British obligation to SEATO, which 'must be regarded as the principal means of safeguarding our vital interests in the Far East'.[69] The precise form of Britain's contribution had to be determined and a specific response could engender similar difficulty to that encountered over NATO – 'Disclosure of the outwardly modest size of our contribution might tend to discourage rather than encourage.'[70] Ministerial consent would be requested for maintaining existing levels of forces in the area and for guaranteeing a swift response should an emergency occur: 'the best contribution that the United Kingdom can make to meet this requirement initially in limited war is the FEAF reinforced by V bombers and carrier aircraft, both eventually with a nuclear capability'.[71] Discussion over possible use of nuclear weapons rumbled on through the months and years. In September 1959 the chiefs of staff approved a report submitted by the British defence coordination committee in Singapore: this emphasised that SEATO ground forces must exploit the shock aroused in the enemy through deployment of nuclear weapons. The high standard of training required for the use of such weapons could not be achieved by the armed forces of friendly states in the region, as currently organised and led. An administrative structure capable of efficient coordination must be created. It was assumed that a high proportion of British tactical nuclear weapons in the Far East would be air-delivered. It was not easy to identify suitable tactical targets for nuclear attack: because of defective maps, indirect fire from ground delivery systems would be inaccurate and radar bombing accuracy could experience problems. Discussion with the United States was needed in order to ensure control of nuclear weapons in a tactical land battle.[72]

British views towards SEATO were ambivalent: the organisation was significant and necessary but there was considerable reluctance to specify the nature of British contributions. Global pressures on resources and the Treasury's powerful emphasis upon controlling expenditure inhibited the Foreign Office and the Ministry of Defence. However, in addition to the financial constraints, political defects in SEATO caused anxiety. Asian members were too few; Anthony Eden's warning that SEATO should not be a 'white man's treaty' echoed down the years. The United States was too dominant and Australia usually followed the American lead. New Zealand showed more independence but did not wish to risk alienating the United States. France frequently adopted a negative stance but France was useful in helping to ensure that Britain was not alone in opposing rash initiatives. The Philippines was ineffectual and Pakistan was obsessed in its confrontation with India and, to a lesser degree, with Afghanistan. Thailand was important for providing the headquarters of SEATO and as the most vital area after Indo-China. The unstable political system, including the ascendancy of military factionalism, accentuated by corruption, raised doubt concerning the reliability of Thailand if a major crisis arose. The role of the United States was basic to the existence and survival of SEATO but there were recurring fears that American military, naval and intelligence personnel could embark on provocative acts, concerning Vietnam and Laos particularly. In March 1956 a report on visits to the Far East by the chairman of the JIC and the assistant chief of the air staff (intelligence) stated that the British authorities in Malaya and Singapore were reluctant to convey delicate information to intelligence agents, 'many of whom have been guilty of wild and inaccurate reporting and indiscretions of various sorts'.[73] It would be preferable to have one American channel for receiving sensitive intelligence. Experienced senior British officials knew this was unattainable. The United States consuls-general in Kuala Lumpur and Singapore should be notified in broad terms about intelligence but without giving details of covert operations.[74] The British held that SEATO should function as a defensive organisation and that potentially dangerous initiatives should be avoided. The Suez crisis bequeathed tensions and suspicions, which exacerbated the strains present from earlier years. This helps to explain Harold Macmillan's enthusiasm for establishing a cordial relationship with the new American president, John F. Kennedy, when the latter assumed office in January 1961. In turn this led to increasing British involvement in Vietnam.[75] However, British reluctance to commit forces in South Vietnam continued to apply.

British strategy for handling the challenges inherent in the extension of the Cold War to Southeast Asia rested upon consistent principles, if with subtle modifications. Nationalism must be accommodated through extending timely concessions and cultivating amicable relations with the leaders of states emerging from colonial empires: to these Thailand had to be added, as a state that had averted the imposition of formal imperialism. This worked quite successfully with certain countries opposed to joining a treaty organisation such as SEATO. India, Ceylon, Burma and Malaya entered this category: Burma declined membership of the Commonwealth in 1948 but relations with Britain were reasonable until General Ne Win's brutal coup in 1962. Malaya's relations with SEATO were equivocal but there was too much hostility to the organisation in Malaya to permit membership. Relations with Indonesia were sometimes strained and grave doubts over the direction of President Sukarno's policy and over the developing power of the Indonesian Communist Party led Britain and the United States to embark on action intended to destabilise Sukarno's regime.[76] A brief prepared in January 1958, for the prime minister's tour of the Far East stated that the time had come to plan secretly with the United States, Australia and New Zealand to support anti-communist elements in Indonesia. The reasons embraced anxiety concerning economic interests; the future of Borneo and Papua New Guinea; subversion supported by Indonesian agents; and a potential (or renewed) Indonesian threat to Malaya. If Indonesia went communist, the repercussions for SEATO would be grave and would create enormous problems for the Commonwealth in the western Pacific and Southeast Asia.[77] Britain was not deeply involved in the Philippines, which was seen as clearly within the American sphere of influence. Interest was shown in the counter-insurgency campaign, associated with Ramon Magsaysay and the 'quiet American', Colonel Edward Lansdale, which had contained the Huk rebellion. Magsaysay's death in an air crash, in September 1957, removed the only Filipino leader of real tenacity.

As regards Indo-China, views within the Foreign Office were ambivalent. Anthony Eden, fully supported by Winston Churchill and the cabinet, made clear in 1954 that Britain would not act militarily and successive governments adhered to this decision. Eden hoped to save Cambodia and Laos and officials felt that this could be achieved, given a combination of sensible compromise all round, discouragement of rash American action (covert or overt), and stimulating a revival of Indian cultural influence. South Vietnam was viewed dubiously but the surprising survival of Ngo Dinh Diem's regime produced limited modification in thinking in the later 1950s and the start of the 1960s, hence the Macmillan government's support for Robert Thompson's advisory military mission in Saigon and the influence Thompson exerted in Washington.

In the main, the trend in Southeast Asia seemed moderately encouraging. Duncan Sandys, the commonwealth relations secretary, told the SEATO Council in April 1959 that the principal threat to SEATO was now a non-military one and this illustrated the success of SEATO in meeting the past, perceived threat of Chinese invasion.[78] This exaggerated the success of SEATO but SEATO, in its early years, had achieved more than has been recognised in confronting the menace of communist expansion. Ideally Britain desired a relationship with the United States in which the latter eschewed adventurism and took adequate account of British representations. However, the reality was that the steady diminution in British power undermined Britain's role more rapidly than was appreciated by the majority of British politicians and diplomats dealing with business in Southeast Asia. The courses of action recommended in Whitehall for achieving positive Western cooperation were sensible. Communism should be contained through improving economic and social conditions and strengthening governance. This should be accomplished through the application of a judicious blend of realism, subtlety and pragmatism. As British power waned, the question loomed ever larger as to how far the United States could implement 'the judicious blend'.

Acknowledgements

I wish to express my deep gratitude to the Leverhulme Trust for awarding me an Emeritus Fellowship, which has enabled me to pursue research in relevant archives. I am also most grateful to the staff of the National Archives, Kew, for their assistance while I conducted research in Kew.

Notes

1 For a brief survey of these issues, see Peter Lowe, 'Change and Stability in Eastern Asia: Nationalism, Communism and British Policy, 1948–55', *Diplomacy and Statecraft*, vol. 15, no. 1 (March 2004), pp. 137–47.
2 See Philip Ziegler, *Mountbatten: The Official Biography*, paperback edition, London: Phoenix Press, 2001, pp. 349–479.
3 See A.J. Stockwell (ed.), *British Documents on the End of Empire*, series B, vol. III, *Malaya*, London: HMSO, 1995, part 1, p. xxviii. Attlee made a statement in the House of Commons on 13 April 1949.
4 Ibid., Introduction, pp. lxix–lxxxi, for a succinct assessment of political–constitutional developments between 1951 and 1957.
5 See J. Pluvier, *South-East Asia from Colonialism to Independence*, Kuala Lumpur: Oxford University Press, 1974, pp. 409–51.
6 Considerable evidence of British dissatisfaction with the policies of the Netherlands and France, particularly for the former, may be found in Foreign Office files, general political correspondence, FO371 series, in the National Archives, Kew.
7 See Christopher Thorne, *Allies of a Kind: the United States, Great Britain and the War against Japan, 1941–5*, London: Hamish Hamilton, 1978, and R.J. Aldrich *Intelligence and the War against Japan: Britain, America and the Politics of Secret Service*, Cambridge: Cambridge University Press, 2000.
8 An interesting example is afforded in the views expressed by the young John F. Kennedy; see Robert Dallek, *John F. Kennedy: An Unfinished Life, 1917–1963*, London: Allen Lane, 2003, pp. 165–7, 185–7.
9 This anxiety is reflected in the despatches and telegrams of Malcolm MacDonald, commissioner-general for Southeast Asia, to be found in FO371 files. See also Karl Hack, *Defence and Decolonisation in Southeast Asia: Britain, Malaya and Singapore, 1941–1968*, Richmond: Curzon Press, 2001, pp. 62–6.
10 See Anthony Short, *The Origins of the Vietnam War*, London: Longman, 1989, pp. 62–97.
11 See Peter Lowe, *Containing the Cold War in East Asia: British Policies towards Japan, China and Korea, 1948–53*, Manchester: Manchester University Press, 1997, pp. 190–210.
12 DEFE 5/24 COS(50)352, 'Staff Discussions with the French Service Authorities in Indo-China', 16–17 August 1950. All references to DEFE, FO and CAB files apply to records held in the National Archives, Kew.
13 Ibid.

14 DEFE 5/24 COS(50)401, 'Discussions between the Commanders-in-Chief, Far East, and General Carpentier', 27–28 September 1950.
15 DEFE 5/41 COS(52)443, 'Discussions in Washington on Global Strategy with the United States Joint Chiefs of Staff and the State Department', COS report, 18 August 1952.
16 On MacArthur, see Peter Lowe, 'An Ally and a Recalcitrant General: Great Britain, Douglas MacArthur and the Korean War, 1950–1', *English Historical Review*, 105, 416 (1990), pp. 624–53.
17 DEFE 5/41, 'Discussions in Washington on Global Strategy with the United States Joint Chiefs of Staff and the State Department', COS report, 18 August 1952.
18 DEFE 5/52 COS(54)98, 'Policy Towards Indo-China', letter from FO to Secretary, COS committee, 29 March 1954.
19 CAB158/15 part 1, JIC(53)5, 'Possible Military Operations in South-East Asia by the Chinese Communist Armed Forces in major war up to the end of 1953', 6 January 1953. The JIC approved a report submitted by the JIC (Far East), which had been endorsed by the British defence coordination committee, Far East.
20 CAB158/15 part 1, JIC(53)12, 'Possible Military Operations in South-East Asia by the Chinese Communists', 12 February 1953.
21 CAB158/6 part 2, JIC(53)119, 'Anti-Soviet Communism', 29 December 1953.
22 Ibid.
23 For Ho's dealings with Nehru in 1954, see W.J. Duiker, *Ho Chi Minh*, New York: Hyperion, 2000, pp. 458, 462–3.
24 CAB158/17 part 1, JIC(54)11(Final), 'Situation in Indonesia', 24 February 1954.
25 Ibid., JIC(54)14(Final), 'Communist Threat to Siam', 4 February 1954.
26 CAB158/17 part 2, JIC(54)49(Final), 'The Political Situation in Malaya in Certain Eventualities', 5 July 1954.
27 Stockwell (ed.), *Malaya*, part 3, no. 391 (pp. 213–25), for the fascinating record of the exchanges between Tunku Abdul Rahman and Chin Peng at Baling. In addition, see Chin Peng, *My Side of History*, Singapore: Media Masters, 2003, pp. 364–91 for discussion of the Baling talks, and C.C. Chin and Karl Hack (eds), *Dialogues with Chin Peng: New Light on the Malayan Communist Party*, Singapore: Singapore University Press, 2004.
28 DEFE 5/64 COS(56)30, 'Japanese Overtures to Obtain an invitation for Chairman of the Japanese Joint Staff to pay an Official Visit to the UK', War Office note, 13 February 1956.
29 Ibid.
30 Ibid.
31 CAB158/24 JIC(56)45, 'The Situation and Outlook in Japan', memorandum, 27 March 1956.
32 FO371/129339 D10323/1/G, de la Mare to Dalton, 24 May 1957.
33 Ibid., Dalton to de la Mare, 11 July 1957.
34 Files in the FO371 series, *c.*1955–58, include significant discussion of a contemplated Indian contribution in blocking the advance of communism in Indo-China. This resulted, to some extent, from Indian membership of the international supervisory commissions, established under the Geneva accords of 1954. The Foreign Office did not believe that India could assist effectively in South Vietnam: Ngo Dinh Diem's government was hostile towards India but in Cambodia and Laos the indications could be regarded as reasonably positive. For a specific reference to India in the context referred to here, see FO371/129339 D10323/1/G, de la Mare to Dalton, 24 May 1957.
35 Ibid., Dalton to de la Mare, 11 July 1957.
36 FO371/129339 D10323/2/G, de la Mare to Dalton, 23 July 1957.
37 Ibid., D10323/3/G, de la Mare to Dalton, 6 September 1957.
38 See Peter Lowe, 'Uneasy Readjustment, 1945–58', in Ian Nish and Yoichi Kibata (eds), *The History of Anglo-Japanese Relations, 1600–2000*, vol. II *The Political–Diplomatic Dimension, 1931–2000*, Basingstoke, Macmillan, 2000, pp. 174–200.

39 See Alan Bullock, *The Life and Times of Ernest Bevin*, vol. III, *Foreign Secretary, 1945–1951*, London: Heinemann, 1983, pp. 746–50.
40 FO371/84594 FZ11013/266, Gaitskell statement, 28 November 1950.
41 FO371/93037 FZ1102/73, FO to Washington, 19 January 1951.
42 Ibid., FO to Washington, 19 January 1951.
43 FO371/101246 FZ1108/26, C.G. Harris minute, 16 May 1952.
44 FO371/101248 FZ1011/10, UK High Commissioner, New Delhi, to CRO, 25 January 1952.
45 Ibid., FZ11011/5, 'Japan and the Colombo Plan', brief for Lord Reading, 16 January 1952.
46 Ibid., FZ11011/24, Singapore to FO, 17 March 1952. See also FO371/101254 FZ11014/134, J.D. Murray minute, 22 April 1952, where Murray noted that Australia had firmly opposed Japanese participation but there were now signs that the Australian approach was undergoing modification, in the sense that Richard Casey believed that Japanese membership could not be delayed indefinitely.
47 FO371/101255 FZ11014/178, Burrows to Murray, 5 June 1952.
48 FO371/160010 DK6115, Joint memorandum by South-East Asia Department and Economic Relations Department, for Lord Lansdowne, in preparation for Colombo Plan Consultative Committee, 30 October–18 November 1961, with covering minute by James Cable, 28 August 1961.
49 FO371/111864 D1074/G, FO memorandum, with covering note by J.G. Tahourdin, 22 May 1954.
50 Ibid., Eden minute undated (23 or 24 May 1954?).
51 FO371/111864 D1074/G, FO memorandum, with note by Tahourdin, 22 May 1954.
52 FO371/111881 D1074/469, Record of meeting held in Treasury, 20 August 1954.
53 FO371/111884 D1074/189/G, Eden to Makins, 6 May 1954.
54 FO371/111863 D1074/46, Geneva Conference Delegation to FO, 22 May 1954.
55 FO371/111881 D1074/456, FO to Washington, 25 August 1954.
56 FO371/111882 D1074/476, FO to Washington, 27 August 1954.
57 FO371/111884 D1071/472, Fitzmaurice minute, 31 August 1954.
58 FO371/116932 D1071/472, Sir Robert Scott to Denis Allen, 29 November 1955.
59 Ibid.
60 Ibid., Malcolm MacDonald to W.A.W. Clark (CRO), 17 December 1955.
61 Ibid., D1071/501, Scott to Allen, 13 December 1955,.
62 Ibid.
63 FO371/129346 D1071/22, J. McCormick minute, 16 January 1957.
64 FO371/129342 D1051/11/G, John Lloyd to F.S. Tomlinson, 19 July 1957.
65 FO371/143745 D1071/225, Sir Richard Whittington to D.F. MacDermot, 19 September 1959.
66 FO371/116933 D1071/502, Scott to Allen, 13 December 1955.
67 'SEATO Military Advisers' Second Meeting', note by secretary, chiefs of staff committee, 25 February 1956. The second meeting of military advisers had taken place between 17 and 21 January 1956: Britain was represented by General Sir Charles Loewen.
68 Ibid.
69 DEFE 5/74 COS(57)45, 'Brief for the United Kingdom Military adviser to SEATO', 22 February 1956.
70 Ibid.
71 Ibid.
72 DEFE 5/95 COS(59)223, 'Control of Nuclear Weapons in the Tactical land Battle', note by secretary, 15 September 1959.
73 DEFE 5/66 COS(56)125, 'Intelligence Organisation in the Far East', report on visits to the Far East by the chairman, JIC, and the assistant chief of the air staff (intelligence), 27 March 1956. It was not feasible for a joint visit to be accomplished and separate visits were made between 8 January and 5 February 1956.

74 Ibid.
75 For discussion of Anglo-American relations under the Kennedy administration, see Peter Busch, *All the Way with JFK?: Britain, the US and the Vietnam War*, Oxford: Oxford University Press, 2003. The longer-term ambivalence in British policy towards Indo-China has to be kept in mind when reading Busch's account, which examines a short, tightly focused period.
76 See Matthew Jones, *Conflict and Confrontation in South-East Asia, 1961–1965: Britain, the United States and the Creation of Malaysia*, Cambridge: Cambridge University Press, 2002.
77 DEFE 5/81 COS(58)2, 'Brief for Prime Minister's Tour of the Far East', COS note, 1 January 1958.
78 FO37/143740 D1071/134, Wellington to FO (tel.), 8 April 1959.

10 The East Asian international economic order in the 1950s

Shigeru Akita

Introduction

The purpose of this chapter is to reconsider the international economic order in East Asia in the 1950s from a new perspective, which focuses on the interconnection between the sterling area in East Asia and the resurgence and development of the Japanese economy in the 1950s. This is part of a larger joint project to reconsider the nature and formation of the 'international order of Asia in the 1930s and 1950s' in the light of new historiographical developments in Britain and Japan.[1]

Recently several Japanese economic historians have offered a new perspective on Asian economic history.[2] They have argued that the economic growth of Asian countries was led by the phenomenon of intra-Asian trade, which began to grow rapidly around the turn of the nineteenth and twentieth centuries. In addition, the British imperial historians, P.J. Cain and A.G. Hopkins have presented their own provocative interpretation, 'Gentlemanly capitalism and British expansion overseas', in which they have emphasized the leading role of the service sector rather than that of British industry in assessing the nature of British expansion overseas.[3] Our joint project has attempted to integrate these two new perspectives in order to present a fresh interpretation of the international order of Asia in the 1930s and 1950s.[4] This chapter seeks to reveal the economic importance of the sterling area for East Asia, and present the economic linkages between Britain, the British Empire and Commonwealth, and East Asian economic recovery and developments in the 1950s. What kind of role did the British Empire and Commonwealth play in the context of the transformation of the international economic order in East Asia? Why did Japan achieve so early and smoothly its economic recovery in the 1950s? The author will specifically analyse the historical role of the Sterling Payments Agreement (SPA) with Japan (1951–57) and its impact on the economic development in East Asia.

The SPA with Japan lacks much scholarly attention even though it played an important role in the process of post-war economic reconstruction in East Asia. Its function was to connect Anglo-Japanese trade relations (export and import of goods or 'visible trade') with the financial ties between the two countries (the exchange of services or 'invisible trade').[5] Looking at the operation of the

Sterling Payments Agreement with Japan is crucial for any comprehensive understanding of economic interests of the British Empire in East Asia in the 1950s.

The only substantial work produced on this topic is by Noriko Yokoi.[6] Yokoi explored Britain's sterling and trade policies towards Japan from 1948 to 1962, and challenged the conventional view that the British had been opposed to Japan's economic recovery in the 1950s. Her excellent detailed work elucidated Britain's complex policies concerning Japan in the 1950s very well. Nevertheless, her extensive research was still dominated by an analysis of the reaction of British home industries against Japanese competition. Especially, she put much emphasis on the attitudes of the Manchester Chamber of Commerce and the Board of Trade to Japan's economic recovery, and their fears of a revival of the severe Japanese competition of the pre-war period. Moreover, her work remained within the framework of the bilateral relationship between Britain and Japan. On the other hand, Kaoru Sugihara has revealed in his recent work that the 1950s saw the revival in the cotton goods markets of the 'intra-Asian competition' that had existed in the 1930s and the rapid recovery of Japanese cotton industries.[7] The author will try to relocate Yokoi's pioneering work into a wider and more global context because the sterling area covered wider areas and regions than East Asia in the post-war era and clearly reflected the economic interests of the City of London and of the British Empire and Commonwealth.[8]

For the reconsideration of British sterling policies in the 1950s, we must refer to recent works in British imperial history. As already mentioned, the work of Cain and Hopkins deals with the post-war international economic policy of Great Britain, the survival of the 'gentlemanly order' and the role of the City, mainly focusing on the role of the sterling area.[9] Receiving a strong influence from their work, Gerold Krozewski presents us with a new analysis of the end of empire in the 1950s, located at the intersection between British imperial policy and international relations. Especially in the late 1940s and early 1950s, when political control was feasible, discriminatory management of the colonies and the sterling area sustained Britain's post-war recovery. However, the emergence of liberal multilateralism, in the new international economic order dominated by the United States, exerted a strong influence on Britain's international position and policies.[10] We had better incorporate the Japanese case and East Asia into these new evaluations of the later stage of the transformation of the sterling area from a global perspective.

From the Open Payments Agreement to the Sterling Payments Agreement

During the Second World War, Britain had lost its gold and dollar reserves as well as overseas assets, and accumulated huge sterling debts (sterling balances) with the sterling area countries in order to finance the war. On 15 July 1947 the convertibility of sterling was restored under pressure from the US government. However, Britain's dollar reserves were soon drastically reduced and the British government was forced to suspend convertibility on 20 August 1947. Therefore, the most important problem for Great Britain in the post-war era was how to strengthen its currency in order to achieve sterling convertibility into US dollars.

After the suspension of the convertibility in August 1947 Britain divided the world into four different account areas: (1) the sterling account (sterling area), (2) the American account, (3) the transferable account, and (4) the bilateral account.[11] The American account group was able to exchange freely its sterling into dollars and vice-versa. The transferable account group countries were permitted to transfer sterling among themselves and with the sterling account countries. However, transfers for the bilateral account group countries were strictly limited; that is, they were able to transfer sterling to sterling account countries only, but if they wanted to use sterling for settlements with another bilateral account country, they had to get special approval from the Bank of England. Those four complicated divisions were initially intended to restrict the amount of convertibility of sterling into dollars, and to prevent a 'shortage of dollars'.

Japan re-opened official trade with Britain and sterling area countries on 31 May 1948 in the form of the Open Payments Agreement (OPA). It was designed as a bilateral annual agreement between SCAP (the Supreme Commander of the Allied Powers) and Britain, which provided that 'trade between Japan and the whole sterling area shall be on a sterling basis and that SCAP may convert into dollars any sterling arising out of that trade which is in excess of his requirements'. This was known as the 'dollar convertibility clause', under which Japan was regarded de facto as a hard currency country like the members of the American account, even if it belonged to the bilateral account group. The OPA was twinned with a Trade Arrangement with Japan, concluded in November 1948, which was different from any other bilateral agreements. The special features of the Trade Arrangement with Japan were as follows:

> Joint negotiation of a single agreement by a group called 'Participants', consisting of the UK (and colonies), Australia, New Zealand, South Africa, India and Ceylon. The most important 'Non-Participants' were thus Pakistan and Burma.
>
> The dominant consideration on our [British] side has been to secure essential requirements from Japan (especially textiles) without paying dollars. The risk of convertibility was ever-present owing to Japan's inability to easily match our full requirements by purchases from us.[12]

Hong Kong was intentionally left out of the OPA with Japan because of concerns that its entrepôt trade with mainland China would lead to a serious dollar drain from the sterling area.[13] Hong Kong therefore separately concluded its own payments and trade agreements with Japan.

The basic principle of the OPA with Japan was to balance the payments between Japan and the sterling area. However, from the first year of the agreement, SCAP accumulated excess sterling, due to the large-scale export of essential goods, especially cotton textiles, from Japan to Britain and the 'Participants' countries, which raised the convertibility issue. For the sterling area, Japan was a major alternative source of cheap non-dollar cotton goods, which complemented the limited manufacturing capacity of Britain. For example, the colonial authority in British Malaya needed a stable supply of cheap Japanese cotton goods in order to maintain the standards of living and welfare of the natives and to justify its colonial rule in the early 1950s.[14] In July 1949, at the request of the British side, SCAP agreed to hold a minimum of £10 million in working sterling balances before it converted excess sterling into dollars. In spite of the devaluation of sterling by about 30 percent in September 1949, Japanese exports to the sterling area continued to increase.

The tendency for Japanese accumulation of sterling changed in 1950 after the outbreak of the Korean War. The internal economic recovery of Japan drove it to seek to increase its trade with the sterling area. Indeed, SCAP wanted it to substantially increase its purchases from abroad as compared with previous years. In view of the nature of Japan's traditional imports and its inability, for political reasons, to obtain supplies from its pre-war sources, Korea and China, Britain expected foodstuffs and raw materials to play a prominent part in this import programme. These changes in the international circumstances necessitated a long-term approach to the sterling area's trade relations with Japan. In July 1950, the Overseas Negotiations Committee (ONC) of the British Cabinet set up a 'Working Party on Long Term Economic Relations with Japan'. In February 1951, the working party completed its report, which met with the approval of the ONC. It contained the following insightful findings about the sterling area:

> Japan is likely, in the long term, to be faced with a shortage of dollars and a surplus of other currencies. They will have to limit purchases of raw materials and foodstuffs from the dollar area (particularly iron ore, coal and cotton) and attempt to buy more food and raw materials from the sterling area and other non-dollar sources.
>
> Japanese competition in textiles may well have a serious effect on Lancashire's trade when world demand for textiles diminishes ... The Japanese should not, however, be so competitive in the heavy industries.
>
> The under-developed countries in the sterling area have a strong interest in buying cheap Japanese goods. It would be inexpedient, now, to ask colonies to impose quota restrictions against Japan along the lines followed in the 1930s. Unless they can be persuaded to abate their likely demands, the dangers of the Japanese earning excessive amounts of sterling which they will seek to convert into dollars (for reasons set out in (a) above) may well become acute.[15]

Based on these findings, the working party recommended to the Cabinet a long-term financial policy towards Japan, first, 'to put sterling area/Japanese payments relations on a non-dollar basis, i.e., by means of a Sterling Payments Agreement', and second, 'to encourage the widest possible use of sterling in the Far East: in view of the importance of Japanese trade, ultimate objective, failing full convertibility, to be the maximum multilateral use of sterling by Japan (e.g., her inclusion in the Transferable Account area)'.[16] The Treasury and the Bank of England had strongly insisted on the need to 'restore and encourage the widest possible use of sterling in East Asia', and their opinions were thus clearly reflected.[17]

From 24 May to 31 August 1951 the first Anglo-Japanese negotiations were held in Tokyo in order to replace the OPA with a sterling payments agreement on normal lines.[18] The focal points of the negotiations were to abrogate the 'dollar convertibility clause' of the OPA and to change Japan's position from a hard currency country to a soft currency one, in order to prevent any further drain of dollars. The Japanese side reluctantly agreed to remove the dollar convertibility clause, accompanying the termination of the occupation. However, another complicated matter was how to incorporate Hong Kong into the new SPA with Japan. SCAP and the Hong Kong government were opposed to the incorporation of the Crown Colony into the agreement by the final stage of the negotiations, but their efforts were in vain.

Within the sterling area, Hong Kong was one of two gaps in a common exchange control system directed against the rest of the world. It is called the 'Hong Kong Gap'. Catherine Schenk explains the unique character of Hong Kong in the sterling area as follows:

> During the 1950s, Hong Kong officially operated a system of foreign exchange restrictions similar to those operating elsewhere in the sterling area. The exchange rate of the Hong Kong dollar was pegged to sterling and the sale of foreign exchange at this rate was restricted to the purchase designated as essential imports, such as cereals, rice, cotton and rayon yarn. [However,] Excess demand for foreign exchange generated a parallel exchange market in which the price of HK dollars was determined freely by supply and demand ... The free exchange market meant that Hong Kong offered an almost unique level of deregulation in the sterling area system of exchange control, at a time when the colony was still ruled by a series of British governments committed to a high degree of intervention in their own domestic financial system.... Hong Kong was a unique gateway between tight exchange controls in the sterling area and the relative convertibility of the dollar area. This position, straddling the sterling and dollar worlds, was a vital factor in Hong Kong's prominence.[19]

As noted above, Hong Kong and SCAP had concluded a separate open payments and trade agreement, payable in HK dollars, under which Hong Kong allowed an annual figure of HK$2.5 million in import licences. Hong Kong's entrepôt trade with China, Taiwan and Macao was important for the Japanese economic recovery in the post-war era, and it also allowed access to Southeast Asian countries as well, such as British Malaya, Indonesia and Thailand. Under this trading system Japan acquired a trade surplus in sterling (HK dollar) and converted it into US dollars under the 'dollar convertibility clause' of the OPA, and thus the 'Hong Kong Gap' enabled it to import essential capital goods and raw cotton from the US. Japan therefore took advantage of the unique status of Hong Kong for its own economic interests. However, from the British point of view, this trade led to a drain of US dollars from the sterling area. By the abrogation of the 'dollar convertibility clause', Japan was thus forced to become a soft currency country, but Hong Kong continued to be an important item in reviews of the sterling payments agreement with Japan in the 1950s.

The interdependence of Japan and the sterling area

The SPA with Japan was originally intended to be valid for one year and to be renewed year by year, according to the results of trade and sterling balances. It was extended on 15 August 1952 to the end of December and automatically for another year on 27 December 1952. After the conclusion of the SPA, Japan's sterling holdings tended to increase, especially in 1952. At the start of the year it reached a level of around £100 million and then continued to increase to £120 million in the middle of 1952. The sterling area, and especially Hong Kong, increased its overall purchases from Japan. Hong Kong's trade imbalance rose to £12.3 million by the end of 1951 and to £12.2 million in the first half of 1952.[20] These trade imbalances were caused by Hong Kong merchants over-importing and the decline of the exchange rates of the HK dollar and sterling against the US dollar.[21] We may recognize here a coincidence of economic interests between the speculative buying of HK entrepôt merchants and the Japanese concern to increase exports through Hong Kong.

However, the rising trend of Japanese sterling balances was reversed in the last quarter of 1952, and tended to drastically decline to the level of around £30 million in 1953, which led to a 'sterling crisis' for Japan. In March 1953 the Japanese government contacted the Bank of England and the Treasury, and asked them to offer sterling credit facilities. After the negotiations, at the end of April, the Bank of England agreed to offer six-month sterling/dollar swap facilities of £25 million to Japan as an emergency measure.[22] Against the background of these violent fluctuations in Japan's sterling holdings and in order to consider Japan's application for GATT membership, in May 1953 the British government decided to set up the Cabinet Committee on Tariff Policy towards Japan. It was tasked with making a study of policies concerning Japan, repeating the exercise carried out in 1951 before the conclusion of the SPA.

The Committee was ordered to consider and report on the following four subjects: (1) Japanese competition with the UK, (2) the interdependence of the trade of the sterling area and Japan, (3) the balance of payments prospects of the sterling area and Japan, and (4) Japanese membership in GATT.[23] The subjects of (1) and (4) have been discussed in previous research, because of the interest in the anxieties of British manufacturing interests about the resurgence of Anglo-Japanese cotton trade disputes. However, the author would especially like to analyse the above subjects (2) and (3), because these two are crucial to revealing the intimate economic relationship between Japan and the sterling area in the 1950s. The specific questions about (2) and (3) were as follows:

Question 4: How far is Japan dependent on the sterling area as a source of supplies and markets for her exports?

Question 5: How far does the sterling area need to look to Japan as a source of supplies, and as a market for exports, including invisibles? In particular, what is the position as between Japan and the UK itself?

Question 6: What are the sterling area/Japan balance of payments prospects and their implications in the short term (i.e. 1953/54) and in the long term?

In regard to questions 4 and 5 on the trade relationship between Japan and the sterling area, the report made by the Treasury clearly pointed out the mutual interdependence on both the supply and demand sides.[24] First, on the supply side, the report mentioned that:

1   For the sterling area, and particularly for the undeveloped territories, Japan is a valuable source of cheap manufactured goods, especially textile and light metal products.

2   Without purchases of Japanese goods (e.g. as a means of avoiding inflation and in view of the poverty of their inhabitants) the underdeveloped territories of the sterling area would suffer and their development be impeded. It is therefore politically impracticable to expect most of the 'new' Dominions and the colonies to do without Japanese goods.

3   If Japanese goods were eliminated, the prices of her competitors' goods would rise.

We can verify here the Japanese role as an essential supplier of consumer goods for the developing sterling area countries in Asia. Second, on the demand side of the exports markets, the report observed that:

4   Japan is now largely dependent on her ability to sell to the sterling area, which took as much as 45 percent of her exports in 1951.... The sterling area moreover has special attractions as a multilateral concern and as an area consisting, to a large extent, of countries which are (a) underdeveloped, (b) well-administered and (c) consciously engaged in economic development.

5   The loss of Japan as an outlet for their products would be a serious matter for a number of sterling area countries, which attach great importance to Japan as a market. Sterling area exports to Japan are about 6 percent of the total exported to destinations outside the area. But, if the UK itself is omitted, the proportion for the R.S.A. alone (in 1952) is 12 percent.

6   How far Pakistan (above all), Australia, India, Hong Kong and Malaya have important interests in exporting to Japan? Pakistan exports 30 percent of her raw cotton to Japan; Australia at least 50 percent of her barley (which in 1952/53 is becoming a big trade); and Malaya practically all her iron ore.

7   Sterling area interests in exporting to Japan are not only in disposing of staple products but in maintaining price levels.
8   While the sterling area as a whole can avoid a reduction in Japanese purchases by maintaining its own imports from Japan, it cannot rely, in the absence of such purchases, on regular substantial sales to Japan.

From these careful observations, the Treasury report concluded 'there is therefore probably a greater measure of interdependence between the two areas than would appear from the figures alone'. In regard to question 6, the report briefly pointed to the Japanese surplus of £30 million with the sterling area in 1950–51, its surplus of £85 million in 1951–52, and deficit of over £100 million in 1952–53.

In October 1953, after the expiration of the sterling/dollar swap arrangement, the Japanese side asked the British authorities to grant other financial facilities to redress the 'sterling crisis' of Japan. The Treasury proposed another £10 million 'swap' to Japan. However, the Bank of England opposed the additional offer of the swap and pointed out that 'the original British aim of fostering the use of sterling in East Asia through Japan was no longer necessary as sterling was standing up on its "own firmer feet" in East Asia due to extensive intra-Asia sterling trade relations'.[25] At that time, the Bank was optimistic about the expansion of intra-Asian trade settled by sterling, and thus took a cautious attitude towards the Japanese government's request for a 'swap'.

Prior to the expiration of the SPA of 1952 the negotiations to renew it took place in London from 3 December 1953 to 29 January 1954.[26] This was the first comprehensive review and negotiation of the SPA since 1951 and took place in the light of the drastic decline in Japanese sterling balances. In order to increase Japanese receipts of sterling, the British negotiators discussed the relaxation of import restrictions on Japanese goods entering the sterling area (quota system), which had been introduced into the colonies in the 1930s and been temporarily tightened in 1952 to redress the Japanese accumulation of sterling.

At the second plenary meeting in the Treasury on 4 December 1953 the Japanese delegate confirmed the three aims of the renewal of the Agreement, as far as Japan was concerned, in the following terms:

1   to provide the framework for carrying on a high level of trade between the greatest multilateral payments area in the world – the sterling area – and some other country. Both parties to the Agreement know that transactions taking place between them will be settled in a mutually acceptable currency of international value – sterling.
2   it [Japan] is prepared normally to hold its working balances – and usually indeed more than its working balances (e.g. as a currency reserve) – in sterling.
3   it provides machinery also for financing international trade over an area still greater than the sterling area itself. This again recognizes that sterling – the

currency in which the greater part of the world's international trade takes place, has a special value and significance which most other currencies, in the nature of things, must lack.[27]

These clear observations on the Japanese side luckily coincided with British intentions. H.L. Hogg of the Bank of England clearly stated the Bank's view on 7 December when he wrote:

> The introduction of the open account arrangements with individual countries was diametrically opposed to the concept of the sterling area as an integral monetary area and to our fundamental policy of expanding the multilateral use of sterling as an international currency. We firmly believed that Japan stood to gain by working with us in the same direction.[28]

The SPA was, however, not regarded by Britain as being intended to be an instrument for the extension of credit and this applied particularly at a time, when the joint efforts of the Commonwealth were directed to strengthening sterling. The representative of the Treasury pointed out that 'the advantage we wish to secure, e.g. in getting the Japanese to take a satisfactory amount of sterling area goods and services, are therefore more likely to be obtained by permitting Japanese access to the colonies (due safeguards being maintained against future need) than by the extension of credit'.[29] The Treasury preferred to see the relaxation of import restrictions on Japanese goods entering the colonies and took a different stance from the more cautious Board of Trade, which wished to see the quotas remain in place.[30]

After the long Anglo-Japanese negotiations, on 29 January 1954 the Agreement was revised and both sides agreed with the target of £209.5 million for trade in both directions. The Treasury and the Bank of England had always borne in mind the use of sterling as an international currency. Japan also finally recognized the possibility of third-party transfers of sterling in the revised Agreement, which gave it further opportunities to increase its holdings of sterling from third-party transferable account countries like Germany, Sweden, the Netherlands, Finland and Thailand. From the British point of view, it welcomed the enlarging of Japan's scope for sterling settlements, which could only enhance the status of sterling as an international currency. At the negotiations in London, the Japanese ambassador to Britain and delegate to the talks, Asakai Kōichirō, described the Bank of England as 'the banker of the sterling area'.[31] He thus precisely grasped the Bank and the Treasury's fixation with maximizing the use and circulation of sterling by other countries outside the sterling area such as Japan.

Transformation of the Sterling Payments Agreements and the shift to multilateralism

The Japanese 'sterling crisis' was relieved by a gradual increase in its sterling balances from the latter half of 1954. From the end of December 1954 to

September 1955 the SPA with Japan was renewed three times, this taking place every three months. However, during these days, the importance of the Agreement tended to decline with the coming prospect of a restoration of convertibility between sterling and the US dollar.

Accordingly, the Bank of England began to take a clear attitude against bilateralism with Japan, and strongly pursued multilateralism in the use of sterling. Soon after, Britain adopted the policy of trying to terminate the various SPAs it had negotiated. In May 1955 the Bank compiled a list of the Agreements which it wished to see lapse. These included:

1   Finland, expires the 30th of June 1955; Brazil, expires the 30th of June 1955; Japan, expires the 31st of July 1955; Peru, expires the 31st of July 1955; Czechoslovakia, expires the 19th of August 1955; Spain, expires the 15th of December 1955; Poland, expires the 31st of December 1956; Austria and Italy, co-terminus with E.P.U. (European Payment Union)

2   Agreements comprising trade as well as payments provisions:
Paraguay, expires the 30th of June 1955 (payments clauses could go); Argentina, expires the 30th of June 1956

3   Other cases:

    a   Non-terminating agreements: USSR (Miscellaneous clauses), Hungary
    b   Lapsed agreements: Chile (No desire for revival), Uruguay
    c   Agreement under notice: Turkey, expires the 30th of June 1955.[32]

However, in 1955 a difference of opinion between the Bank of England and the Treasury became apparent during negotiations with the Japanese delegate in Tokyo. The Bank presented an aide-memoire to the ONC on 20 May 1955 in which it protested against restrictive trade policies being linked to the SPA. It argued that:

1   the problem of sterling balances cannot nowadays be considered in terms of the holdings of one country or another but rather in terms of the total amount of sterling held abroad and whether that amount is increasing or decreasing.

2   bilateral relation with Japan is out of accord with British multilateral stand in the OEEC (Organization for European Economic Cooperation).

3   we should clear our minds on our attitude towards Japan in the light of the approach of convertibility.

4   the point at issue with Japan is that she is maintaining restrictions on imports from the sterling area when her balance of payments with the sterling area is strongly favourable. This is a trade question which it is proper to discuss with the Japanese but which ought not to be linked with the level of Japan's sterling balances.... The Bank of England feels strongly that attempts should not be made to justify any restrictive trade practices on the grounds of our sterling payments agreement. In fact we should prefer to see the Sterling Payments Agreement and the letter attached to it disappear.[33]

From this aide-memoire, we can clearly see the Bank's aims. The Bank of England insisted that it must be for Japan to use sterling as widely as possible and to trade generally on a non-discriminatory basis so that it could compete freely. Its views were reiterated in August 1955 when it noted that:

> It does more good in promoting the multilateral use of sterling to encourage her to hold and use the currency than to indicate to her that we do not wish to see her holding any more sterling than she strictly needs as a working balance.... The bilateral approach on payments is wrong in principle, dangerous in its effect on other good users of sterling, and provides no proper reason for restricting colonial imports.[34]

In 1955, when the restoration of the convertibility of sterling finally came into view, the character of the SPAs therefore changed for British financial interests, especially for the Bank of England. The latter put much emphasis on the overall balance of payments position and the total amount of British sterling liabilities to countries outside the sterling area, and the inappropriateness of looking too narrowly at the particular sterling position of individual countries.

As already mentioned, the SPA with Japan was closely related with the Trade Arrangements. When the increase of the Japanese trade deficit towards the sterling area and the sharp drop of sterling balances occurred in 1953–54, there were often discussions at British Cabinet meetings about the causes of the trade imbalance and its relation with the quota system. Although the British government reached a consensus on the necessity of adjusting the Japanese trade deficit, the various ministries concerned differed from each other about a practical solution. For example, the Secretary of State for Commonwealth Relations proposed the enlarging of Japan's quotas and the expansion of imports from Japan for re-export from Hong Kong and Singapore and the Chancellor of the Exchequer supported his stance.[35] As a practical adjustment, in 1954, the quota for Japanese grey cotton goods exports to the UK was increased by one million in exchange for a decrease in Japanese exports to Nigeria (five million reduction in grey goods) and British East Africa (2.5 million reduction in grey goods), which were two colonies in which the Lancashire cotton industries still occupied a dominant position. By adjusting the home quota at the expense of reducing the colonial ones, the British government managed to coordinate the British industrial interests with the import of Japanese cotton goods.[36] This adjustment policy set a precedent for a more general relaxation of the quota system against Japanese goods. A majority within the British government was now opposed to restrictions on Japanese imports, and the Board of Trade was increasingly isolated in its insistence on the need to maintain a tight quota system in the British colonies.

In spite of the strong opposition of the Bank of England, on 17 October 1955 the SPA with Japan was renewed for another one year to the end of September 1956. However, thereafter in 1956 the Treasury's attitude to the Agreement also changed, and the SPA lost its original meaning as a way of balancing the trade between Japan and the sterling countries. The linkages or mutual connections between the trade relations and financial ones on the British side were completely weakened, and the SPA became an impediment to the convertibility of sterling and the revival of sterling as a world currency. Therefore, at the end of March 1957 the SPA with Japan was finally abrogated. Thereafter, only the Trade Arrangement was left and it was renewed year by year until November 1962 when the Anglo-Japanese commercial treaty was signed.

Conclusion: the sterling area and transformation of the economic order in East Asia

The author has tried in this chapter to reveal the changing character of the SPA with Japan in the 1950s as a model for perceiving the characteristics of the international economic order of East Asia in the 1950s. First, we may identify a similarity between the international order of Asia in the 1930s and that of the 1950s, especially concerning the role of the sterling area for assisting the economic development or the economic recovery of East Asia. During the period of the OPA, the 'dollar convertibility clause' and the 'Hong Kong Gap' played important roles for Japan in getting access to precious US dollars under the world-wide phenomena of a severe shortage of this currency. The Japanese economic recovery also, in turn, provided great benefits to the developing sterling area countries in Asia, such as Burma, Pakistan and British Malaya. On the one hand, for these Asian countries, the purchase of primary products by Japan via SCAP, that is, the Japanese importation of Burmese rice, raw cotton from Pakistan and iron ore from Malaya, gave them important outlets for their products, which contributed to the increase of their sterling balances. On the other hand, the Japanese exportation of consumer goods to Southeast Asia, especially of cotton goods, was a non-dollar cheap source of manufactured goods, which were essential for maintaining the social welfare standards of poor Asian ordinary people in these regions. Therefore, the sterling area in Asia and Japanese economic recovery were complementary to each other, at the level of the transactions of goods.

Second, by the middle of the 1950s Britain played the role of 'the banker of the sterling area'. The records of the Bank of England, as well as those of the Treasury, reflect the financial value of sterling as a world currency. Especially, in the first half of the 1950s, the existence of the SPA was a symbol of sterling's declining but still powerful influence in the capitalist world economy. The inclusion of Japan as a soft currency country into the sterling area contributed to the extension of the financial influence of sterling in Asia and enhanced status as a world currency versus the US dollar. However, in the second half of the 1950s, when the Bank of England tended to adopt multilateralism and shifted its focus from the sterling area to Europe and inter-industrial trade among the advanced nations of the North, the SPA with Japan, as well as with other countries, became an impediment to the maintenance of Britain's financial influence. The global trend towards multilateralism was thus reflected in the changing nature of the SPA with Japan.[37]

Third, we must, of course, identify the difference or transformation of the international order of Asia between the 1930s and 1950s. The prominent factor leading to change was the growing presence of the US and its pursuit of international order in post-war Asia. Especially, after the Chinese Communist Revolution in 1949 and the outbreak of the Korean War in June 1950, the US government changed its policy towards the non-communist countries in Asia, and started to offer military and economic aid to these countries.[38] The main focus of US strategy was to sponsor Japanese trade recovery and the restoration of the status of Japan as 'the workshop of Asia'.[39] In the process, the US started to adopt military Keynesianism to contain the spread of communism in Asia.[40] We have to recognize the influence of these changing factors on the international order of Asia in the 1950s. However, the predominant influence of the US would only come into existence in Southeast Asia in the early 1960s, for the British presence in the region still exerted its influence as a 'structural power' in the first half of the 1950s, when political decolonization progressed with the rise of Asian nationalism.[41] This means that the age of 'Pax Americana' must be dated a little later than usually assumed.

Notes

1 For the work already produced, see Akita Shigeru and Kagotani Naoto (eds), *1930-nendai Ajia kokusai chitsujo*, Hiroshima: Keisui-sha, 2000; and Shigeru Akita and Nicholas White (eds), *International Order of Asia in the 1930s and 1950s*, London: Ashgate, forthcoming 2010.
2 Sugihara Kaoru, *Ajiakan bōeki no keisei to kozo*, Kyoto: Minerva, 1996; Kagotani Naoto, *Ajia kokusai-tsusho chitsujo to kindai Nihon*, Nagoya: Nagoya daigaku shuppankai, 2000; and Akita Shigeru, *Igirisu teikoku to Ajia kokusai-chitsujo*, Nagoya: Nagoya daigaku shuppankai, 2003.
3 P.J. Cain and A.G. Hopkins, *British Imperialism, 1688–2000*, Harlow: Longman, 2001.
4 For the debate on 'Gentlemanly Capitalism' and East Asia, see ibid., pp. 16–17; and Shigeru Akita, 'British Informal Empire in East Asia, 1880–1939: A Japanese Perspective', in Raymond E. Dumett (ed.), *Gentlemanly Capitalism and British Imperialism: The New Debate on Empire*, London: Longman, 1999, chapter 6; and S. Akita (ed.), *Gentlemanly Capitalism, Imperialism and Global History*, Basingstoke: Palgrave-Macmillan, 2002.
5 Janet Hunter and S. Sugiyama (eds), *The History of Anglo-Japanese Relations, 1600–2000*, vol. IV, *Economic and Business Relations*, Basingstoke: Palgrave, 2002.
6 Noriko Yokoi, *Japan's Postwar Economic Recovery and Anglo-Japanese Relations 1948–1962*, London: RoutledgeCurzon, 2003.
7 Kaoru Sugihara, 'International Circumstances Surrounding the Post-war Japanese Cotton Textile Industry', in D.A. Farnie and D.V. Jeremy (eds), *The Fibre that Changed the World: The Cotton Industry in International Perspective, 1600–1990s*, Oxford: OUP, 2004, chap. 17.
8 C.R. Schenk, *Britain and the Sterling Area: From Devaluation to Convertibility in the 1950s*, London: Routledge, 1994; and Economic Cooperation Administration Special Mission to the United Kingdom, *The Sterling Area: An American Analysis*, London, 1951.
9 Cain and Hopkins, *British Imperialism*, chap. 26.
10 Gerold Krozewski, *Money and the End of Empire: British International Economic*

166 *Shigeru Akita*

Policy and the Colonies, 1947–58, London: Palgrave, 2001; and ibid., 'Gentlemanly Imperialism and the British Empire after 1945', in Akita (ed.), *Gentlemanly Capitalism*, chap. 4.

11 Schenk, *Britain and the Sterling Area*, pp. 8–10.
12 Bank of England Archive (BOE), OV16/61, Minister of State for Economic Affairs, JAPAN: Trade and Payments Negotiations, 20 May 1950, pp. 1–2. See also Gaimushō/Tsusanshō Kanri-Bōeki Kenkyukai (ed.), *Sengo Nihon no Bōeki/Kinyu Kyotei*, Tokyo: Jitsugyō no nihonsha, 1949.
13 Yokoi, *Japan's Postwar Economic Recovery*, p. 19.
14 Nicholas J. White, 'Britain and the Return of Japanese Economic Interests to South East Asia After the Second World War', *South East Asia Research*, 6–3, 1998; and John Weste, 'Britain, Japan and South-East Asia in the 1950s: Anglo-Japanese Economic Relations in the De-colonizing Empire', in *Aspects of Japan's Recent Relations with Asia, STICERD Discussion Paper*, no.IS/00/403, LSE, 2000.
15 BOE, OV16/69, 135, Japan, 21 February 1951, p. 1.
16 Ibid.
17 The National Archives, Kew (TNA), CAB134/264, ES(51)7, Economic Steering Committee (ESC) memorandum on long-term economic relations with Japan, 6 February 1951.
18 *Nichiei Bōeki Shiharai Kyotei Ikken*, reel B'0020, Public Release Series 8 (25 March 1985), Diplomatic Records on Microfilm (hereafter DRM), The Diplomatic Record Office of the Ministry of Foreign Affairs, Tokyo (hereafter MOFA), B5.2.O.J/B2.
19 C.R. Schenk, *Hong Kong as an International Financial Centre: Emergence and Development 1945–65*, London: Routledge, 2001, pp. 72–3, 133. See also Schenk, *Britain and the Sterling Area*, p. 10.
20 BOE, OV16/79, Heasman to Loynes, 25 January 1952; and Yokoi, *Japan's Postwar Economic Recovery*, p. 52.
21 BOE, OV14/8, Hong Kong Working Party: Working Paper No. 1, The Exchange Control Problem in Hong Kong, 20 February 1952.
22 *Nichiei bōeki shiharai kyotei ikken* [Japan–UK Trade Payments Agreement], reel B'0021, Public Release Series 8 (25 March 1985), DRM, MOFA, B'5.2.0.J/B2.
23 TNA, T236/3439, ON(53)128, 'Memoranda on long term economic relations – Japan & GATT', Overseas Negotiations Committee/Japan, 11 July 1953; and Yokoi, *Japan's Postwar Economic Recovery*, pp. 77–80.
24 TNA, T236/3439, Treasury redraft, 10 July 1953, no.T.1030–53.
25 BOE, OV16/90, Hogg note, 16 October 1953.
26 TNA, T236/3891, Anglo-Japanese payments talks (1953) file.
27 TNA, T236/3891, 'Minute of 2nd plenary meeting held in the Treasury on 4th December, 1953'.
28 BOE, OV16/92, 'Japanese payment agreement, Overseas & Foreign Office', Hogg note, 7 December 1953.
29 BOE, OV16/92, Serpell (Treasury) to Armstrong (Treasury), 7 December 1953.
30 TNA, CAB128/26, Part II, C(53)341, CC(53)77(7), 'Japan: trade with the sterling area', Chancellor of the Exchequer memorandum, 8 December 1953.
31 TNA, T236/3891, Asakai statement to Armstrong, 10 December 1953.
32 BOE, OV44/10, 'Sterling payments agreements, a list', BOE memorandum, 11 May 1955.
33 BOE, OV16/99, 'Japan' ONC aide memoire, 20 May 1955.
34 BOE, OV16/101, 'The Bank's view on policy for Japan', 12 August 1955.
35 TNA, CAB129/59, C(53)88, 'Sterling Area Trade with Japan 1953', Secretary of State for Commonwealth Relations memorandum, 6 March 1953; CAB128/26, Part 1, CC18(53), 'Japan. Trade with the Sterling Area', 10 March 1953; CAB129/64, C(53)341, 'Trade and Payments Policy with Japan', Chancellor of the Exchequer

memorandum, 7 December 1953; CAB128/26 Part 2, CC(81)53, 'Japan. Trade with the Sterling Area', 29 December 1953.

36 TNA, CAB129/65, C(54)30, 'Japan: Trade with the Sterling Area', President of the Board of Trade memorandum, 27 January 1954; CAB128/27 Part 1, CC6(54), 'Japan. Trade with the Sterling Area', 28 January 1954.

37 The Bank of England made a comprehensive review of sterling area policies with the Treasury in 1955–56; see BOE, OV44/33–392, 'Problems of the sterling area: report by a working party of the Treasury and the Bank of England', 25 June 1956.

38 Andrew J. Rotter, *The Path to Vietnam: Origins of the American Commitment to Southeast Asia*, Ithaca: Cornell University Press, 1987.

39 William S. Borden, *The Pacific Alliance: United States Foreign Policy and Japanese Trade Recovery, 1947–1955*, Madison: University of Wisconsin Press, 1984; and Aaron Forsberg, *America and the Japanese Miracle: The Cold War Context of Japan's Postwar Economic Revival, 1950–1960*, Chapel Hill: University of North Carolina Press, 2000.

40 Bruce Cumings, 'The American Ascendancy, 1939–1941', in Shigeru Akita and T. Matsuda (eds), *The Proceedings of the Global History Workshop Osaka, 1990, Looking Back at the 20th Century: The Role of Hegemonic State and the Transformation of the Modern World-System*, Osaka: Osaka University of Foreign Studies, March 2000.

41 For the arguments about structural power in the 1930s, see Akita, *Igirisu teikoku*, and Yamamoto Yuzo (ed.), *Teikō no kenkyu: genri, ruikei, kankei*, Nagoya: Nagoya daigaku shuppankai, 2003.

11 'Complementarity', decolonization, and the Cold War

British responses to Japan's economic revival in Southeast Asia during the 1950s and 1960s

Nicholas J. White

Introduction: Britain, Japan and 'anti-communism on the cheap'

During July 1951 a joint economic mission composed of Japanese technocrats and US officials in the SCAP (Supreme Commander for the Allied Powers) administration of Japan visited various countries in Southeast Asia. This delegation was headed by Kenneth Morrow, a senior administrator in SCAP's Economic and Scientific Section. As the UK Liaison Mission (UKLIM) in occupied Tokyo soon discovered, the Morrow mission was part of a grand American design to 'stem the advance of communism' in Pacific Asia, but without incurring too many additional US costs. Washington had recently informed SCAP officials that raw materials for Japan's industries to assist the general 'rearmament' of the 'free world' could no longer be met from the dollar area. This withdrawal of US largesse was in anticipation of the complete cessation of US aid to Japan at the planned termination of the Occupation in 1952. Hence, the Morrow mission's particular brief was to stimulate increased Japanese purchases of Southeast Asia's commodities.[1]

Indeed, John Foster Dulles regarded commercial linkages between Japan and Southeast Asia as central in his negotiations for the peace treaty between 1950 and 1952, and subsequently in his role as US secretary of state after 1953. Moreover, in articulating the 'domino theory' in April 1954, President Eisenhower emphasized that Japan 'must have' Southeast Asia as 'a trading area or Japan ... will have only one place in the world to go – that is, toward the Communist areas in order to live'.[2] Given its ongoing heavy commitments in terms of foreign aid, the Eisenhower administration was not particularly enthralled by the proposal of Japan's prime minister, Kishi Nobusuke, for a Southeast Asian Development Fund during 1957 – a scheme described by the British ambassador in Tokyo as a 'marriage of convenience between American capital and Japanese technical skill and industrial power'. Nevertheless, US officials continued to argue that 'unless this idea, or something fairly like it, is realized the pressure on the present Japanese Government to come to terms with the communist Asiatic mainland will prove irresistible'.[3]

With such American blessing, Japan's economic re-penetration of Southeast Asia was certainly noticeable and wide-ranging by the end of the 1950s. This applied even to those areas most closely coveted by British policy-makers, such as the dollar-earning bastion of the Federation of Malaya, which achieved independence in August 1957, but where Britain retained considerable post-colonial commercial and strategic sway.[4] In May 1960 a most-favoured-nation trade agreement was concluded between Japan and the Federation. Since the early 1950s there had been no significant expansion in Japanese exports to Malaya, but a qualitative shift in the pattern of Japan's trade with the Federation (as well as Singapore) stood out. Sales of textiles were on the decline given competition from newly industrializing economies in the rest of Asia. Yet, radios, photographic equipment and consumer durables had shown dramatic progress – for example, Japan could now claim 71 per cent of the Malayan market for battery radios. New intrusions were being made in the capital goods market also at the expense of British engineering sales, and Japanese industrialists were predicting an exponential proliferation of capital and technical investment in the Federation and Singapore. For example, a Japanese company in 1960 had already been formed to build a sugar refinery at Perai opposite Penang Island, with 55 per cent of the capital – in the form of 'know how' and plant – being supplied by Japanese firms. Other Malayan–Japanese joint ventures had received pioneer industry certificates from the federal government to produce asbestos, galvanized iron, and toothpaste at Petaling Jaya, the purpose-built industrial township outside Kuala Lumpur. In primary production, meanwhile, Malaya had become the largest supplier of iron ore to Japan's steel factories, making up for the 'loss' of China.[5]

In this re-expansion of Japanese economic interests in Malaysia and beyond, Britain had not necessarily acted as Washington's 'poodle'. Sensitive towards public opinion, both in the region and in the UK, and utilizing capital controls and visa restrictions to try and ensure the gradual return of Japanese businesses to Southeast Asia, British governments had tempered the worst excesses (as they saw them) of the US–Japan alliance. But, it is now widely recognized by both Japanese and British scholars that British bureaucrats and ministers did not substantially obstruct the process whereby Japan re-emerged as a significant economic player in the Southeast Asia region.[6] Indeed, in 1961, when British timber concessionaires protested about a possible direct investment by Mitsui in the forests of North Borneo, the last British governor of the colony, Sir William Goode, intimated that 'the infiltration of Japanese [was] an inevitable development, and not something to be resisted'.[7]

The first part of this chapter re-examines why British officialdom took a relatively liberal attitude towards the return of Japanese economic interests to Southeast Asia. As such, an on-going debate concerning the economic and geo-political underpinnings of Anglo-Japanese 'complementarity' in the region is re-visited. We then move on to consider an overlooked aspect of Anglo-Japanese relations in Southeast Asia – namely, the linkages re-forged, from the early-1950s onwards, between British trading, shipping and investment groups and Japanese business interests.

Finance versus geo-politics: Anglo-Japanese 'complementarity' in British official thinking

Another essay by the present author has been criticized (in a friendly manner) by Shigeru Akita on the grounds that it overlooks the financial imperative in British policy in Southeast Asia during the era of decolonization: as Akita tells us, in the negotiations for the Sterling Payments Agreement (SPA) with Japan during 1951, the Treasury and the Bank of England 'expressed a strong desire "to restore and encourage the widest possible use of sterling in East Asia"'. Such a policy reflected 'the survival of British financial influence in East and Southeast Asia in the 1950s and the strategy of extending British economic interests through the expansion of the sterling area'.[8] This line of argument suggests a revival of the 'complementarity' between British finance, or 'gentlemanly capitalism', and Japanese industrialization, and hence Japanese-led intra-Asian trade, dating back to the late-nineteenth century and even surviving the troubled 1930s.[9]

Noriko Yokoi's extensive interrogation of the British archives tends to support the Akita thesis: Britain's guarded encouragement of Japanese economic recovery was motivated 'entirely by self-interest' and was concerned primarily with the revitalization of the sterling area, and thus Britain's financial interests in the Asia-Pacific region. Hence, in the expanded SPA of 1954, for example, the Treasury ignored Board of Trade and Ministry of Transport objections, as well as an uproarious House of Commons, in an attempt to persuade Japan to convert its dollar reserves into sterling in return for the lifting of restrictions on Japanese goods in the British colonies. The encouragement of Japan's trade with the Asian sterling area to provide cheap manufactured goods for the 'under-developed' colonies of the region, and so stabilize their societies and polities, was merely an 'additional benefit' according to Yokoi.[10]

There is certainly evidence to support the 'sterling-first' argument. Britain's commissioner-general in Southeast Asia, Malcolm MacDonald, was a particular advocate of Japan's commercial resuscitation in the countries under his remit. In a despatch to the Foreign Secretary in September 1951, MacDonald emphasized the gains in Southeast Asia for Britain, arising from a new financial and commercial agreement with Japan. Indeed, as the Morrow mission had likewise appreciated, here lay the 'largest contribution' that Britain could make to the fostering of Japanese trade with Southeast Asia. SCAP was confident that an Anglo-Japanese payments agreement would allow Japan to accumulate sufficient sterling to expand trade with Southeast Asia, and therefore relieve the direct burden on the US economy. The sterling area obviously included the colonies and protectorates of British Malaya and British Borneo. Despite refusing to join the Commonwealth, Burma also remained inside the post-colonial exchange regime. Moreover, Thailand, as a member of the transferable account area, would be able to trade much more freely with Japan, now that there was no danger of a consequent 'dollar drain'. In MacDonald's view, Japan should be encouraged towards multilateral trading with the Southeast Asian countries and away from Tokyo's existing policy of barter transactions financed through open accounts.[11]

This strategy appeared to pay off for British financial interests in Southeast Asia. During 1956 Thailand and Japan finally abandoned their open account, barter dealings for a new trade and payments agreement, which permitted the use of sterling, dollars or any other mutually agreed currency, for making payments. In the short term, however, Bangkok and Tokyo decided to use only sterling, since the British currency was 'less hard' than the US dollar. This was good news for the status of the pound as an international currency and, moreover, any sterling that Japan acquired from Thai trade was likely to be spent in the Asian sterling area, thus strengthening the empire–Commonwealth bloc in South and Southeast Asia.[12]

However, MacDonald's principal, longer-term concern in the autumn of 1951 lay beyond the realms of economics: it was to provide Japan with 'such opportunities for contact and trade with the non-Communist world as will discourage her from becoming too dependent upon her relations with Communist China'. The 'paramount aim' of a 'liberal policy towards Japan' in the British territories of Southeast Asia was 'the retention of Japan in the anti-Communist fold'.[13] In Whitehall, the Foreign Office was not completely convinced by the commissioner-general's line of thinking on Sino-Japanese relations: there was no historical basis for believing that the existence of close economic ties between the two countries was bound to lead on to political and military intimacy.[14] However, the Foreign Office did agree that 'Japan's trade with the Chinese mainland is certainly not likely in the near future to attain anything like its pre-war dimensions'. Japan was therefore 'urgently faced with the prospect of finding new markets for her manufactures, and new sources of supplies for raw materials and foodstuffs'. In this, Britain 'fully accept[ed] the fact of Japan's need for viability'.[15]

In 1957 news of Kishi's plans to visit various Southeast Asian countries, as well as Washington, to discuss schemes for economic cooperation in the region, caused some alarm in British diplomatic circles in Tokyo and in the Foreign Office in London. There were fears that a re-invigorated US–Japanese anti-communist alliance in the region might result in 'our military and naval withdrawal from the Pacific' being 'followed by a commercial retreat'. But Britain's principal interest remained lodged in the avenues of geo-politics: so long as Japan did not emerge as either politically or economically paramount in Southeast Asia, the British felt obliged to encourage:

> any honest and non-discriminatory Japanese attempts to improve relations with South East Asia, both from the point of view of strengthening those countries economically and of countering communist attempts at economic penetration and from that of assisting Japan in her efforts to maintain a secure and prosperous post-war economy.[16]

Indeed, what made the Japan–Southeast Asia economic link all the more crucial from a political point of view, for British mandarins and proconsuls alike, was the contribution which Japanese trade and investment could make towards stabilizing Southeast Asia, and hence defeating left-wing militancy in the new and decolonizing nations of the region. As the commissioner-general had elucidated to the Foreign Office in 1951, increased trade with Japan would benefit Southeast Asia because of the wide demand for the cheap consumer goods that Japan could offer. Such a development would also reduce inflationary pressure in sterling-area Southeast Asia, given the ongoing tightness of supplies from an increasingly uncompetitive industrial Britain. The Foreign Office needed no persuading here, since six months earlier it had resisted demands for a restriction on the production of Japanese cotton goods in the peace treaty on the grounds that 'Japan must be able to pay its way in the world' and that 'there was a large demand for textiles in South-east Asia and the British industry was incapable of meeting it'.[17] Moreover, to meet the economic development plans of both the British and foreign territories of Southeast Asia, plentiful quantities of capital goods were required. Japan would be crucial here given that Britain and Western Europe were currently engaged in expensive rearmament programmes, preventing British factories from supplying capital goods at the delivery dates required.[18]

British officials noted also that Japanese government and business increasingly viewed the economic relationship with Southeast Asia in a new, less exploitative light by the end of the 1950s. No longer were the economies of the region viewed exclusively as markets for Japanese consumer and capital goods in exchange for dollar-saving raw materials. Rather, Japanese interests were increasingly sensitive to the nationalistic ambitions of Southeast Asian governments to develop their own manufacturing industries – 'the opinion is growing that Japan will not lose by helping in the establishment of ... [import substitution] ... provided that her own industries continue to outpace those of her Southern neighbours and adapt themselves to the changing nature of external demands'.[19] Such developments were welcomed by British officials, given the role which Japanese direct foreign investment could play in providing employment for Southeast Asia's rapidly expanding and youthful population. Hence, in November 1957 talks with Kishi, Sir Robert Black, the governor of Singapore, endorsed plans for greater Japanese involvement in the island's industrialization 'with the object of countering increasing Communist influence in the region'.[20]

And, beyond the bounds of British direct control, Japan's trade was also seen as crucial in stabilizing societies and polities. In Thailand, Japan's cheap consumer goods were 'essential for the welfare' of the rice-producing peasantry whose purchasing power was still limited. Moreover, the US's Economic Cooperation Administration was fostering development projects which called for large-scale import of capital equipment: for the British embassy in Bangkok, Japanese participation in this area would also prove 'essential' and certainly 'desirable'.[21] In similar vein, Whitehall and Westminster became concerned during 1954 at the breakdown of reparations negotiations between Japan and Indonesia, given the desperate need of economic aid in the archipelago's postcolonial financial debacle. In October, Douglas Dodds-Parker, joint parliamentary under-secretary of state for foreign affairs, returned from Jakarta and reported that there were 'big opportunities' for Japanese exports with plentiful supplies of 'foodstuffs, rubber etc. in return if only the problem of Japanese reparations payments could be cleared'. Dodds-Parker even went so far to suggest that Britain might offer its 'good offices' to negotiate both reparations and trade agreements between Indonesia and Japan.[22] In Burma too, British diplomats became concerned at the end of 1959 by a brief breakdown of economic relations with Japan, despite the signing of a reparations agreement in 1954. The government in Rangoon put into effect a complete embargo on Japanese imports, following Japan's refusal to increase both its reparations shipments and its rice purchases. The embargo might result in Burma eventually purchasing more consumer and capital goods from Britain. But a ban on imports from Japan was 'even more foolish than an embargo on our imports ... since Japan is in a position to retaliate by stopping all reparations shipments'. This 'would quickly result in some serious shortages' in a country faced with a chronic balance of payments deficit, a schism in the Buddhist–Socialist government, armed revolts in the non-Burman fringe, and an on-going border dispute with communist China.[23]

Indeed, British financial, as well as industrial, interests were often ignored in what Junko Tomaru has characterized as the 'development-first' strategy for stabilizing Southeast Asia.[24] Hence, in Malaya, a desperate desire to encourage economic development to win 'hearts and minds' in the face of the communist insurrection, and so aid the political management of decolonization, came to supersede the strict enforcement of sterling-area rules. In the re-development of the peninsula's iron mines, the Treasury described Japan's barter deals and bilateral trading methods as 'objectionable'. But the views of the Federation's assertive expatriate Member for Economics, Oscar Spencer, prevailed:

> [T]he over-riding requirement is the rapid development of Malaya on a sound economic basis; providing this is achieved we consider we must be prepared to compromise, if necessary, by accepting foreign plant and machinery to a greater extent than we would really like.... We recognize of course that there is a foreign exchange aspect to be considered, and that it is an important one ... [B]ut this objective should be secondary to the really important issue of development.[25]

In the course of the 1960s, utilizing Japanese capital to underpin Southeast Asian prosperity became even more urgent for British policy-makers as the Malaysia territories were viewed as an increasing drain on scant British resources. In the late 1940s and early 1950s the Malaya region was the dollar earner *par excellence* of the sterling area. By 1960, however, the Macmillan government was well aware that rubber and tin were no longer vital to Britain's balance of payments, and, indeed, there was no material asset in Southeast Asia to compare with the importance of Middle Eastern oil, while less than three per cent of its world-wide exports ended up in the region. Hence, the promotion of 'Greater

Malaysia' – the extension of the Federation of Malaya to incorporate Singapore, Sarawak, Brunei and North Borneo (Sabah) – offered a solution 'to a particularly knotty problem of maintaining regional stability at minimum cost to the British taxpayer'.[26] Lord Selkirk, the last British commissioner-general in Southeast Asia, was thus happy to give encouragement to a high-powered Japanese economic mission comprised of leading industrialists and bureaucrats, and led by the president of Mitsubishi Electric, which arrived in Singapore in September 1962. Notwithstanding Japan's balance of payments difficulties, the government in Tokyo was encouraging its entrepreneurs to take a long view of the economic potentialities of Malaysia, particularly in secondary production, given that the population of the area was expected to rise by ten times in sixty years.[27]

Japanese industrial investment was therefore seen by the last of the British administrators in Southeast Asia as a means of making Malaysia function as a viable economic unit. This was especially the case given the growing hostility of Treasury and Bank of England officials in London towards free flows of capital within the Commonwealth, which allegedly deprived domestic industry of funds for renovation and exacerbated Britain's balance of payments difficulties. This financial critique culminated in the Wilson government's swingeing budget of 1965 (which removed tax concessions for overseas investors), the refusal of additional defence and development aid for Malaysia in 1966, and an accelerated run down of British forces 'East of Suez' from 1968.[28] Hence, when Japan emerged as the major trading partner for Malaysia in the course of 1966 and Japan's prime minister, Satō Eisaku, visited the country in September 1967, the British high commissioner in Kuala Lumpur, Sir Michael Walker, believed that closer Malayo-Japanese commercial links should be welcomed 'as a factor contributing towards Southeast Asian stability. Even though this will no doubt ... lead to more severe competition in the future for our own exports.' Indeed, disappointment was expressed that Japan had not been able to take up more of the aid burden in Malaysia – beyond an £18 million loan offer in 1966 – given Tokyo's continuing balance of payments problems. Moreover, although the 'blood debt' issue appeared solved by the donation of two Japanese ocean-going cargo ships, worth about £3 million to the Malaysian national shipping line, Malaysia–Japan relations were still 'not particularly close'.[29]

'If you can't beat them, join them': Anglo-Japanese business connections in Southeast Asia

Attitudes towards Japanese manufacturers amongst industrial circles in post-war metropolitan Britain – with accusations of copyright infringements, dumping and exploitation of labour – bordered on an unpleasant xenophobia, and replicated the 'yellow peril' mentality of the 1930s.[30] The right-wing and protectionist Commonwealth and Empire Industries Association launched its anti-free trade slogan in 1953: 'Do you want a Jap to take your job... GATT would make it easy for him.'[31] More progressive opinions in Birmingham, Bradford and Bolton only emerged after the visit to Japan of the director-general of the Feder-

ation of British Industries, Sir Norman Kipping, in October 1961.[32] On the spot
in Southeast Asia, however, the British agency houses woke up to the opportunities of doing business with Japanese industrial and commercial firms from the
early 1950s. The British trading and investment behemoths retained their dominance of local economies in maritime Southeast Asia well into the 1960s, and
despite political decolonization. But this dynamism was often sustained through
the agency houses divorcing themselves from a stagnating industrial Britain.[33]
When Kipping visited Malaya in early 1959 he discovered that, 'The old established British merchant houses have an international spread of agencies and
many of them have found their foreign or continental principals more competitive than their UK opposite numbers.'[34]

   The managers of one of the largest British importers in Singapore, the Borneo
Company Ltd. (BCL), boasted of their great success 'post-war in attracting new
agencies'. However, this entailed a 'steady drift of our business away from the
UK as the principal source of supply'.[35] This certainly proved to be the case with
Japanese manufacturers, who were increasingly wooed by BCL during the
1960s. One of BCL's core businesses was automobiles, distributed through a
cluster of subsidiary companies in Thailand, the Federation of Malaya, Singapore, Brunei, Sarawak and North Borneo. The most important contract here was
the right to market the Austin cars and commercial vehicles of the British Motor
Corporation (BMC). However, in 1962 BCL managers could not help noticing
that Japanese Toyota 700 class cars achieved an 'instant success' in Penang.
Moreover, representatives of the BCL motor group were impressed by the
quality of vehicles on display at the Tokyo Motor Show of 1962, and thereafter a
Japanese franchise for Malaya was actively sought, despite the inevitable negative reaction from the BMC.[36] Indeed, from the mid-1960s, the Inchcape group –
the world-wide British trading conglomerate which would effectively take-over
BCL in 1967 – 'began to evolve as one of Toyota's largest distributors'.[37] Moreover, as a prelude to a 'Top Brass visit' to drum up more business in Japan
during 1965, BCL secured the agency to sell Sanyo's electrical products – refrig-
erators, transistors and radios, vacuum cleaners, washing machines and pressure
cookers – throughout East Malaysia and Brunei. As part of the deal with Sanyo,
a BCL technician was to be sent to Osaka for training. Links with Japanese
trading companies, such as Ikemura & Co. of Osaka, were further facilitated by
BCL's take-over of the Hong Kong-based import–export firm, Gibb, Livingston
& Co. in 1961.[38] From as early as 1952 BCL had also acted as the Malayan
agents for Japan's premier shipping line, the Nippon Yusen Kaisha (NYK), and
during 1955 NYK opened a resident representative office within BCL's Southeast Asian headquarters in Singapore. As such, by the early 1960s BCL managers were scouting around for suitable primary exports – such as kaolin from
Johor and the Borneo territories – which could be carried by NYK vessels on
their homeward voyages to Japan.[39]

   Other leading British agency houses in the Malaysia region were soon to be
involved with Japanese enterprises too. It was Boustead & Co. which joined
together with the British shipping line, Andrew Weir & Co., the Kelantan state

government, and the Japanese mining firm, Kokan Kogyo, to form the locally registered Oriental Mining Co. Ltd. for exploitation of the Temangan iron-ore deposits after 1954. Bousteads and Weirs would come to hold 51 per cent of the shares in Oriental Mining, and, to the relief of the Colonial Office, 'the standing of the British partners and their financial stake' would prove sufficient to prevent the Temangan operation becoming 'no more than a British front for Japanese capital'.[40] During 1954 the premiere British agency house in Malaya, Guthrie & Co., had opposed the removal of quotas on Japanese cement imports, fearing 'dumping' on Malayan ports at the expense of its British principals – this being one local government response to the liberalization of Japanese trade with the sterling area generally. Yet, by 1957, when the Federation of Malaya became independent, the Guthrie head office in Singapore was acting as the surveying and settling agent for two Japanese financial institutions – the Yasuda and Nisshin insurance companies.[41]

Another British merchant firm of note, which was prepared to cooperate with Japanese interests in the re-expansion of intra-Asian commerce, was Jardine Waugh Ltd., the Malaysian subsidiary of the Hong Kong giant, Jardine Matheson. In the course of 1961 a powerful group of Japanese mining interests descended upon Sarawak to examine the possibility of opening up the Silantek coalfields. The principal interest was the Nippon Coal Mining Co., associated with the Yawata Iron and Steel Company and backed by the Steel Making Raw Materials Committee of the Tokyo government. Jardine Waugh was involved in discussions with the Sarawak secretariat and the British firm was set to provide – with local interests – about 40 per cent of the financing for the Silantek project.[42] Here was a classic symbiosis or 'complementarity' between the British merchant firm and Japanese industrial interests. Jardines had suffered the 'hostage capitalism' and 'slow-motion nationalization' of its commercial and manufacturing operations in mainland China, following the communist takeover in 1949.[43] It was anxious, therefore, to forge new business in the relatively safer political environment of Malaysia. For the Japanese mining and steel combines, their raw material sources had been thrown into disarray by the Chinese civil war and the advent of the People's Republic. As it turned out, the Sarawak coal enterprise came to nothing – the demands of the Kuching secretariat proved rather too stringent for the Japanese firms, while, as was often the case in late-colonial Sarawak, transport difficulties undermined the cost-effectiveness of development plans.[44] Yet, the Jardine group remained as a significant link in a commercial chain that increasingly integrated the economies of Japan and East Malaysia. By 1958 timber surpassed rubber as North Borneo's principal export, thanks largely to the massive expansion of the Japanese market. In the 1960s 70–80 per cent of the colony's hardwood logs were destined for Japan. The Bombay Burmah group may have complained about the intrusion of Japanese firms in Sabah's logging industry, but the bulk of the British conglomerate's output was sold by Jardines in Japan.[45]

The enthusiasm with which the agency houses embraced these alliances with Japanese enterprises might seem bizarre, given torrid wartime experiences. BCL was 'practically closed down' for three and a half years after the fall of Singapore in February 1942 – all of its overseas branches were in enemy hands, and eighteen BCL staff died either during the Japanese invasions or internment.[46] Yet, the visit of BCL's managing director, W.K. Young, to Tokyo in the spring of 1965 was facilitated by long-standing connections with Teishima Yoshio, the manager of Ikemura. Teishima had worked for the *sogo shosha* (general trading company), C. Itoh, in Bangkok before 1941 and had conducted a number of dealings with BCL's branch in the Thai capital.[47] As early as 1910, BCL had acquired the NYK agency in Singapore, alongside the leading British shipping lines.[48] Indeed, after 1934 some 80 per cent of European merchant firms on the island were distributing competitive Japanese goods in British Malaya and the wider Southeast Asia region.[49]

It would seem therefore that agency house executives were able to make a distinction between the excesses of the Japanese military and the peaceable *sarariman*. At the least, this was a pragmatic readjustment to the realities of intra-Asian trade and investment; another phase in the re-invention of the British multinational trading companies.[50] As Shimizu and Hirakawa have claimed for the 1930s, so in the 1950s and 1960s, the agency houses appreciated that 'if you can't beat them, join them'.[51]

This was also the experience of British shipping interests in East and Southeast Asia. The Ocean Steam Ship Company (OSSCo; otherwise known as the Blue Funnel Line or Alfred Holt & Company) was the first British concern to place orders in Japan for the construction of cargo liners, turning to Mitsubishi Heavy Industries in Nagasaki to build two highly automated vessels, which were delivered in the course of 1967.[52] Into the 1970s this Liverpool-based group occupied the leading international shipping position in a trading realm which traversed an arc from Sri Lanka to Japan.[53] In the early 1950s OSSCo's most important route in terms of vessel earnings was the Straits, China & Japan service. As such, Blue Funnel, and its agents in Hong Kong and Japan, Butterfield & Swire, and in Singapore, Mansfields, were key emissaries in the revival of Japan–Southeast Asia linkages, and the 'still non-existent' nature of Japanese commerce had been regarded by OSSCo's executive as a factor holding back the group's full rehabilitation in January 1947. Indeed, a prime explanation for Blue Funnel's weathering of the inter-war depression lay in the group's increasing carriage of Southeast Asian raw materials to Japan on outward sailings, and Japanese manufactures to Southeast Asia on homebound voyages.[54] Admittedly, one of OSSCo's senior executives had forebodings about the 'doubtless ... reintegration' of the *zaibatsu* on the re-gaining of Japanese sovereignty in 1952, sardonically commenting that Japan had been 'extraordinarily lucky – thanks to the Russians – to be treated so generously'. Nevertheless, the Ocean and Swire groups fully supported the readmission of Japanese shipping companies to the Europe–Far East Freight Conference after 1953. Even Mitsui's attempt to operate outside this ring was contained in 1956 by inclusion of the *zaibatsu*'s shipping interests under the NYK's wing.[55] Moreover, it had been recognized by Blue Funnel directors in the early 1950s that Japan's accumulation of sterling balances would substantially boost OSSCo's carryings to East and Southeast Asia,[56] especially as mainland China was proving an increasingly troublesome destination for Holt's vessels.[57]

Conclusion: the official and the commercial

An Anglo-Japanese 'complementarity' clearly proved a significant element in the post-war revival of Japan's economic linkages with Southeast Asia. Yet, on an official level, the symbiotic relationship between British and Japanese interests in 1950s and 1960s Southeast Asia derived primarily from geo-political rather than exclusively economic concerns. There is no doubt that British policy-makers saw advantages for the strengthening of the sterling area, and reviving Britain's financial influence in the Asia-Pacific region. But these considerations were largely ancillary to the 'bigger [geo-strategic] picture', namely the containment of communist China and the stabilization of decolonizing Southeast Asia. This tendency points to the centrality of policy-making 'on the spot', not in London. The main issues for expatriate diplomats and administrators in Southeast Asia were local and regional and largely political in nature rather than metropolitan and economic.

In reassessing Anglo-Japanese economic relations in Southeast Asia we also need to move beyond 'macro' official matters to examine the 'micro'-scale partnerships of Japanese commercial and manufacturing concerns with British agency houses and shipping lines. It is here that we can be more certain about acknowledging 'complementarities' – the British trading, shipping and investment groups sought more competitive supplies of both goods and services, while Japanese industrialists and raw material extractors relied on the expert local knowledge of the agency houses, and particularly their skills in navigating through vast swathes of expatriate and indigenous red tape. In addition to US Cold War strategy, it is more usual to stress the triangular relationship between Japanese big business, overseas Chinese entrepreneurship, and indigenous politics in the long-term, post-war reintegration of the Asia-Pacific economy.[58] However, for the 1950s and 1960s, at least, British firms also played a significant role in reviving Japan's links with Southeast Asia.

Notes

1 The National Archives, Kew, London (hereafter TNA), CO537/7353, Clutton to Foreign Secretary, 10 July 1951.
2 Ronald Pruessen, 'John Foster Dulles and Decolonization in Southeast Asia', in Marc Frey, Ronald Pruessen and Tan Tai Yong (eds), *The Transformation of Southeast Asia: International Perspectives on Decolonization*, Armonk: M.E. Sharpe, 2003, pp. 234–5; extract from *Public Papers of the Presidents of the United States: Dwight D. Eisenhower, 1953*, Washington, DC: Government Printing Office, 1958, pp. 381–90 reproduced in Frederik Logevall, *The Origins of the Vietnam War*, Harlow: Longman, 2001, p. 102.
3 TNA, CO1030/559, 'Brief on Japan for the conference of UK representatives in the Far East, Eden Hall, Singapore, 16–19 January 1958', HM Ambassador, Tokyo, 13 December 1957.

4 Federation politicians chose to remain within the Commonwealth and the sterling area on independence, and later signed the Anglo-Malayan Defence Agreement, which permitted the continued stationing of British troops on Malayan soil.

5 TNA, DO35/9974, Woodruff (UK Trade Commissioner, Kuala Lumpur) to Phillips (Board of Trade), 19 May 1960 and enclosures; extract from Malayan Fortnightly Summary, 17 February 1960.

6 Junko Tomaru, *The Postwar Rapprochement of Malaya and Japan, 1945–61: The Roles of Britain and Japan in South-East Asia*, London: Macmillan, 2000; ibid., 'Japan in British Regional Policy Towards South-East Asia, 1945–1960', in Caroline Rose, John Weste, Makoto Iokibe and Junko Tomaru (eds), *Japanese Diplomacy in the 1950s*, London: Routledge, forthcoming; John Weste, 'Facing the Unavoidable – Great Britain, the Sterling Area and Japan: Economic and Trading Relations, 1950–1960', in Janet Hunter and S. Sugiyama (eds), *The History of Anglo-Japanese Relations, 1600–2000: Volume 4: Economic and Business Relations*, London: Palgrave, 2003, pp. 283–313; Nicholas J. White, 'Britain and the Return of Japanese Economic Interests to South East Asia after the Second World War', *South East Asia Research*, 6, 3 (November 1998): 281–307; ibid., 'Malaya and the Sterling Area Reconsidered', paper presented at the XIII Congress of the International Economic History Association, Buenos Aries, July 2002; Noriko Yokoi, *Japan's Postwar Economic Recovery and Anglo-Japanese Relations, 1948–62*, London: RoutledgeCurzon, 2003.

7 Inchcape Archives, Guildhall Library, London (hereafter IA), Ms. 27281, MacEwen, Managing Director, Borneo Company Ltd., London to Pearson, General Manager, Kuching, 3 March 1961.

8 Shigeru Akita, 'Comments' on Nicholas J. White, 'The Aftermath of Empire: British Influence and the Decolonisation of Southeast Asia', in *Report of Workshop on The End of Empire and the Transition of Hegemony in the Asia and Pacific Areas, Sendai, 1–2 November 2003*, pp. 64–5.

9 Shigeru Akita, ' "Gentlemanly Capitalism", Intra-Asian Trade and Japanese Industrialization at the Turn of the Last Century', *Japan Forum*, 8, 1 (1996): 51–65; Shigeru Akita and Naoto Kagotani, 'The International Order of Asia in the 1930s', in Shigeru Akita (ed.), *Gentlemanly Capitalism, Imperialism and Global History*, London: Palgrave Macmillan, 2002. For a critique see Antony Best, 'Economic Appeasement or Economic Nationalism? A Political Perspective on the British Empire, Japan and the Rise of Intra-Asian Trade, 1933–37', *Journal of Imperial and Commonwealth History*, 30/2 (2002): 77–101. The 'gentlemanly capitalism' thesis is associated with P.J. Cain and A.G. Hopkins; see their *British Imperialism, 1688–2000*, Harlow: Longman, 2002.

10 Yokoi, *Japan's Postwar Economic Recovery*, pp. 3–4, 32–3, 39–40, 91–2, 158; see also the chapter by Professor Akita in this volume.

11 TNA, CO1022/218, copy of despatch no. 73, 24 September 1951.

12 TNA, FO371/123657, DS11323/3, Chancery, Bangkok to SE Asia Department, FO, 28 March 1956; DS11323/5, Mocatta (Board of Trade, hereafter BOT) to Hurrell (Bangkok), 7 May 1956.

13 Ibid., despatch of 24 September 1951

14 TNA, CO1022/218, Johnston to MacDonald, 16 November 1951. For one Colonial Office mandarin, MacDonald's despatch contained 'an unsuitably large amount of rot, especially about Sino/Japanese relations' see ibid., Watt minute, 12 November 1951.

15 Ibid., Johnston to MacDonald, 16 November 1951.

16 TNA, FO371/127552, FJ1121/4, Harpham (Tokyo) to Selywn Lloyd, 30 May 1957; FO minutes of 6 and 8 June 1957.

17 TNA, CO1022/218, despatch of 24 September 1951; Peter Lowe, 'Great Britain, Japan, and the Future: The End of the Allied Occupation, 1948–52', in Richard Aldrich and Michael Hopkins (eds), *Intelligence, Defence and Diplomacy: British Policy in the Post-War World*, London: Frank Cass, 1994, p. 191.

18 TNA, CO1022/218, despatch of 24 September 1951; telegram from MacDonald to Colonial Office (hereafter CO), 8 February 1952.

19 TNA, FO371/127552, FJ1121/4, Harpham to Selwyn Lloyd, 30 May 1957.

20 Hiroshi Shimizu and Hitoshi Hirakawa, *Japan and Singapore in the World Economy: Japan's Advance into Singapore, 1870–1965*, London: Routledge, 1999, p. 161.

21 TNA, CO1022/218, Wallinger to Eden, 23 December 1951.

22 TNA, FO371/110488, FJ1491/3, Scopes (Jakarta) to Eden, 17 February 1954; and FJ1491/4, Dodds-Parker minutes, 12 and 13 October 1954.

23 TNA FO371/141463, FJ11379/2, Commercial section, British Embassy, Rangoon to Commercial Relations & Exports Department, BOT, 23 December 1959; Hugh Tinker, 'Burma', in Guy Wint (ed.), *Asia Handbook*, Harmondsworth: Penguin, 1969, pp. 291–4.

24 Tomaru, *Postwar Rapprochement*, p. 107.

25 Letter to CO, 26 June 1953 cited in Tomaru, *Postwar Rapprochement*, p. 108; TNA, CO1030/184, Dalton (Treasury) to MacKintosh (CO), July 1954; Dalton to Harding (CO), 3 September 1954; Colonial Secretary to Kuala Lumpur 13 September 1954; and CO1030/184, Ryan, Bank of England to Dalton, 31 August 1954.

26 A.J. Stockwell, 'Introduction', in ibid. (ed.), *Malaysia*, London: HMSO, 2004, pp. xlvi–xlvii.

27 TNA, DO189/219, Reynolds (UK Trade Commissioner, Malaya) to Richards (BOT), 28 August 1962; and Lushington (Office of the UK Commissioner, Singapore) report, 17 September 1962, enclosing note of a meeting with selected members of the Japanese Economic Mission to Malaysia, 5 September 1962.

28 See Nicholas J. White, 'The Survival, Revival and Decline of British Economic Influence in Malaysia, 1957–70', *Twentieth Century British History*, 14 (2003): 222–42.

29 TNA, FCO24/247, despatch to Commonwealth Secretary, 4 October 1967.

30 See Yokoi, *Japan's Postwar Economic Recovery*, pp. 95–6; Best, 'Economic Appeasement or Economic Nationalism?', pp. 80–1

31 Cited in Philip Murphy, *Party Politics and Decolonisation: the Conservative Party and British Colonial Policy in Tropical Africa, 1951–1964*, Oxford: Clarendon, 1995, p. 102.

32 Yokoi, *Japan's Postwar Economic Recovery*, pp. 149–50.

33 Nicholas J. White, 'The Diversification of Colonial Capitalism: British Agency Houses in Southeast Asia in the 1950s and 1960s', in Ian Cook *et al.* (eds), *Dynamic Asia: Business, Trade and Economic Development in Pacific Asia*, Aldershot: Ashgate, 1998.

34 Confederation of British Industry records, Modern Records Centre, University of Warwick, Mss. 200/F/3/D3/6/75, D/5527.

35 IA, Ms.27298, Donald to Managing Director, London enclosing copy of Chaplin to Young, 14 November 1959; and Young to Simpson, 26 July, 26 August, 19 and 22 September 1960.

36 IA, Ms.27189, minutes of Motor Group Meetings, 9 November and 8 December 1962, 27 February and 2 November 1963.

37 Geoffrey Jones, *Merchants to Multinationals: British Trading Companies in the Nineteenth and Twentieth Centuries*, Oxford: OUP, 2000, p. 142.

38 IA, Ms.27280/4, General Manager, Kuching to the Managing Directors, London, 24 November 1964; Pearson to Heath, 20 January 1965; and Ms.27178/26, Board of Directors minutes, 9 February 1961.

39 Shimizu and Hirakawa, *Japan and Singapore*, p. 177; and IA, Ms. 27281, Stovold to Pearson, 30 January 1962.

40 White, 'Britain and the Return of Japanese Economic Interests', pp. 301–2; and TNA, CO1030/183, MacKintosh to Spencer, 11 March 1954.

41 Arkib Negara Malaysia, AE/99/M, Penang Chamber of Commerce Confidential Minute Book, 18 November 1946 to 8 July 1958; Confidential Minutes, 9 February 1954; *Straits Times Directory of Malaya and Singapore 1957*, pp. 66–7.

42 TNA, CO1030/1226, Sussex minute, 21 April 1961; Nield minute, 17 June 1961; notes of a meeting between representatives of the Sarawak Government and the Japanese Coal Team, 4–8 September 1961; and IA Ms.27275, Combe, Borneo Motors (Singapore) Ltd. to Pearson, BCL, Kuching, 8 June 1962.

43 Aron Shai, *The Fate of British and French Firms in China, 1949–54: Imperialism Imprisoned*, Basingstoke: Macmillan, 1996; and David Clayton, *Imperialism Revisited: Political and Economic Relations Between Britain and China, 1950–4*, Basingstoke: Macmillan, 1997, chs 6–7.

44 IA, Ms.27275, Pearson to Combe, 21 August 1963.

45 Edwin Lee, *The Towkays of Sabah: Chinese Leadership and Indigenous Challenge in the Last Phase of British Rule*, Singapore: Singapore University Press, pp. 7, 23; and IA, Ms.27281, MacEwen to Pearson, 5 April 1962.

46 Stephanie Jones, *Two Centuries of Overseas Trading: the Origins and Growth of the Inchcape Group*, Basingstoke: Macmillan, 1986, pp. 233–4.

47 IA, Ms.27280/4, Pearson to Heath, 20 January 1965.

48 Jones, *Inchcape Group*, p. 216.

49 Shimizu and Hirakawa, *Japan and Singapore*, pp. 88–9.

50 On the remarkable adaptability of the British trading companies, irrespective of relative UK industrial decline, see Jones, *Merchants to Multinationals*.

51 Shimizu and Hirakawa, *Japan and Singapore*, p. 89.

52 Ocean Archive, National Museums Liverpool, Maritime Archives & Library (hereafter OA), 554, Glen Line News Release, 15 March 1967; OSSCo. News Release, 27 November 1967. With a production capacity of around half of all Britain's yards put together, Mitsubishi was able to deliver these ships six months ahead of the swiftest of the UK shipbuilders contracted to construct equivalent vessels. Malcolm Falkus, *The Blue Funnel Legend: A History of the Ocean Steam Ship Company, 1865–1973*, Houndmills: Macmillan, 1990, p. 330.

53 Graham Turner, *Business in Britain*, Harmondsworth: Penguin, 1971, p. 307.

54 OA, 4003/8, Annual Meeting, 27 April 1953, Chairman's Report for 1952; Annual Meeting, 27 January 1947, Chairman's Report for 1946; Falkus, *Blue Funnel Legend*, pp. 176, 219.

55 OA, 671, 'British Interests in Eastern Asia', University of Liverpool Lecture by Sir John Hobhouse, 26 May 1952; 1131; Alfred Holt & Co. to Butterfield & Swire (Japan) Ltd., Tokyo, 12 November 1951; Falkus, *Blue Funnel Legend*, p. 302; Turner, *Business in Britain*, p. 313.

56 OA, 4003/8, Annual Meeting, 25 April 1952, Chairman's Report for 1951.

57 See Nicholas J. White, 'Liverpool Shipping and the End of Empire: The Ocean Group in East and Southeast Asia, *c*.1945–*c*.1973', paper presented at the 3rd Annual Conference of the Centre for Liverpool and Merseyside Studies, Merseyside Maritime Museum, Liverpool, 21 April 2006.

58 See, for example, Rajeswary Brown, *Chinese Big Business and the Wealth of Asian Nations*, Basingstoke: Palgrave, 2000.

12 Concluding remarks

Akira Iriye

One of the pleasures of reading recent monographs in international history, of which the studies included in this book are excellent examples, is to realize the long distance that historians have travelled in their quest for original insights and novel interpretive schemes. The study of East Asian international relations, which serves as a broad framework for most of the chapters, till recently focused on wars: the wars between China and Japan, between Russia and Japan, between Germany and Japan, the Second World War, and the Cold War. Origins of wars were the starting point, even the principal preoccupation, of many a volume, and alliances, wartime diplomacy, peace treaties, and the like provided the meat of the story. Periods between wars were understood as preludes to another war, or else conceptualized in terms of a search for a new balance of power. All such themes took the nation state as the key unit of analysis. International relations were considered to consist of interactions among nations, and their relations with one another, whether in peacetime diplomacy or in war, were minutely examined in archival sources. In such a situation, there was little beyond nation-centred themes and arguments in the depiction of international history.

It is only during the past twenty years or so that historians have begun to go beyond such traditional frameworks. First, there has been a shift away from a preoccupation with wars, hot and cold, toward a concern with what may be termed non-geopolitical phenomena. For instance, instead of comprehending the history of the 1920s as an inter-war period, which assumes that another war was just around the corner, historians have turned their attention to such topics as the League of Nations' efforts to promote cultural communication among nations, to provide for the relief of refugees, or to eradicate communicable diseases. Or, to take another example, post-1945 history has begun to be examined not in the usual framework of the Cold War, but in terms of other themes like de-colonization and economic globalization. It is entirely possible to view the history of the second half of the century in the framework of globalization. In such a perspective, the Cold War would be relegated to a footnote, not the master narrative. Moreover, the Cold War-centric perspective privileges the super-powers and their military weapons, whereas these other topics pay attention to smaller countries as well as to the non-Western parts of the world. To move away from the Cold War framework, then, is also to overcome the conventional understanding of modern history that privileges the West and to bring the East or the South their due.

Second, related to the move away from the focus on international conflict is to stress international cooperation and interdependence. This can best be illustrated by studies that focus on economic integration, as exemplified by regional communities. Nations give up part of their sovereign rights to enter into customs unions, work out schemes for common-border enforcement of law and order, or otherwise develop shared policies. We may also note the growingly popular subfield of 'borderlands history', a study of those areas in the world that cannot be entirely identified with nations or national boundaries, such as the areas overlapping the United States and Mexico, the United States and Canada, Pakistan and Afghanistan, and indeed most parts of the world in which national boundaries have never meant national identities. Such identities are less important than the sharing of life styles and destinies on all sides of boundaries. Regional history and borderlands history have thus come together to weaken the traditional preoccupation with national sovereignty.

Third, many international (as well as national) historians now emphasize the roles played by non-state actors as makers of history. Instead of examining the modern past in terms of how governments and military forces behaved, historians have begun to trace the evolution of business enterprises, non-governmental organizations, religious institutions, and the like that are not interchangeable with states or confined within state boundaries. This stress on non-state actors has resulted in the popularity of transnational history, an inquiry into the past not in terms of states but of forces, movements, and interactions across national boundaries. Transnational phenomena such as migrations, diseases, environmental hazards, and the like cannot be studied within national frameworks. The recently published *Palgrave Dictionary of Transnational History* contains over four hundred entries, not one of which is definable within traditional conceptions of national or international affairs.[1] Moreover, the fact that these articles were contributed by 350 writers from twenty-five countries suggests the growing practice of transnational scholarly collaboration. That in turn ensures that historical writing that focuses only on one or two nations will no longer be adequate. Instead of endlessly discussing when and how decisions for war were made, for instance, transnational historians tend to pay equal, even greater, attention to how individuals and non-state actors met, thereby creating transnational moments as another reality besides that defined by states.

Fourth, larger transnational entities such as religions, races, and civilizations have also claimed increasing scholarly attention. In part under the influence of social history and culture studies that gained influence during the 1970s and the 1980s, international historians also began to notice race, gender, ethnicity, civilization, and other non-national subjects as important components of world 'realities'. Instead of focusing on domestic 'sub-cultures' consisting of microscopic, local phenomena, however, historians of international relations have, since the 1990s, been paying attention to global interracial, gender, or trans-civilizational interactions. Historians today appear much more interested in these other categories which, when combined with transnational phenomena such as climate change and the fate of endangered species, produce fascinating new perspectives in international history.

All such historiographic developments seem to be related to, and promoted by, the recent vogue of world history and global history. Reflecting the awareness that it makes little sense to examine in close detail what happens within a country without relating it to the rest of the world, historians have been embracing these larger frameworks with increasing enthusiasm. World history as a genre has, of course, been around for a long time. William McNeill and other world historians had, since the 1960s, devoted their intellectual energies to examining such phenomena as diseases, demographic trends, money flows, and even crime (such as drug trafficking and piracy) as worldwide phenomena that cannot be separated from any discussion of national or international history. For a long time theirs had been a lonely endeavour, but in the 1990s other historians – Bruce Mazlish, Raymond Grew, Patrick Manning, Gerry Bentley, Christopher Bayly, to name but a few – joined the pioneering scholars and began to teach and write their versions of world history. World historians and global historians have been exploring movements that establish connections among nations and regions, as well as making comparisons across nations and regions. It is not surprising that, as a culmination of all these developments, globalization – economic, social, cultural – has emerged as a new conceptual scheme within which to trace historical developments, especially in the last two centuries.

Many of the chapters in this volume fit admirably into one or more of these scholarly trends. To state the obvious first, the book is a product of transnational collaboration. British and Japanese historians have been undertaking scholarly cooperation for over thirty years, in the process broadening not only their respective intellectual horizons but also those of scholars from other countries. It may also be noted that while many of the chapters deal with the bilateral (British–Japanese) relationship, which is a very traditional framework of analysis, that relationship is put in many perspectives – regional, international, transnational, global – that go far toward enriching our understanding of the past.

To specify some of the valuable and fresh insights offered by the chapters, Antony Best gives an important analysis of the racial and cultural foundations – or rather, lack thereof – of the Anglo-Japanese alliance. Robert Bickers provides a systematic analysis of a vital institution that has tended to be neglected in studies of Asian international affairs: China's Imperial Customs Administration. The article shows how an institution established in China but initially controlled by British officials eventually grew more transnational, with the addition of Japanese and other nationals to its staff.

Several articles offer new readings of Japan's foreign affairs before the Second World War. Harumi Goto-Shibata's study of Japan's role in the League of Nations' Opium Advisory Committee (OAC) throws light on a little understood aspect of the nation's relationship with the League. Although it is customary to consider that relationship as having come to an end when Japan withdrew from the League in 1933, the author shows that the nation remained quite active at the OAC. Our understanding of Japan in world affairs during the 1930s would have to take such information into consideration. That decade has also been studied in terms of the Japanese ideology of pan-Asianism, but Masataka Matsuura makes an important contribution by introducing the roles played by Indians in Japan. On the other hand, Hans van de Ven's excellent chapter on the Japanese bombing of Chinese cities in 1937 refers to an essay by an Indian scholar who noted that 'while Indian nationalists would welcome anything weakening the British, most had been appalled' by the bombings. Whatever moral authority Japan may have enjoyed in the rest of Asia would seem to have evaporated after 1937. By referring to Japan's 'nauseating hypocrisy', Anthony Eden may have been pointing to the restoration, to some extent any way, of British prestige in Asia as the other side of the coin of Japanese barbarism.

British–Japanese relations, as even such an episode reveals, were quite central to the Asian regional order. Most studies of Asian-Pacific international relations have focused on just one player, in particular examined as an aspect of the imperial history of Britain, Japan, or the United States, but some of the chapters in this book point to the importance of the bilateral British–Japanese connection as a major component, even key, to regional order. The Anglo-Japanese relationship, as Joseph Maiolo's excellent discussion of the naval treaties shows, played such a role during the 1920s and the 1930s. But other chapters extend the perspective to the post-1945 years. While Britain tends to disappear or be slighted in most accounts of the immediate aftermath of the Second World War, the chapters by Tomoki Kuniyoshi and Peter Lowe show that Britain was very much present even at such U.S.-dominated scenes as the San Francisco peace conference and the formation of the Southeast Asian Treaty Organization, in both of which, as these authors demonstrate, London and Washington were more often in disagreement than acting in unison within the Cold War framework. The final two chapters in the book, studies of British–Japanese economic relations by Shigeru Akita and Nicholas White, round out the picture of postwar British–Japanese relations. These chapters note the complementarity (Akita) as well as competition (White) between the two economies, but, despite their different emphases, the authors help us understand the transition from prewar economic nationalism to postwar globalization.

In sum, then, the chapters in the book invite us to overcome our preoccupation with conventional themes (war, cold war, imperialism) and broaden our understanding, first, by noting multiple dimensions (economic, ideological, medical) of the Asian regional order, second, by taking the bilateral British–Japanese relations to the level of global and transnational frameworks, and, third, by conceptualizing a new chronology of world history of which the various episodes depicted here will form integral parts.

Note

1 A. Iriye and P. Saurier (eds), *Palgrave Dictionary of Transnational History* (London: Palgrave/Macmillan, 2009).

Index

Bevin, Ernest (British Foreign Secretary) 120, 140

Black, Sir Robert (post-WWII British Governor of Singapore) 172

Bland, J.O.P. (*The Times* correspondent in Shanghai and later Peking) 38, 50

Blue Funnel Line (British shipping company) 177

Bombay Burmah Group 176

Borden, Sir Robert (Canadian Prime Minister) 59

Borneo 148; *see also* North Borneo

Borneo Co. Ltd. (BCL) 175–7

Bose, Rash Behari (Indian nationalist exile) 83, 88–90, 102

Boustead & Co. 176

Bowra, C.A.V. (Acting Inspector-General, CMCS) 44

'Boxer' uprising *see* China

Bredon, Sir Robert (appointment to CMCS Inspector-General obstructed) 46

Britain 1, 4; and appeasement 13, 17, 27; and naval armaments limitation 4–5, 69, 71–4; and opium control 57–8, 60–3; and pan-Asianism 83, 86–92; and the CMCS 100–1; and the naval treaty system 76–7; and the Pacific War 9–10, 64–5; Anglo-Japanese History Project 3, 9; 14, 19; Order of the Garter 26

British armed forces: Air staff (intelligence) 147; Army 36; Chiefs of Staff 121, 125, 138, 146; Royal Navy 22, 28–9, 36, 69, 71, 73–7

British economic policy *1. General:* and the Colombo Plan 140; Anglo-Japanese 'complementarity' 169, 176, 178; Anglo-Japanese economic relations 153–6, 158–9, 170, 178; Anglo-Japanese Trade Arrangement (1948) 155, 163–4; British Trade Arrangements 163; competition from Japan 87, 88; currency multilateralism 161–2, 164; financial account areas (1947) 155; financial interests in Southeast Asia (1950s to 1960s) 169, 171, 175; importance of British service sector 153; post-WWII economic recovery in East Asia 11–13, 153; *2. Sterling:* and British interests 154, 164; and East Asia 153; and Hong Kong 157; and Japan 153–4, 156–7; and the OPA 155–6; convertibility 154–5, 157–8; Sterling Payments Agreements (SPA) (1951–7) 157–8, 160–4, 170; sterling policies

154–5, 160; sterling usage in East Asia 156, 160, 164

British Empire (later Commonwealth): 13, 25, 35; and naval armaments limitation 71, 74, 77; and opium 58, 62, 65; and pan-Asianism 91–2, 94; and post-WWII security 119–20, 122–6, 128–9; and post-WWII trade with Japan 170–1; and sterling policies 153–4, 159, 161, 163, 170–1, 174; and the Colombo Plan 140–2; and the OPA 155; and the SPA with Japan 153–4; British Borneo 170, 175; British Commonwealth Conference (1947) 120; British Commonwealth Conference and Working Parties (1950) 123, 140; British Commonwealth Conference (1951) 124; colonies 7, 87; Commonwealth membership 170; overseas expansion 153; post-WWII colonial independence 134; pre- WWII Japanese exports to 87

British foreign relations: China 3, 7; 62–3; France; discussions on colonial rule post-WWII 135; Germany 27, 41; Japan 7, 61, 81–2, 86, 88–9; 'a Japanese– British war' 91; Anglo-Japanese alliance 3, 8; 13–16; Chapter 2, 82, 114; Anglo-Japanese political relations 3–4, 6; 10, 12–17, 19, 84; Britain seen as an enemy 92–3, 95; business connections in SE Asia 174; commercial treaty (1962) 164; post-WWII British Liaison Mission 123; post-WWII distrust of 138–40; post-WWII peace treaty 118–29; League of Nations 60; United States: and the second London Treaty 77; little co-operation at the post-WWI peace conference 3, 15; different reactions to Japanese aggression 17–18, 32; post-WWII peace treaty 118–29; support for a US/Japanese security pact 6

British government organizations: Admiralty 36, 69, 71, 73, 77; Board of Trade 36, 59, 143, 154, 161, 163, 170; Cabinet 156, 163; Cabinet Committee on Tariff Policy towards Japan (1953) 158; Colonial Office 36, 62, 143, 176; Commonwealth Relations Office 143, 163; Defence Coordination Committee (Singapore) 146; Foreign Office 22, 28, 36, 45–6, 59, 120–2, 124, 136, 139–40, 142–5, 147–8, 171–2; India Office 36; intelligence services 36, 88; Joint Intelligence Committee 136–8, 147;

For Product Safety Concerns and Information please contact our EU
representative GPSR@taylorandfrancis.com
Taylor & Francis Verlag GmbH, Kaufingerstraße 24, 80331 München, Germany

www.ingramcontent.com/pod-product-compliance
Lightning Source LLC
Chambersburg PA
CBHW050435280326
41932CB00013BA/2124

* 9 7 8 0 4 1 5 6 2 5 0 4 3 *